CW00591269

Dan Bell

Ps. 91vl

"Fire on the Mountain"
The Story of the Darkley Church
Northern Ireland

*Where three Church Elders died during the 1983 massacre
in Mountain Lodge Pentecostal Church.*

AMBASSADOR INTERNATIONAL
GREENVILLE, SOUTH CAROLINA & BELFAST, NORTHERN IRELAND

www.ambassador-international.com

Mountain Lodge Pentecostal Church

"Fire on the Mountain"

Celebrating 60 years of faithful Christian witness

1953 – 2013

Pastor David Bell

Mountain Lodge Pentecostal Church
27 Mountain Lodge Road, Darkley, Keady, Co Armagh, BT60 3BT.

www.mlpc.co.uk

Fire on the Mountain
The Story of the Darkley Church Northern Ireland

Paperback ISBN: 978-1-62020-141-1
Hardback ISBN: 978-1-62020-143-5

Printed by Bethel Solutions

Unless otherwise indicated, all Scripture quotations are taken from the King James Version (KJV) of the Holy Bible.

Ambassador International
Emerald House
427 Wade Hampton Blvd
Greenville, SC 29609, USA
www.ambassador-international.com

Ambassador Books and Media
The Mount
2 Woodstock Link
Belfast, BT6 8DD, Northern Ireland, UK
www.ambassadormedia.co.uk

CONTENTS

I Dedicate this Book

To the glory of God, and –

To my wife Sally, a living expression of Proverbs 31 and to my daughter Esther – you both are God's priceless gift to me. Your unfeigned love, wise council, and continual encouragement have sustained me through 23 years of Christian ministry.

To the congregation at Mountain Lodge, who have been my spiritual family for more than thirty-seven years. It has been my privilege to serve you as your Pastor for twenty-three of those years, in the call that God has given me. You have stood with me every time I took a step of faith into the unknown, went out on a limb spending finances we didn't have, or just simply believed God! We are "risk-takers" together for His glory!

To the memory of three very special friends who were shot dead during the Sunday evening church service on 20ᵗʰ November 1983. Each one of them helped shape the course of my life –

Harold Browne, a mature father-figure to a young believer,

Victor Cunningham, whose vivacious smile and untiring zeal for God impacted me on my first visit, and

David Wilson, my best friend and spiritual mentor, whose memory I will treasure forever.

Pastor David.

ACKNOWLEDGEMENTS

I gratefully acknowledge the following sources of photographs, newspaper editorial and other general information which have proved invaluable in compiling this account of the life of Mountain Lodge:

The Ulster Gazette.

The Belfast Telegraph.

The Belfast Newsletter.

Pacemaker International Limited.

Marie Allen, Photographer.

Old Mill Heritage Centre, Keady.

Irish Reference Library, Armagh.

Griffiths Valuation 1864.

Ulster Counties Directory 1880.

Hansard Publications.

'A Typographical Dictionary of Ireland,' by Samuel Lewis, first published 1837.

'Armaghbreague Presbyterian Church, 150 years of Christian Witness,' by Trevor R. Geary, first published 1997.

I am also indebted to the many members and friends of Mountain Lodge Pentecostal Church from far and near, whose contributions are such a central part of this story.

A special word of thanks to Esther's English Literature teacher, Mrs Carol Day, for so freely offering your time to edit the manuscript, as you sought to bring clarity to the finished work. *"God speed the plow."*

FOREWORD

On the Sunday evening of 20ᵗʰ November 1983, those who had gathered to worship the Lord in Mountain Lodge Pentecostal Church, near the village of Darkley in South Armagh, could never have anticipated the events which would unfold before their very eyes. Events which were far removed from anything associated with a church service.

Sinister forces had also planned to attend the service that evening. Their visit, which was not to worship God, would result in the indiscriminate murder of three church elders, and leave seven members of the congregation seriously wounded. The 'Troubles' in Northern Ireland had reached an all time low, when not even the house of God was regarded as sacred in the minds of depraved terrorists.

'Fire on the Mountain' is a compulsive read. The church's sixty year history is well documented in a readable and most interesting manner. The chapter headings allow the reader to easily engage with the free flow of the story as the author, who is the present Pastor, seeks to put in print the life story of the fellowship, in a warm and intimate style.

The church, having commenced with the vision of one man, Thomas Hunniford, has in spite of various uphill battles, made its own distinctive contribution to the work of God, and has retained its unique witness and testimony, far beyond the remote geographical location in which it is situated.

Two malicious fires, and a horrendous terrorist attack, have not put out the spiritual fire that still burns brightly today in the hearts of its people. God has blessed and honoured their faith, as He has worked among them in ordinary and extraordinary ways.

It was when the congregation were singing the last verse of the opening hymn, ably led as always by Pastor Bob Bain, in his own unique manner, that the terrorists struck. In an act of wanton murder and cowardice, they took the earthly lives of three real heroes of the cross.

That evening, Harold Browne, David Wilson and Victor Cunningham paid the ultimate sacrifice. Yet, before the terrorists had left the church building to escape into the darkness of night, God's three servants had already entered into His presence. Bullets can kill the body but never the soul.

In reading *'Fire on the Mountain,'* I am reminded of a statement attributed to Queen Victoria; *"Please understand that there is no depression in this house. We are not interested in the possibilities of defeat; they do not exist."*

That is the kind of spirit that has driven the fellowship in Mountain Lodge during the past sixty years.

I heartily recommend the reading of this book and trust that you will be inspired by its story.

Pastor Eric McComb.

(Superintendent of the Elim Pentecostal Church in Ireland, 1979-2011)

ENDORSEMENTS

Jesus said, *"I will build my church, and the gates of hell shall not prevail against it."* Mountain Lodge Pentecostal Church is living proof that Jesus told the truth. Hell has thrown everything it's got at this church, yet it stands as a beacon of light, illuminating the darkness with the truth of God's eternal Word. A 'Book of Acts' style story. Great faith building reading.

Bob Gass, Author of 'The Word For Today'.

~~~

A few years ago, while on an Irish tour, I was invited to sing at the Mountain Lodge Pentecostal Church along with my friends in the local Country Gospel band, 'Live Issue.' Our evening together was one that I often recall with great fondness.

From the moment I entered the building, I felt God's presence all around me, and the members of the church openly displayed a genuine love and concern for each other, and for the wider community. The welcome and hospitality given not just to me - but to everyone who visited the church that night - greatly encouraged and challenged me.

I believe that the Mountain Lodge Pentecostal Church is a ministry which is not confined to the walls of a building, but reaches out across the island of Ireland and beyond, with a message of hope. In my opinion it is an example of what Christ intended His church to be. May God continue to bless Pastor David Bell and everyone associated with this very special church.

George Hamilton IV, USA.

It takes a certain individual, with a strength of character, to persevere and navigate through the extremities of life that to the average person would seem unsurpassable. This book will lift your faith, as you journey through those extremities, with one such person who proved God faithful in the face of many extreme challenges. If you have the tenacity and determination to hang in there no matter what or who comes against you, it may come down to the last wire, but God comes. I believe Pastor David Bell has demonstrated God's faithfulness, remonstrated throughout the pages in this book.

Pastor Bill Wilson, Metro Ministries, New York.

~~~

It has always been a blessing to minister alongside Pastor David Bell, a man who has a passion for souls, who earnestly contends for the faith and who under God, is building a Church that is in line with New Testament doctrine and practice. Gun fire and natural fire have been seen and heard in this church on the mountain, but the words of Christ have proved to be true – *"I will build My Church and the gates of hell will not prevail against it," (Matthew 16:18).* I sincerely pray that God will richly bless everyone who reads *'Fire on the Mountain'* and I pray that the fire of the Holy Spirit will continue to burn as long as there is a church on the mountain.

Rev Jim Patterson, Presenter on Revelation TV.

~~~

This book shouts out the great news that God is with us in the highs and lows of life. It reminds us of Paul's testimony in Philippians 1:12 when he wrote from prison; *'The things that have happened to me have fallen out rather to the furtherance of the Gospel.'* David Bell and the story of Mountain Lodge gives us all hope, and shows us that even on our worst days, Jesus is still Lord. Thank you so much Pastor David for your faithfulness, commitment and vision. We hold you in the highest esteem and honour you for your integrity. You have left us with no option but to shout aloud 'Amazing Grace!'

Dr Cecil Stewart, O.B.E.

'Fire on the Mountain' is a must read! Not only for the Irish, but for every child of God who has heard of the tragedy of sectarianism that has ravaged what is otherwise one of the most enjoyable places on earth to visit! The Author has personally lived through the tragedy that is chronicled in the book. It is one of those books that you cannot put down! I highly recommend this true story!

Dr. Martin G Tharp, D. Lit., Ph.D.

~~~

Mountain Lodge Pentecostal Church, always known to me as the Darkley Church, is one of the most important witnesses for the Lord Jesus Christ in Ireland – for the members labour and worship in a crucial area, right on the border. Their history and background is known and admired by all. They remind me of the "Smyrna Church" in Revelation Chapter 2, where *"brethren were faithful unto death!"* Also, in spite of suffering two satanic fires, still they are there.

To me it's amazing that a small work like this can be so effective, and, above all, so faithful. I pray that all who read this book, and especially Pastors and those who would desire to go into God's work, will be inspired and challenged through the witness of this church. Pastor David Bell has written the account of this Assembly very well. Our prayer is that God will continue to bless him and use him in this very important part of the Lord's vineyard.

Dr. James McConnell, Whitewell Metropolitan Tabernacle, Belfast.

~~~

For the pastor and church leadership seeking to build an effective church amidst difficult times, in a difficult area of the community, within the pages of this book you will be encouraged not to give up. As miracles supersede magic, as fact supersedes fantasy, so likewise the spirit of perseverance that always supersedes the spirit of discouragement comes shining forth from this interesting good read.

Pastor Bill Dunn, BA, Elim Minister.

The Three Martyrs

The Pentecostal church stood on a Darkley hill
A tribute to a godly flock, who did their Saviour's will.
Each week in Mountain Lodge they met to worship, praise and sing
In humble adoration to their Saviour, God and King.
Their mission wasn't politics, for this they were not sent -
It was to open up the gospel that sinners might repent.

Lord's Day November twenty, in the year of '83
An act of sheer brutality we never thought we'd see.
A tiny congregation met to worship God and King
Young and old, their voices raised as they began to sing.
"Would you be free from your burden of sin?"
The question was posed in their opening hymn.

Everyone was seated, 'cept three elders by the door;
Soon two were lying lifeless, shot to death upon the floor.
A third though mortally wounded staggered in to warn the flock
But another burst of gunfire caused pandemonium and shock.
That third Christian life was ended in the twinkling of an eye,
As God called His murdered martyrs, to His mansion up on high.

Gunmen kept on firing both from within and from outside
Leaving men and women lying wounded side by side.
Little children screamed in terror, not knowing what to do
As they watched their stricken parents blood-spattered in the pew.
Three souls dead, seven wounded, little children scarred for life
Just another chapter in fourteen years of hideous strife.

God is not mocked, His scripture makes it known
Evil men will one day reap the harvest they have sown.
If only wicked men would bow and Jesus' mercy crave
He would reach down in tenderness, their sinful souls He'd save.
Three Darkley Martyrs have gone home to be with Christ the King
Forevermore they'll reign with Him and His great praises sing.

John J. Somerville.   Sun 4th Dec.1983.

This poem, together with 800 letters sent from all over the world, arrived at Pastor Bob Bain's home in the days following the church massacre, which occurred on Sunday 20th November 1983.

INTRODUCTION

"Forasmuch as many have taken in hand to set forth in order a declaration of those things which are most surely believed among us, even as they delivered them unto us which from the beginning were eyewitnesses, and ministers of the word; it seemed good to me also, having had perfect understanding of all things from the very first, to write unto thee in order, most excellent Theophilus, that thou mightest know the certainty of those things, wherein thou hast been instructed." (St Luke 1:1-4.)

It is obvious that St Luke, as he penned these opening words of the gospel that bears his name, felt a very real burden to prepare an accurate account of the events that eventually led to the formation of the early church, so that not only the *"most excellent Theophilus,"* but also you and I, might know *"the certainty of those things wherein we have been instructed."*

Most theologians place the writing of Luke's gospel around 60-62 AD, and so it would seem good to me as the third successive Pastor of this church that, as we celebrate sixty years of faithful ministry on this mountain, this is also an appropriate time to compile a similar record from the beginning until the present day, of the work that is now known as Mountain Lodge Pentecostal Church, since its formation sixty years ago.

It is important that those who eventually take up the mantle, should the Lord tarry, are provided with an accurate point of reference as to the salvations, miracles, healings, blessings and visitations witnessed by past generations in this place. It is my earnest prayer that they will also take courage from the knowledge of past battles fought and victories won, and that they will remain steadfast to the call of God in His service in this place, as they are reminded of those who made the ultimate sacrifice. *"We wrestle not against flesh and blood, but against principalities, against powers, against the rulers of the darkness of this world, against spiritual wickedness in high places." (Eph. 6:12).*

My sincere desire is that this book will serve to re-kindle a fresh flame within those more mature souls among us, who have worshipped faithfully in this place over the years, as we remember some of the mighty visitations of the Lord in our midst. I also hope that it will also be a source of inspiration and encouragement to our younger members, as they discover the rich heritage that the saints have sought to preserve for them through overcoming various trials and tribulations down through the years.

As for you the reader, whether you are a member of Mountain Lodge, one of the very many 'friends' who have been in fellowship with us from time to time, or a brother or sister in the Lord whom we have not yet met, my prayer is that this book will be such a source of blessing to you that you will feel personally compelled to seek a fresh anointing of the Holy Spirit upon your life and ministry. And for those who do not yet know the Lord Jesus as Saviour, the writing of this book will have been more than rewarded if something contained within its pages compels you to *"seek the Lord while He may be found,"* as you join us on this epic journey.

This book is not intended to be a theological masterpiece, or a guide on creed or doctrine, for as Pentecostals we simply believe that Jesus died for us, and that through repentance and faith we can have eternal life in Him. We believe that He desires to baptize us in His Holy Spirit that we might be endued with power to serve Him, and while we know what and Whom we believe, we fellowship with all who know and love Him as Saviour.

Instead it is simply the story of an amazing journey of faith, of spiritual hills and valleys, of mountains to climb and rivers to cross, of times of abundant blessing and times of overcoming immense trials, hardship and testing, proving in all things that He is still Lord.

Enjoy the journey!

Pastor David Bell.

Chapter 1

Magoregan's Field

An Auction Notice dated 1924 is displayed in the 'Old Mill' local history library, in the border town of Keady, some eight miles south of the city of Armagh (the ecclesiastical capital of Ireland). It provides details of a proposed sale of the contents of Mountain Lodge House. Local auctioneer Thomas Mallon officiated on behalf of the owner at that time, H. G. Douglas, Esq., J.P. So extensive were the contents offered for sale, that two days' viewing were organised on Friday and Saturday 5th and 6th December 1924, with the auction taking place on the Monday, Tuesday and Wednesday of the following week, commencing at 11 o'clock each day.

Some of the items for sale included: from the Dining Room 'A massive marble mantle-piece clock' and 'Very fine old Spanish mahogany sideboard'; from the Study '1000 volumes of books'; from among the contents of six bedrooms 'Massive Spanish mahogany wardrobe' and 'two Spanish mahogany canopy beds'; from the kitchen 'Three large kitchen tables, Crocks, Mangle etc'; from the Motor House 'An English built 1914 motor car'; and lastly from the Yard '2 five year old horses, 20 horned ewes, 20 cross-bred ewes and about 20 store bullocks'.

Of course, the history of Mountain Lodge House and Estate goes back much further than 1924, as will be revealed later. The Estate is situated in the picturesque townland of Aughnagurgan (meaning 'the field of Magoregan'), an area of hill and bog in the south west of County Armagh.

Mountain Lodge House and the Pentecostal church which

bears its name are, as the name of the church aptly depicts, located near the top of a mountain at 749 feet above sea level.

The nearby Carrickatuke Viewpoint (meaning the rock of the Hawk) stands at 1203 feet above sea level and on a clear day offers some outstanding views - from Dundalk Bay to the South Armagh hills, including Forkhill; the Gap of the North; Sleve Gullion (an ancient volcano); Camlough Mountain and Cooley Peninsula; the Mournes; Slieve Croob (some 40 miles distant); the Black Mountains; the Antrim Plateau, and Slemish on a clear day; Lough Neagh; the Sperrins (including Bessie Bell); the Monaghan hills, and right down through counties Cavan, Westmeath and Meath, covering the flat Bog of Allen (ten counties in total). Nearby Tullyneill Hill in the townland of Tullyvallen rises to 1024 feet above sea level and is said to be the highest cultivated ground in Northern Ireland.

There are a number of lakes within walking distance of the church, including Aughnagurgan Lake, Darkley Lake and Tullynawood Lake. Also, a small gold nugget found in the local Clea (or Clay) Lake has been placed in the Belfast museum.

The local village of Darkley lies some half a mile to the north west of Mountain Lodge, while the city of Armagh lies some ten miles directly to the north. There are also splendid views of Armagh's two historic cathedrals from the back of the church.

According to Samuel Lewis's 'Topographical Dictionary of Ireland 1837': "the mountains abound with clay-slate and there are also indications of lead and copper ores, but no attempt has yet been made to work either. About two miles from the village [of Keady] is Mountain Lodge, the residence of Hugh Garmany."

Mountain Lodge Estate historically consisted of a large gentleman's residence, with a gate lodge and some 260 acres of land, most of which is now planted by the Forest Service in Norway Spruce, Larch and the occasional clump of Lodgepole pine. As you will read later, this Pentecostal pioneer work started in the front Drawing Room of the 'Big House'. The present Mountain Lodge Pentecostal Church is still situated on the estate just a few hundred yards away from the original site, where it all began. The forest today surrounds the church on three sides.

The Mountain Lodge House and Estate changed hands several times over the years before finally being purchased by the Forest Service around 1990. I have already alluded to Hugh Garmany who appears to have occupied the estate in the early 1800s and there is anecdotal evidence to indicate that the Garmanys were related by marriage to the Douglas family who later lived at Mountain Lodge.

According to Griffiths 1864 Valuation, it would appear that Mountain Lodge House and Lands were the property of the Earl of Charlemont, who rented them to a Mr John Douglas. Again according to Griffiths, this John Douglas appears to have been the owner of the small cottage (to the north east of the church) on Mountain Lodge Road, together with a two acre field on the opposite side of the road. (This cottage, in more recent times the home of the Warmington family, was purchased by the church in August 2013). The records indicate that John Douglas rented his cottage out to a Mr William Preston, while Douglas in turn leased the Mountain Lodge House and lands from the Earl of Charlemont. This would have been a fitting residence for John Douglas who (according to the 1880 Ulster Counties Directory) was a local magistrate.

The 1864 Griffiths Valuation also indicates that a Mr William Bigham owned and occupied a small cottage sitting on 4 acres 1 rood 20 perches (approximately 1.7 hectares) immediately adjacent to and northwest of the Mountain Lodge estate. We have discovered that this old cottage once stood on the site of the present church. A local woman, Hannah Coulter (nee Ward) was born in this house. Hannah has attended many of the meetings and testifies of mighty times of blessing in the present Mountain Lodge Pentecostal Church.

The 1901 Census indicates that Mountain Lodge House was occupied during the early 20th century by a Hugh G. Douglas who is also listed in the entry as a local magistrate.

There is also anecdotal evidence to suggest that an orphan, Miss Minnie Higgins, born in Monaghan in 1883, was placed by the Board of Guardians, in Mountain Lodge House for a time as a maid. (Minnie also had two brothers, James and William). Minnie later emigrated to Canada in 1904, where she married an Isaac Warmington later that year. Isaac, who was an uncle of Albert Warmington (a member of Mountain Lodge Pentecostal Church until his death in 2012), had emigrated to Canada some time before. However, Isaac obviously still had feelings for Minnie because, when his brother, James Warmington, was emigrating to Canada in 1904, Isaac arranged for Minnie to travel out with James.

According to the 1911 census records, a Hugh Garmany Douglas, JP (aged 56) lived with his wife Roberta Douglas (aged 50) in the townland of Aughnagurgan (at Mountain Lodge). They employed one servant, Hannah Monaghan, who was a single woman, aged 30 years. While the records indicate that the Douglas family attended the Church of Ireland, they show that Miss Monaghan was a Presbyterian.

It appears that Hugh Douglas eventually sold the lease to Mountain Lodge Estate to a Mr Kilpatrick, who in turn sold it to Bob Flanagan, from whom Thomas John Hunniford later purchased it in 1949.

Mountain Lodge is situated on an 'unapproved road' in South Armagh, just one and a half miles from the border with the Republic of Ireland. During the 'Troubles' such roads were so named, because the British Army demolished culverts and bridges on these minor roads, to prevent direct access over the border between Northern Ireland and the Republic by terrorists seeking a safe haven. However, this action on the part of the British Army proved to be very inconvenient for local farmers (Catholic and

Protestant alike) who oftentimes owned land in both jurisdictions. Consequently the farmers would eventually make the road passable again. This course of remedial action by the locals, would work greatly to the church's disadvantage in later years.

When travelling to Mountain Lodge from the direction of Keady, one must negotiate 'the Slither' (a winding hilly S-bend) on the main Newtownhamilton Road, just prior to turning in at 'Donnelly's Quarry,' (long since filled in and used as reclaimed land). Not a journey for the faint hearted on an icy wintry evening!

Access to Mountain Lodge church is via a narrow, steep and winding country road which meanders along the mountain, by the edge of Aughnagurgan Lake. The road is so steep that usually one or two church services have to be abandoned each winter as the elements of nature take their course.

The natural beauty of God's creation in this part of the world makes a fitting backdrop for a church where many have gathered over the years to experience the presence of God.

MOUNTAIN LODGE

KEADY, CO. ARMAGH.

ANTIQUE & MODERN

FURNITURE & EFFECTS

Old Spanish Mahogany Sideboards, Secretaire with glass top, Rosewood Drawing Room Suite, Rosewood Davenport, Rosewood Card Tables, Baize centres; Very Fine Rosewood Cheffonier, Old Sheffield Plate, Old Silver, 20-Piece Wedgewood Fruit Set, Cut Glass, Steel Engravings, Oil Paintings, &c., &c.

I have received instructions from H. G. DOUGLAS, Esq., J.P., Mountain Lodge, Keady, to Sell by Public

AUCTION

ON THE PREMISES,

On Monday, Tuesday & Wednesday, 8th, 9th & 10th December

Commencing at the hour of ELEVEN o'clock, a.m., each Day,

DINING ROOM—Very Fine Old Spanish Mahogany Sideboard, Rosewood Davenport, Tapestry Banner Screens, Old Spanish Mahogany Arm Chair, Old Spanish Mahogany Telescope Dining Table, Old Spanish Mahogany Couch, 6 Old Spanish Mahogany Dining Room Chairs, 2 Old Mahogany Carving Chairs, Double-end Mahogany Couch, Wicker Arm Chair, Massive Marble Mantel-piece Clock, Bronze and Metal Ornaments, Plaques, 20-Piece Wedgewood Dessert Set, 1 pair Old Sheffield Plated Candlesticks, 1 pair Entree Dishes, Plated Cake and Fruit Baskets, Plated Salvers, Fish and Fruit Sets, Old Silver Spoons and Forks, China, Cut Glass, Engravings, Oil Paintings, Steel Fender and Irons, Coal Box, Lamps, Carpet, Rugs, Window Poles and Drapery, &c., &c.

DRAWING ROOM—2 Rosewood Cheffoniers with marble tops and plate-glass backs, Piano, Rosewood Piano Stool, 2 Rosewood Circular Tables on pillar and claw, 2 Rosewood Card Tables on pillar and claw, baize centres; 9-Piece Rosewood Suite, Rosewood Settee, Lady's Scroll-back Chair in Rosewood, Foot Stools, Cushions, 2 Large Overmantels in gilt frames, 1 pair Lustres, Tapestry Banner Screen, Walnut Needle-work Foot Stool, Ball-framed Chairs, Brass Curb, Fire Irons, Bronze Table Lamp, Fire Screen with painted panel, Black Lacquer Chair inlaid with Mother-of-Pearl, Carpet, Hearth Rugs, Tapestry and Lace Curtains, Brass Poles and Rings, &c., &c.

HALL, STAIRS & LANDING—Old Mahogany Grandfather Clock, 2 Old Spanish Mahogany Hall Chairs, Mahogany Side Table, Barometer, Metal Hall Stand, Mahogany Circular Table on pillar and claw, 2 Hall Lamps, Horns, Plant Stands & Pots, Stair Carpet and Rods, Linoleum and Mats, &c., &c.

STUDY—Old Mahogany Secretaire, glass case on top; Old Mahogany Sideboard, Book-case, sliding door, 9ft. x 7ft.; 1,000 Volumes of Books, Mahogany Card Table, 6 Spanish Mahogany Chairs, Gramaphone, 60 Records, Smoke Chair, Engravings, Oil Paintings, Prints, Steel Fender and Irons, Gun Case, Ornaments, &c., &c.

Contents of 6 BEDROOMS, containing the following:—Massive Spanish Mahogany Wardrobe, Spanish Mahogany Set of Drawers, Mahogany Dressing Tables, Mahogany Washstands, Mahogany Toilet Glasses, Mahogany Pedestal with marble top, Walnut Overmantel, 2 Spanish Mahogany Canopy Beds, Hair Mattresses, Bedding, Iron Bedsteads, Mahogany Towel Rails, Rosewood Table on pillar and claw, Walnut Side Table, Deal Presses, Lobby Drawers, Pine Dressing Tables and Washstands, Child's Collapsible Chair, Wall Mirrors, Boot Rack, Carpets, Linoleum, Rugs, Pictures, Ornaments, &c., &c.

KITCHEN & PANTRIES—Dresser and Plate Rack, 3 Large Kitchen Tables, Windsor Chairs, Clothes Horse, Delph, Pots and Pans, Dish Covers, Crocks, Kitchen and Culinary Utensils, Oil Drum, 50-gal. Oil Tank, Oil Cooker, Mangle, Oil Barrels, &c., &c.

WORK SHOP—3 Carpenters' Benches, Lathe, Carpenter's Tools, Sundries, Sweep's Brush, Chairs, Table, &c.

MOTOR HOUSE & HARNESS ROOM—English Built Ford Motor, 1914, Motor Car, Gent's Bicycle, Saddles, Bridles, Saddle Stands, &c., &c.

YARD & OUTSIDE EFFECTS—2 Five-year-old Horses, Cow in full milk, 1 Year-old Calf, 2 Farm Carts, Metal Roller, Hay Cutter, Pierce Mowing Machine, Tumbling Machine, 2 Double Harrows, Swing Plough, Turnip Sower, Light Grubber, 3-horse Cultivator, Drill Plough, Hay Cutter and Pulper, Metal Rick Stands, Cattle Racks, 2 Metal Boilers, 2 Slipes, Cross-cut Saw, Axes, Hedge Shears, Sand Riddle, Grains, Wheelbarrows, Shovels, Ladders, 1 Stock of Oats, Hay, 1 Ton Potatoes, 30 Load of Turf, 3 Tons Best English Oral Coal, Scrap Iron, Fire Wood, 2 Garden Seats, 50 Plants and Pots, &c., &c.

LIVE STOCK—20 Horned Ewes, 20 Cross-bred Ewes (between 2 and 3 years old), and about 20 Store Bullocks (1 to 2 years old).

ORDER OF SALE : 1st DAY—Dining Room, Drawing Room & Hall; Sale of Motor Cars at 1 o'clock, p.m.
2nd „ Study, Bedrooms, & Workshop.
3rd „ Kitchen & Outside Effects.

VIEW DAYS : FRIDAY & SATURDAY, 5th & 6th DECEMBER, 1924, from 11 till 3.

TERMS—Prompt Cash and 5 per cent. Auction Fees.   Admission to Sale by Catalogue, Price 1s., Refunded in Purchase.

THOMAS MALLON,

OBJETTE PRINTERS, ARMAGH.   AUCTIONEER, KEADY.

Mountain Lodge House Auction Notice dated December 1924

Chapter 2

Winter of Discontent

It happened in the winter of 1948. It seemed that the rain couldn't have come at a worse time. The Cloonroot area of Portadown consisted of good fertile land, with one drawback – some of it was low-lying ground.

Thomas John Hunniford was a member of a small Pentecostal church, just a few miles from the farm he worked at Clonroot with his wife Margaret Jane. A father and a husband, he had a desire to raise his children in the ways of the Lord and would be found at the Lord's Table breaking bread with his fellow believers at the Battlehill Apostolic Assembly every Sunday morning. He was a man of prayer and earnestly sought the Lord's mind on all the 'day to day' issues of life.

But recently Thomas John had been restless in spirit. Like Abraham of old, he felt that the Lord was prompting him to pack up his tent. And so Thomas John Hunniford put his house and farm up for sale. George Allen, a local auctioneer from Portadown, and a fellow believer, was entrusted with the sale of the farm. Like Abraham, Thomas John had no idea as to where he would move to; he only knew that if God was leading him in this decision, then God would provide.

A billboard went up and adverts were placed in the local newspapers, and Thomas John and his family waited with anticipation to see what God would do.

The weeks of waiting turned into the months of winter, yet no one came forward to buy the farm. Was it possible that he had not heard from God?

He had just decided to take the farm off the auctioneer's books when George Allen contacted him. "I have a man from Buckingham Gate in London, and he wants to invest money in Northern Ireland; would you still be willing to sell?"

George brought the gentleman over, but it was now wintertime and much of the farm was under water! The gentleman from the exclusive London suburb, just a stone's throw from Buckingham Palace, took his binoculars out of his bag and surveyed the land that might soon belong to him.

What he saw impressed him greatly – the flooded fields were as picturesque as beautiful lakes, and he immediately fell in love with Clonroot! The man from London made an offer for the farm that very day, offering far beyond what Thomas John anticipated. It was a real miracle – the farm was sold there and then!

But oftentimes one miracle just creates an opportunity for another. Now Thomas John had another problem! He asked George Allen, "What am I going to do now? I have no farm and no home."

Everyone knows that a farmer can't farm without a farm. But Thomas John's dilemma would soon be resolved in an equally remarkable manner. George Allen once again came to the rescue. George said to him, "Thomas John, I have the perfect farm for you," and so the two men travelled the twenty miles or so to view Mountain Lodge House and estate.

Bob Flanagan owned Mountain Lodge at the time, but had decided to sell up and move into the nearby village of Darkley, where he and his wife May would reside well into their latter years.

The big house was indeed an impressive affair, with its twelve foot high corniced ceilings and an arched window on the landing. A grand entrance consisting of three sandstone steps flanked by wrought iron railings on either side, led to the four panelled front door. White Georgian windows and a slated hipped roof added to the grandeur. It came complete with servants' quarters, stable block, carriage house and courtyard, and an impressive avenue lined on both sides with rhododendrons. Oak and beech trees, and rose bushes and lilac trees proudly adorned the grounds at the front of the house.

Along the back lane to the courtyard, the stone wall flanking the lane is diverted over the adjacent stream which spreads out into a wash bay sort of affair. A dam had been formed and this is reportedly known as Ireland's first car wash! It was where the servant would wash the carriage after it returned home.

At the entrance to the main avenue to the House stood a Gate Lodge, a peculiar hexagonal shaped building, sporting living quarters with a pony house attached to the rear. This little building would play a pivotal role in the Lord's plans for Thomas John in due course.

Along with the house and grounds came some 260 acres of farmland, which at some 800 feet above sea level would surely never flood! This land, unlike the fertile land of Clonroot, was near the top of a mountain and consisted largely of rock or bog. One hundred acres of the farm formed part of the mountain. However, just as Abram left the well watered plains of Jordan to his nephew Lot, in favour of the lands of Canaan, Thomas John was destined to leave the watery fertile farm at Clonroot, and make his way to the heathery hills of Darkley.

Just as the man from Buckingham Gate, London had sealed the purchase of the farm at Clonroot on the day he viewed it, before he left Mountain Lodge that day, Thomas John Hunniford agreed the price and bought the lease to the farm.

Clonroot is close to Portadown, and Portadown has often been known as the 'Hub of the North.' Although the Second World War had just recently ended, even in 1948 all the services and public utilities you required were close at hand and there was always the train from Portadown to Belfast for a shopping day out, or to pursue those things not readily available in the local town.

Mountain Lodge and the village of Darkley, on the other hand, were situated in what could only be described as 'the back end of nowhere.'

Thomas John brought the family to view his purchase, but some of them were not very happy at the prospect of living in such an isolated area. There was no electricity or gas lighting in the house at that time, only paraffin (kerosene) tilley lamps. However, the house did have a telephone, which was unusual for those days, and a wholesome water supply, which was pumped from a nearby well supplied by mountain springs.

Darkley had a very poor bus service (some would argue that it still has), and the nearest telephone was a couple of miles away at the 'Breague Crossroads. The main mode of transport was a bicycle, but at least it was downhill all the way to Armagh! (There was always the slim possibility of hitching a ride on a horse and cart on the return trip home!)

Thomas John Hunniford and his wife Margaret Jane

(Emily Greenow's parents)

Country houses such as this always have their own unique piece of history, and Mountain Lodge House is no different. As long as anyone remembers, stories have existed about this house being haunted. Thomas John's daughter, Emily Greenow, remembers the rumours well but says that in all the years she lived there, she never saw or heard anything untoward, although walking up or down the avenue at nights could be eerie enough, as the owls hooted at each other across the trees!

And so in the early part of 1949, Thomas John Hunniford moved his wife Margaret Jane and their children, Robin, Jim, Dinah, Maisie, George and youngest daughter Emily, up to Mountain Lodge.

Emily still remembers being assigned the task of painting all the large Georgian timber sash window frames throughout the house. Not a job for the faint hearted – indeed a good head for heights was called for! She recalls climbing out through the first floor windows and sitting on the window sill, while painting the outside of the big upstairs windows, applying the paint in long flowing strokes of the brush! Well, it would have been a heavy task to cart a ladder from window to window, and it was probably faster to climb out on the window sill anyway!

One of the first things Thomas John did on arriving at Mountain Lodge, was to arrange to have the telephone disconnected. It proved to be too expensive a commodity, with six young people in the house attempting to maintain contact with the outside world! However, in due course, he did have gas lighting installed in the house.

Later in the autumn of that year Thomas John's daughter Maisie was married from Mountain Lodge House.

Some of the Hunniford family standing on the front steps of Mountain Lodge House

Emily with her sisters on Maisie's Wedding day

Chapter 3

Chicken Houses and Pony Stalls
:: Seeking His Presence ::

Thomas John immediately sought opportunity to join himself and his family to a local fellowship of believers, where he could worship the Lord and break bread together with other brothers and sisters of like mind, who also knew and loved the Saviour. He found that there was no Pentecostal witness in the area, and so he visited a number of local churches and fellowships in the coming weeks, including a Brethren hall that then existed at Caramoyle crossroads (on the outskirts of Keady, a local town some three miles distant). However, not being one of their usual number, he wasn't permitted to participate in Communion with the Brethren, and so he continued to seek the mind of the Lord as to where the family's spiritual home should be.

For the time being, Thomas John continued to travel back to Portadown at weekends, to fellowship with the believers at the little Pentecostal Hall at Clonroot. During the week, he also started to attend a number of Faith Mission meetings in the local Keady area and, before long he met other Christians in the locality, to whom he offered encouragement and inspiration in all things concerning the scriptures.

It wasn't long before Thomas John began to arrange prayer meetings in the front Drawing Room in Mountain Lodge House, and of course some of those men whom he had met in the Faith Mission meetings were only too eager to attend. These were meetings filled with the Holy Ghost, and full of the presence of God. According to Thomas John's daughter Emily, "nobody went home until everyone had an opportunity to pray."

Mountain Lodge House
(the room to the right of the front door is where the prayer meetings began)

Those early days saw Jimmy, Sammy and Willie Gibson, along with Tommy Warnock and John Blackstock come in to the Mountain Lodge prayer meetings. Jimmy and Annie Gibson cycled across the border from McKelvey's Grove, a round trip of some ten miles! These people were passionate for the power of God and for the lost. They had a desire to see God break through in the area, and they sought the face of the Lord night after night, sometimes well into the early hours. They didn't know it then, but God was about to exceed their greatest expectations. Shortly, a new 'work' would be born out of prayer.

The prayer meeting in the house was now well established, and the men met to pray EVERY night during the winter months. By now, the quaint little gate lodge at the entrance to the front avenue had become vacant. And so the Lord began to unfold the next stage of His divine purpose to Thomas John.

The gate lodge had two bedrooms. Thomas John demolished the wall between the bedrooms, and also knocked out the back wall between the gate lodge and the pony house. He then dismantled a disused wooden hen house on the farm, and used the timber to make long benches to serve as seats. The benches didn't have any backs so there was little chance of anyone falling asleep, not that anyone would have been afforded the privilege of sleeping in those early Holy Ghost meetings anyway!

Two of the hen house windows were installed in the side wall of what was previously the pony house, and timber from the old pony stalls was used to make a small platform at the front. Two tilley lamps powered by paraffin oil provided the light, and a small pot belly stove produced some heat.

And so 'The Gate Lodge' was ready for the Lord's service. Thomas John would come over to the Gate Lodge early in the evening, and stoke up the stove so that the hall was warm when everyone arrived. On occasions, the old stove would smoke them all out of the hall!

Previously there had been no Pentecostal witness in this area. For the next two to three years a prayer meeting was held in the Gate Lodge two or three nights a week as other locals started to come in and join their number. His daughter Emily remembers these meetings well. According to her, those gatherings were rowdy prayer meetings.

In Acts19: *'Paul came to Ephesus, and finding certain disciples, he said unto them, "have ye received the Holy Ghost since ye believed?" And they said unto him, "we have not so much as heard whether there be any Holy Ghost." And when Paul had laid his hands upon them, the Holy Ghost came on them; and they spake with tongues, and prophesied.'*

Like these New Testament believers, the early members of this prayer meeting in the Gate Lodge were excited about their new found faith, and their freedom in the things of the Spirit.

Emily recalls, "There was no clock on the wall and no finishing time. The meeting never ended until every one had prayed. Most people came on bicycles, there weren't many cars in those days. There were a lot of bicycles around the Gate Lodge every night."

Some people began to come from further afield, from over the border (the Republic of Ireland) in cars. Some nights they would leave the meeting so full of the Holy Spirit, they would have to stop and 'sober up' before crossing the Customs Post!

Such an explosion of power and prayer was sure to attract the odd casual onlooker as well – not in the meetings, but lying around the bushes outside the Gate Lodge, listening to the commotion inside! Such was the volume of prayer going up inside the Gate Lodge that one such lad listening outside, reportedly shouted through the window, "Are you lot alright in there?" On another evening, the volume of prayer going up to the Throne of Grace was reportedly so urgent and so loud, that it was virtually impossible for one to begin to pray, before another would have seized the opportunity. One anxious soul eventually cried out loudly, "I want to pray!" Much to everyone's surprise the answer did not come from within but from without. "Pray like h***!" came the response from one of the country lads lying in the bushes outside the window listening to the prayer meeting!

Oh that as believers we would be so convicted, that we would be stirred in our spirit to seek the face of the Lord in such a manner once more! How this nation, more than ever, needs men and women of God who will learn the art of intercession! I believe the Lord gives the gift of intercession to certain believers, but I also firmly believe He calls each of us to intercede before Him for our families, our friends, our nation and our world. Oh that we would desire to wait upon Him, to seek afresh the anointing of the Holy Spirit upon and within our lives; that we would press beyond the Gift of Tongues and desire the remaining Gifts of the Spirit to be operational within our lives! In other words, a true Baptism of the Holy Spirit, giving power to witness as the scripture promises.

Pastor Kane from the Apostolic Church, along with two other men, came to the Gate Lodge to hold some meetings. They stayed in a caravan, and visited throughout the district during the daytime. Bob Flanagan (the previous owner of Mountain Lodge House) walked into the meeting one night. He had a daughter who was unable to attend school owing to illness, and asked the preacher if he thought God could do anything for her. Bob was from a Brethren background and really knew very little of God's power to heal. The preachers went to Bob Flanagan's house after the meeting that night and prayed for his daughter. She was completely healed and as a result the family came in and joined the fellowship.

A gospel mission was planned to take place during 1953, in Armaghbreague Presbyterian Church, just a short distance from Mountain Lodge. Once they became aware of this, Thomas John and Bob Flanagan began to meet in the Gatelodge EVERY night to pray for the area, imploring God to move in the mission.

In his book 'Armaghbreague Presbyterian Church – 150 Years of Christian Witness' local historian and author Trevor Geary, states:

"However, 1953 continued to be a busy year as a mission was also held. Mr Lockhart recalled, 'We had a mission in Armaghbreague which lasted 3 weeks. It was conducted by Mr David Hamilton, Secretary of the Belfast City Mission. He was an awfully nice fellow, and a great preacher. He's now deceased. He came to preach and as the weeks went by the attendance built up you know. We had a full church in 1953.'"

This mission in Armaghbreague Presbyterian Church produced a number of new converts. The Rev. Lockhart's report above testifies to this, as the Presbyterian church was filled in those days. Jim Clarke, a local man with little or no interest in spiritual matters, was invited to this mission. Both he and his wife Violet committed their lives to the Lord during these meetings. A little later they found their way to the Gate Lodge.

The 'Gate Lodge' at the entrance to Mountain Lodge House
(the original 'Pony House' is visible to the left of the photo)

Chapter 4

The Gate Lodge Days
:: 1953 – 1959 ::

The Mountain Lodge fellowship was now firmly established with a small band of Spirit-filled born again believers, and Thomas John encouraged them to meet with him and his family around the Lord's Table in the Gate Lodge on Sunday mornings. The converted building was capable of seating approximately fifty people.

A number of other local families joined themselves to them, including: Harold and Lizzie Browne; Albert Warmington; Tommy and Lily Warnock; The Johnstons; the Duffys; sisters Maud and Hannah Ward (now Maud Riddle and Hannah Coulter); Sam Joe Smith and family; Sam Wallace and others from across the border in the Republic of Ireland.

New people continued to turn up at the meetings week by week. Cecil Stewart, his brother Herbie and several others from the Monaghan area began to attend some of the services at this time.

Herbie, now an international evangelist pioneering new churches and digging wells in many impoverished areas of the world, from his base in New Holland, Michigan, USA, still remembers those early meetings in the Gate Lodge. He recalls:

"Early in my Christian experience, I heard about a small group of Believers who were meeting for communion on Sunday mornings. I started to attend regularly. That was my introduction to a new kind of living. Soon we discovered other meetings in Northern Ireland; one in Armagh, another in Portadown, then in Belfast. We were hungry. Very hungry.

Then another, yes another different kind of meeting. A friend, Sam Wallace, brought a few young people to a series of meetings in a 'Gate Lodge' on an estate called Mountain Lodge. The small Gate Lodge would originally have been the home of the security person. I can still picture the pillars, the big windows, the solid brick architecture inside, and the homemade benches (seats with no backs). Only a few country people attended. The location was in County Armagh - on the edge of our own home county, County Monaghan. This was on the border crossing between the then Irish Free State and Northern Ireland. Yet we had to motor for several miles, because of the unapproved road. A huge ditch and a large 'Road Closed' notice forced us to drive through the town of Keady.

A few tambourines, an accordion and joyful singing made the rafters ring. Then, a man by the name of Hunniford spoke on Ecclesiastes 4:12, *'If one prevail against him, two shall withstand him; and a threefold cord is not quickly broken.'* These meetings surely had a profound impact on my life, and placed a Gospel concept within my heart that has motivated me in the work of God for many years. This would later open a door to me, for preaching ministry in Mountain Lodge Pentecostal Church, even to this day."

The first international preacher to grace the platform of the Gate Lodge was Dick (Keith) Iverson from Portland, Oregon, USA. According to a report given in 1990 by the late Pastor Robin Hunniford, "Dick Iverson was greatly used, and the anointing of God was on him, and God honoured His Word with signs following. My mother (Thomas John's wife Margaret Jane) had arthritis in her hand and could not open it, and after prayer she was able to open it straight away. Each time Dick was in the country, he would come up and speak at the Sunday evening service. The place was packed; we couldn't get them all in." (Robin Hunniford was Thomas John's son and pastor of a Pentecostal church in Belfast known as the Railway Mission).

Another preacher who visited Mountain Lodge regularly in those days was Frank Bray from Cork, who always brought a team of about twenty others with him in a mini bus. Harold and Lizzie Browne would always have them for tea – a lot of hungry mouths to feed after a four or five hour journey from the southern tip of the Republic of Ireland all the way to Mountain Lodge!

John Houston, who as a young boy would travel from Belfast city to Mountain Lodge with his parents as they came to speak, remembers spending his entire summer holidays on the Brownes family farm – what a difference from city life! The Brownes, along with others in the fellowship, would regularly provide hospitality to visiting preachers during those formative days of the church.

Albert Chambers, a young Pentecostal preacher from Portadown, was a regular speaker at Mountain Lodge in those early days. He travelled to the meetings on his motor cycle, his young fiancée Dolly travelling pillion on the back! Eventually Albert popped the question and Dolly said 'yes' to marriage! Following the wedding, they spent their honeymoon on the Browne family farm. Harold, a bit of a comedian, made sure the marital bed was not conducive to a good night's rest – upon entering the bed, the young lovers found a layer of whins (gorse) neatly arranged under the sheets! A prickly start to married life!

Later in 1953, two young evangelists, Bob Mullan and David Greenow, came to the Gate Lodge to conduct a mission which lasted three months. This was a tremendous time of visitation and blessing. The meetings were packed each night. The gospel was preached and the sick were prayed for. Mrs Mullan made cushions stuffed with hay to soften the impact for those kneeling in prayer on the floor.   Emily remembers the condensation rising out of the cushions each night, once the stove got fired up. No double glazing or central heating in those days! The Pentecostal Assembly was now well established as a work of God in its own right.

The fellowship then decided to hold a one day tent rally in the field to the right of the avenue leading to Mountain Lodge House.

A large marquee was erected, and a preacher from Nigeria was invited to preach. Outside caterers were brought in to provide food. Hundreds of people came to the all day meeting. Joan Owens (nee Montgomery) from Antrim, now 73 years old, remembers being invited along to sing by Alex Scofield. She recalls standing as a teenager inside the tent, on a hay cart for a platform, with her sister Molly and two cousins Sandra Goudy and Gladys Montgomery. She said it was a great day.

During the months (and years) that followed, much more was seen of the young evangelist David Greenow as he continued to frequent the meetings long after the mission ended! Romance was blossoming and in October of 1956, David married Thomas John's youngest daughter Emily. One might well wonder if there was an ulterior motive in the mission lasting so long! When Emily approached the minister of Armaghbreague Presbyterian Church to set a wedding date, he directed her to Second Keady Presbyterian Church in the town instead. He said her guests would never find 'The Breague' Church! David Greenow, who originally came from Herefordshire, was a popular young preacher who would live his entire life in service for his Master. David was also an excellent Bible teacher and came to be known all over the British Isles and further afield, in Pentecostal circles. He came to be in high demand as a speaker in Canada, USA and Germany, to name but a few countries. David, who passed into the Lord's presence on Friday 4th May 2012 aged 84 years, was to remain a lifelong friend of the Assembly at Mountain Lodge right up to his death.

In February 1957, a mission was organised to take place in Darkley Orange Hall, just one and a half miles away on the main Keady – Newtownhamilton Road. The mission was conducted by farmer, John Reid, locally known as the 'Prophet of the Moy' (Moy being a small village in Co Tyrone, close to where Mr Reid resided). Such was this preacher's desire for the things of God, that should someone arrive at his house for prayer, he would immediately leave the hay field or the farm yard to attend to the more pressing matter on hand – a soul to be saved or a body in need of prayer for healing!

David & Emily Greenow in more recent years

A local farmer, living two miles away, was invited to attend the mission by his neighbour, Harold Browne (Harold was one of the founding members of the Mountain Lodge Assembly). Bob did not really want to go to the mission but Harold was persistent, calling regularly at Bob's house to invite him along. Eventually, he gave in; he would go along one night. He heard, as he said, the four square gospel which he had never heard before; that Jesus was the Saviour, Healer, Baptiser and Coming King. He heard testimonies of healing and of the power of the Holy Spirit not only in salvation, but also in our personal lives to witness.

Bob went home that night and took the Bible down to check for himself whether these things were true. Like the Thessalonians in Acts 17, he *"received the word with all readiness of mind, and searched the scriptures daily, whether those things were so."* He continued to attend the mission each night along with some of his children. His oldest son Tommy remembers those meetings well, as at the mission on the evening of 20th February 1957, he made a personal commitment to the Lord and became a Christian.

And so Bob Bain and his wife Margaret started to attend the meetings at the Gate Lodge, and with a family of young children they certainly swelled the numbers! About that time Bob's sister Lily, his brother Tommy and wife Eileen also started to attend the meetings.

Bob's daughter recalls that her father took John Reid and another man called Ben Beattie up to Newtownhamilton, to visit a woman dying in the final stages of cancer. The men prayed for her, laying hands on her in accordance with the scriptures (Mark 16:18; James 5:14). She made a full recovery and lived well into old age.

Bob Bain's life and that of his family was to take a new direction. He could not have known it then, but God was already raising up a future leader in Bob, a leader who would face some of the greatest challenges any church leader has ever encountered. Before 1958 would draw to a close, Bob's brother, sister and sister-in-law would all go home to be with the Lord: three deaths within a period of six months.

Bob felt like selling up the farm and moving away but instead he remained steadfast. However he was to face even more difficult times, but that would not be for some years to come.

John Reid, the 'Prophet of the Moy'

Chapter 5

Moving on with God
1959-1970 :: The First Hall

By 1956, Thomas John Hunniford saw the need to make provision for the future establishment of the work. The Gate Lodge was fast out growing its purpose. He asked a surveyor to map out a parcel of ground which fronted the Mountain Lodge Road, just a few yards from the Gate Lodge, for the construction of a future building. (Obviously at some earlier time the cottage and four acres previously referred to as in the ownership of William Bigham had been purchased by the owners of the Mountain Lodge estate).

Under the leading of the Holy Spirit, Thomas John then appointed the following trustees; James Clarke, Thomas Warnock, Samuel Gibson, Harold Browne and himself. The fellowship continued to meet in the Gate Lodge until they felt the time had come to erect a hall on the piece of land Thomas John had given them.

A new hall, capable of seating around seventy people, was opened in 1959.

This was a new chapter in the history of Mountain Lodge as the work went from strength to strength.

Willie Gibson played the organ, and at times the accordion, and thus provided the music. Willie would introduce new hymns on a regular basis, and visiting speakers often brought new choruses which would have been sung sufficiently often for everyone to learn the words off by heart, before the meeting ended. No need for modern multi-media projectors back then, folk just sang the song until they knew it – but what an anointing came down! Roy Turner (England) wrote many of the four line choruses at that time, which are still a blessing to so many today.

Another mission was held shortly thereafter, conducted by the late Miss Edith Neville and Miss Sadie Carson (now Mrs Billy Davidson of Markethill Elim Church). A number of children came to the Lord during that mission, many of whom are still going on with the Lord today, and some have entered Christian ministry.

One local lady who sang regularly at Miss Neville's missions, was the late Madge Foster (nee McGeeney). Madge was well known for singing the gospel, and often spoke fondly of the meetings in Mountain Lodge. She talked of the 'early days' and especially of the mission conducted by Miss Neville, whom she described as a forthright, fiery, faithful preacher of the gospel! Sally Bain (the current pastor's wife) was one of those who became a Christian in that mission. In the words of Florence McGeeney, the song that Madge often sang during the mission proclaims the ministry of Mountain Lodge:

I dreamed I searched heaven for you;
Searched vainly through heaven for you:
Friend, won't you prepare to meet me up there,
Lest we should search heaven for you.

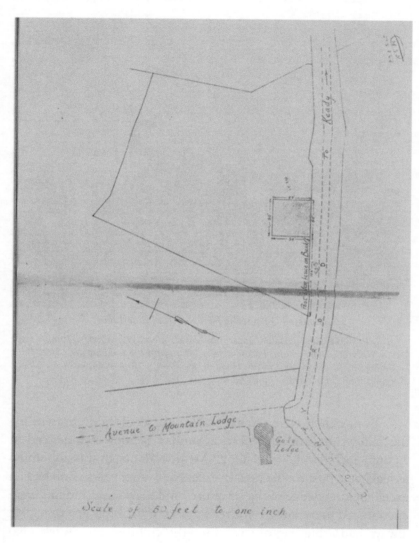

The Surveyors map of the Plot for the first new Hall

Gathered Outside the First New Hall (late 1960s)

<u>L-R:</u> *Willie Gibson; Willie Frazer; Jim Clarke; Albert Warmington; Tommy Bain; David Williams; Bobby Bain; Pastor Robert Bain (with the tambourine); Sally Bain; Louie Frazer; Mrs Browne; Marion Hadden; Mr Priestly; Ann Williams; Jean Clarke; Margaret Bain; Mrs McAfee; James Gibson.*

By now there were a considerable number of children attending the fellowship, and therefore a Sunday School commenced at 3.00pm each Sunday afternoon. Mr Bob Flanagan was appointed as teacher, a position he held in excess of twenty years. Bob had an excellent knowledge of the scriptures and his young students were encouraged to memorize entire chapters of the Bible at a time! He always had a big bag of sweets for the children each week. No thoughts of gum disease back then!

When Bob retired from the Sunday School Alex Frazer and Barbara Bain were appointed in his place.

Pentecostal preachers from all over the world began to turn

up at Mountain Lodge Pentecostal Assembly, as the work had now become known from countries as far away as Australia, USA and Canada as well as from all over the British Isles and the Republic of Ireland.

Others began to frequent the meetings at Mountain Lodge from time to time as well, like the Cuddy family from Dungannon and Fred Hopper from Moy. The blessing of God was flowing in fullest measure and people had a desire to be in His presence.

Then just as suddenly as God had spoken to Thomas John in the first place, so the Lord was to speak to him again. The ordering of church business during the previous years was not without a reason.

The Lord had other plans for Thomas John, which would necessitate him returning to the Portadown area once more. Thomas John would soon be on the move again. His son George, who was now married, was to be given charge of the Mountain Lodge House and land.

Chapter 6

A Tambourine and a Song Book
:: 1969 ::

No two meetings were ever the same in those days – and the same is still true today! Different folk would be moved to share a scripture or start a chorus. This particular meeting just started out like any other normal Sunday morning service for Bob Bain. Then it happened. Thomas John handed Bob a hymn book and told him to go up and lead the meeting. Nervous though he was, Bob was not one to back away from a challenge. He had a good singing voice and before long he was not only leading the meeting but also playing the tambourine. It was no ordinary tambourine. Bob's tambourine was nearly as large as a side drum and was arrayed with a ring of tuning keys around its perimeter, and it sported a number of colourful ribbons which flowed in the warm air as Bob kept the beat. Bob is remembered for many things, some of which will be recorded later, but one of those is most definitely his ability to play the tambourine in his own unique way.

Now that Bob Bain was leading the meetings on a regular basis, Thomas John felt it was time to relocate to Portadown again. Bob was appointed as pastor to lead the flock.

Bob was thrown in at the deep end. He was a farmer, without the benefit of any Bible College training, but it soon became very evident that the hand of the Lord was mightily upon his life. Not only was he a good singer, but also a capable leader, and one who spent much time seeking the Lord in prayer.

One lady recalls how she came under conviction of sin in the meeting, as Pastor Bob led the hymn, '*When the roll is called up yonder, I'll be there.*' He threw out the challenge, "Don't sing the words of the hymn unless you know that you are going to be there!" This lady, who was only 13 years old at the time, was so convicted of her need of the Saviour that she returned home in tears and promptly repented, asking the Lord Jesus Christ into her life as Saviour, and she still faithfully walks with Him today.

The Rev Anderson, a Presbyterian minister in Armagh, was greatly used of God in a divine healing ministry at that time. Pastor Bob would have regularly taken him to pray with those who were sick. On one occasion Pastor Bob received a request from a man who was seriously ill. Bob had no telephone in his home in those days. He therefore attempted to phone the Rev. Anderson from a public telephone at Armaghbreague crossroads, about two miles away. The Rev. Anderson was unable to come, and Pastor Bob was now in something of a dilemma – the man was far from well! Bob felt the Holy Spirit say to him, "Why don't you go and pray for him yourself?" So Bob set off for the man's house, and began to pray the prayer of faith, according to the scriptures. The man was completely healed and lived for many years. This was the beginning of a healing ministry that would become a major part of Pastor Bob's life.

The Assembly began to hold conventions at Easter and at Christmas, each of them spanning two days. The people travelled for miles to enjoy the blessing of God. Two meetings were held each day, with tea between. The new hall had gas lights and a gas heater. Water was transported in aluminium milk churns from Bob Bain's house to make the tea. Loaves of sandwiches were made by the ladies and four hundred buns were usually ordered from McCullagh's home bakery in Keady. When announcing the Convention meetings Pastor Bob would usually say, "If you don't come in time, there will be nothing left but bun papers!" Cups had to be taken home and washed: there was no such thing as disposable cups in those days. It would be some years yet before the church would have the benefit of running water, but as long as the 'new wine' was in abundance, folk didn't mind having to fetch water.

Such was the anointing in those meetings that Florence McGeeney from Loughgilly, Markethill, remembers her introduction to Mountain Lodge very well. Florence, who has been a member of Mountain Lodge for many years, tells her own story:

"I was saved in 1955 during a mission run by Mr Boland and Mr Grant in Glenanne Orange Hall, and then a little later my Auntie and I were invited to Pentecostal meetings in Mountain Lodge.

These meetings were new to us. We loved the singing, powerful preaching and praying. I remember being so conscious of God's presence in the Saturday night meetings. I told friends and family and some of them came with us. Bobby Herron and others gave us a lift in their car, and so we made many new friends over the years.

I remember Jimmy Gibson, his brother Willie on the accordion, the Clarke family and all the others, many of whom are in the Glory now.

In 1959, I had the most wonderful experience (after salvation). I went along to the Mountain Lodge convention with my cousin Kathleen, and remember so well sitting in the fourth row up. Walker Gorman prayed for us after the first meeting. We were immediately baptized in the Holy Spirit and lay under His power all during the tea break. Then the second meeting started and we have often laughed that we missed our tea. Fifty three years later I am still rejoicing that I missed my tea but received the power! As I travel to Heaven rejoicing in salvation, I often thank God for a place called Mountain Lodge."

Oh that such wonderful times of blessing might continually flow in abundance within our churches!

Many visiting speakers came not only to the conventions, but also to speak at the Sunday meetings, some of them travelling to Mountain Lodge to minister at both Sunday services. Those stopping for both meetings would usually be treated to lunch at Pastor Bob's house. Most Sunday evenings the visiting preachers would be invited back to the home of Jim Clarke, Harold Browne or Bob Bain for supper. Very often, other members of the congregation would be invited back as well, for a time of singing and ministry, especially if some were still seeking the Baptism in the Holy Spirit. Pastor Bob would entertain the preachers afterwards, while many a night his daughters would fetch the cows in for milking! You see, Pastor Bob was not only a pastor, he was also a full time farmer and life had to go on.

Such English and Scottish preachers included Eddie Smith, David Willows, Brian Smithyman, David Nellist, Jackie Ritchie, Arthur Burt, Louie Cardno, Ken Harwood and others.

From these local shores, Pastor Roy Kerr, Herbie Stewart, Cecil Stewart, Keith Gerner, Alex Scofield, Billy Shearer and the Victory Testimony Team, Willie and Lillie Worthington, Mrs Foster, Harry Creighton, Eddie Moir, Sidney and Meta Greer, Sid Murray, Alan Williamson, Harry Wright, Bob Gilmore, Freddie Hopper, Ernie Busby, David Ervine and Jimmy Horner preached regularly in those early days. All who came into the meetings were greatly blessed, the anointing was flowing, people were getting saved and many experienced healing after prayer.

One such preacher was Jimmy Stafford from Belfast, who was well known for his prophetic ministry. On one such visit around 1969, he prophesied during one of the meetings that the Lord was going to fill the vacant seats, and bring in a people we had never known. The church saw the fulfillment of this prophecy unfold before their eyes within three months!

The Whytes from Castleblayney, the Dougan families, David and Doreen Wilson, Gary and Hilary Anderson, the Agnews, the Hughes, Alex Frazer, the Lowe family from Crossmaglen and many others all came in around this time. Adele Lowe played the piano in Mountain Lodge for a number of years, a position she took over from Heather Warnock. Wesley Walker played the drums at that time. Many others from local churches began attending the Sunday evening meetings, as they did not have an evening service in their own church. Many of these local families still frequent the meetings on a regular basis today, including the Giffin families, Iris McBride, Alex and Eileen Patterson and Ken Gordon.

Pastor Robert (Bob) Bain with his colourful tambourine

Chapter 7

"This was Real!"

:: Away 'Till after Midnight ::

Gary Anderson, now pastor of Lisnadill Full Gospel Church, like many others, was introduced to Mountain Lodge through a friend, in this case, a Mr Sam Agnew. Gary recalls:

"One Tuesday evening in January 1970, I entered for the first time a tiny wooden Gospel Hall on a South Armagh hillside, an event which would dramatically alter the shape and course of my life. Having been converted just four months earlier from within a fairly predictable evangelical setting, this would come as a quite dramatic culture shock.

I was immediately struck by the spontaneity and the unbridled enthusiasm of the noisy worship. Men and women with their hands aloft, singing unrestrained to the accompaniment of an accordion and Pastor Bob Bain's decorative tambourine. Besides Bob and his wife and family, Jim and Violet Clarke were there, Jimmy and Annie Gibson, Willie and Louie Frazer, David and Doreen Wilson, Rita Lester and Bob Flanagan. Many of these have gone to be with the Lord whilst others have remained lifelong friends.

I can still remember the hymn being sung over and over again - *"Is not this the Land of Beulah?"* This type of scenario was all entirely new to my experience and although I was somewhat apprehensive at the start because of the unstructured simplicity of the worship, there was no denying of the tangible presence of the Spirit of Almighty God in the midst of His people. I was smitten! Here the bible was presented not just as an historic book but its promises were available by faith today! Now! In the everyday situations of life!

Testimonies were shared, stories of answered prayer last month! Last week! Yesterday! Credible testimonies of life-changing crisis situations. This was real! I learned about the Holy Spirit giving a 'Baptism' of power in the believer's life and the wonderful availability of the 'Gifts of the Holy Spirit' today.

I remember fondly also the Easter and Christmas conventions, with so many visiting preachers and singers. There was Eddie Moir, Billy Shearer, Brian Smithyman and Eddie Smith. There was Robert McDowell a simple soul from Tandragee with his unusual falsetto singing voice, and a host of others too numerous to mention.

I remember also in the year 1975 bringing an 18 year old called David Bell, none of us realising that his future would be linked with Mountain Lodge as their Pastor in the years ahead, and also as a member of the Bain family through marriage.

In conclusion, I can also vividly remember in November 1983, waking up one Monday morning as a patient in the high dependency unit of an Enniskillen hospital, and learning of the horrors of the terrorist shooting the night before, and the untimely deaths of three good friends. I also remember, on behalf of the church, replying to a sample of the hundreds of letters received from across the world and, in particular, one from Prime Minister Margaret Thatcher who wrote a very personal note to Pastor Bain, offering her sincere condolences. I thank God for those days of great fellowship and the effect that many of these wonderful people had on my life."

"Away till after midnight"

In those days, as stated previously, most of those who found their way to Mountain Lodge did so through the invitation of a friend or work colleague. This is also true of the late Sinclair Halliday from Mountnorris, who was introduced to Mountain Lodge in 1969 through a Mr George Jamison. Sinclair's son,

Pastor Barrie Halliday, now the pastor of Fivemilehill Pentecostal Church, with the help of his mother, recalls the story of the night his father first attended Mountain Lodge:

"The story my father, who was born and bred a Baptist, gave us when asked of his introduction to Pentecost is as follows. During the late 1960's he found the going tough and lonely on the road to Heaven. Then God moved in, through my father meeting a Mr George Jamison, who was selling grain. One night they got talking, and my father felt 'Here is a man who understands.' George Jamison invited my father to a wee place called Mountain Lodge where they prayed for the sick.

Here my mother takes over. "Sinclair was away to past midnight and I wondered what was happening but when he arrived home he put my mind at rest, saying 'I have met people with love and joy who believe the whole bible.'" Mum says he talked the whole night long of there being more than just being saved.

After much persuasion, Mum (who was from a Brethren / Baptist background) agreed to go to Mountain Lodge. She often says, 'I thought they were mad, but they had love and compassion like I'd never seen in a church before. Glyn Greenow and David Greenow spoke and prayed with power and Holy Ghost help'.

The Bain, Clarke and Gibson families all reached out to my parents. Those early days made an impression on my father. When the Baptists moved from our land into Newry town in 1970, my father with the help and guidance of David Greenow, Jim Clarke, John Nabi, Sam Agnew and David Wilson, who all shared the vision for a Pentecostal witness in the Whitecross to Bessbrook area, began holding some meetings, and so the work began, with many coming to faith and multitudes prayed for and filled with the Holy Spirit.

As children we found it fascinating watching Bob Bain playing the tambourine and singing choruses many times over. A game we played as children, I'm told, was stamping on the devil, like Bob Bain told us to do! Fivemilehill Pentecostal Fellowship still maintains a Pentecostal witness in the Mountnorris area.

We say with thankfulness, a visit to Mountain Lodge nearly forty five years ago changed our lives and also the lives of many of our neighbours."

Chapter 8

Don't put down your Spoon
:: 'Til You've Stopped Suppin! ::

Many local Presbyterian and Church of Ireland folks began to attend the gospel services in Mountain Lodge, as their own church didn't have an evening service. One such couple who attended the meetings regularly were Thomas and Mrs McBride. Their daughter Iris, who for many years served as a missionary to India, takes up the story:

"My association with Mountain Lodge Pentecostal Church goes back as far as 1970. As our own church, Second Keady Presbyterian Church, didn't have a regular evening service and my mother didn't feel up to attending a morning service, my parents attended the six o'clock evening service at Mountain Lodge. I have to say that a Pentecostal church wouldn't have been my father's choice, but once introduced, he got to enjoy the hearty singing of the good old gospel hymns. When I returned home from India on furlough, I too went along in Dad's wee Morris Minor car.

My memories are of Pastor Bob Bain walking back and forth with his tambourine, and singing verses, not just once or twice. Sometimes he would ask for a volunteer to read a verse which meant a lot to them, of the hymn we were singing, and then we'd sing that verse again - and maybe the others after it - to the end of the hymn. Worship at Mountain Lodge was both enthusiastic and genuine.

There was usually a visiting speaker each night, and when we'd sung ourselves hoarse, we settled down to listen to an interesting message, with maybe a testimony or a solo. Sometimes we picked up practical advice too. I recall one business man, telling a story about his son. He told how his son's wife had left him – and emptied his bank book. He recounted how he was thankful that he hadn't yet handed over his own business to his son. That's a long time ago. He expressed it in this way, 'Don't put down your spoon 'til you've stopped suppin'!'

I was out in India at the time of the attack on the Mountain Lodge church. I heard about it on BBC, but the location wasn't specified. A couple of weeks passed, and I got a letter from home. My parents had not been present at Mountain Lodge that night. It so happened that two weeks previous to the attack, Dad's car had mounted the pavement on the way home coming through Keady, and my mother refused to go with him the following Sunday. Dad went along by himself. But the next Sunday, he too didn't go. That was the night of the attack. Thank God for His mercy.

I have mentioned the good singing already. Nowadays, we are led in singing by a youth group plus organ, piano and drums. Then however, it was Pastor Bob himself with the tambourine, and the organ and piano, played by two of his family.

Mountain Lodge has always been strong on healing and the Gifts of the Holy Spirit. People are invited to come out for prayer for healing, or to receive the Holy Spirit, or to respond to the Gospel.

There weren't too many long faces in the meetings. People enjoyed the services and felt welcome. There were always a few leaders at the door to greet us, and give us a hymn book. Apart from the welcome and the warmth and comfortable seating, Mountain Lodge was more than generous in giving to God's work. I myself, though not a member, received several generous gifts while on the mission field. They had a great interest in mission (and still have) and I had opportunities on home leave, (or furlough as it was known then), of telling about the radio work I was doing in India and Nepal.

I thank God for Mountain Lodge. My life has been enriched by the fellowship I received there."

Chapter 9

Fire on the Mountain
:: *1971* ::

The blessing of God was flowing in abundance. New folk were coming into the meetings. People were getting saved and baptized in the Holy Spirit. Keith Gerner from Holywood, Co Down was a regular speaker at the meetings and, when the need arose, he would bring a portable swimming pool with him, which would be erected at the back of the hall to facilitate the baptism of believers by full immersion. The tank was filled using 'clean' water transported in a slurry tanker! Many believers were baptized at this time. Pastor Robin Hunniford, Thomas John's son, was also a regular speaker in those early days.

Among the many new people who came into the meetings at that time was a young woman whose heart was touched by the Holy Spirit. She began to attend regularly for a time.

On the morning of Friday 9th July 1971, Harold Browne came running down into Pastor Bob's farmyard. "The hall is on fire!" he said. Pastor Bob's immediate reaction was – "We are always looking for the fire!" (He was referring to the fire of the Holy Spirit). Harold said, "I'm not joking – there's a fire on the mountain!" The two men travelled the short distance to the Mountain Lodge hall where they witnessed the building collapse before their eyes! They were devastated by what they saw. The new hall was gone!

The boyfriend of the young lady who had recently begun to attend the meetings was convicted by the authorities for burning the hall down. He was sentenced to two years imprisonment. The police investigation was recorded in the local newspaper, where the church was referred to as the Aughnagurgan Pentecostal Church. Now the believers who faithfully met there each week were left without a building in which to worship.

The fellowship therefore immediately began to look for alternative places where they could meet in the meantime, while they considered their options. They were able to borrow a disused Hall at Corkley, just a short distance away, which was kindly loaned by Jimmy Reaney, a local farmer. The fellowship set to and cleaned the hall up, borrowed some seats and had their first service in it the following week. Johnny and Molly Wilson arranged for the loan of some 'Songs of Victory' hymn books from Camagh Mission Hall. Corkley Hall would become the new spiritual home to the fellowship for the next eleven months.

This new venue presented challenges all of its own. There weren't many facilities in the hall that had just been burned down, but there were even less in the Corkley Hall. The ladies were fortunate in that there was one toilet on site but the brethren had to find refuge elsewhere!

The blessing continued to flow; there was a very real sense of the Lord's presence in every meeting. Wonderful fellowship was to be had around the Lord's Table on Sunday mornings and two conventions were also held in the hall during those eleven months.

One young man who came in to the meetings at that time in Corkley Hall was Victor Cunningham. Victor had never been in a Pentecostal meeting before, and had never heard anyone speak in tongues. The praise and worship was lively. Brian Smithyman from England was preaching, and Victor said he "left with a sore head and wouldn't be back!" But he was convicted. He was back within days for more. Victor soon realised that these Pentecostal people had something he did not have, but desperately wanted. It wasn't long before he was saved, baptized in water and baptized in the Holy Spirit. Victor and his wife Edna were to become valued members of the fellowship.

Meanwhile, the fellowship had been seeking God as to what to do about the future of the work. Corkley Hall was just a temporary solution, and they knew God would supply their need.

Corkley Hall today

Chapter 10

House of Cedar

:: 1972 ::

"... the house which king Solomon built for the LORD... So he built the house, and finished it; and covered the house with beams and boards of cedar." 1 Kings 6:2, 9.

David Wilson had a dream. In the dream he saw a new cedar-wood building. What was unique about the building in the dream, was the fact that the cedar wood boards covering the exterior of the walls were fixed horizontally, while at that time it was customary for the boards on a building of this nature to be fixed vertically.

According to Willie Frazier (now living in Scotland), eight or nine of the men travelled to Lisburn to view buildings being manufactured by 'John McGowan & Sons Ltd,' a firm who specialised in the construction of timber-framed modular units. A price was agreed and the firm were appointed to manufacture and erect the new hall.

Noel Robinson, a local surveyor, was asked to prepare plans for the new building and obtain Planning Permission, which was duly granted on 15th February 1972.

The new hall cost £2150, a lot of money back in those days for a small fellowship to find but a faithful God supplied every need. All the families gave £100 each, and the cost was quickly met, so David Wilson offered to pay for the new fence along the roadside in front of the hall.

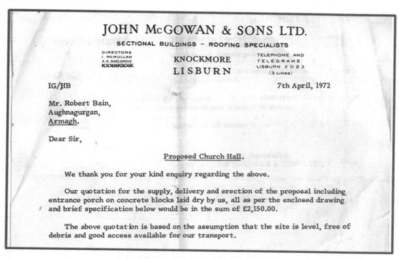

JOHN McGOWAN & SONS LTD.

SECTIONAL BUILDINGS - ROOFING SPECIALISTS

DIRECTORS
I. McMULLAN
A.C. SNELGROVE
XXXXXXXXX

KNOCKMORE
LISBURN

TELEPHONE AND
TELEGRAMS
LISBURN 2 0 2 3
(3 Lines)

IG/HB   7th April, 1972

Mr. Robert Bain,
Aughnagurgan,
Armagh.

Dear Sir,

Proposed Church Hall.

We thank you for your kind enquiry regarding the above.

Our quotation for the supply, delivery and erection of the proposal including entrance porch on concrete blocks laid dry by us, all as per the enclosed drawing and brief specification below would be in the sum of £2,150.00.

The above quotation is based on the assumption that the site is level, free of debris and good access available for our transport.

The original Quote for the New Hall

On 24th June 1972, less than one year after the fire, the new hall was opened on the site of the previous one, having taken just three days to erect!

The local newspaper advertisement in the Armagh Gazette for the previous week, states that Pastor Aubrey Whittal (of Armagh Elim Church) officially opened the new building. Pastor Whittal, David Greenow and Sid Murray were the main speakers and some of the older members of the congregation still remember David Greenow's text on that day from the Old Testament book of Haggai relating to the dedication of the temple –

'Then came the word of the LORD by Haggai the prophet, saying,

Is it time for you, O ye, to dwell in your ceiled houses and this house lie waste?...Go up to the mountain, and bring wood, and build the house; and I will take pleasure in it, and I will be glorified, saith the LORD ... and they came and did work in the house of the LORD of hosts, their God... **In the four and twentieth** *day of the sixth month, in the second year of Darius the king.'*

David emphasised that, just as the Old Testament temple was completed on the twenty fourth day of the sixth month, so the members and friends of Mountain Lodge Pentecostal Assembly opened their new church building on the twenty fourth of June!

The new hall was to be known as 'Mountain Lodge Pentecostal Assembly'.

SPECIAL OPENING RALLY
MOUNTAIN LODGE PENTECOSTAL ASSEMBLY
will open their New Church

ON SATURDAY, 24th JUNE at 6.30 p.m.

Speakers—Pastor WHITTAL,

Evangelists DAVID GREENOW, SIDNEY MURRAY.

Everyone Warmly Welcomed

Notice contained in the Armagh Gazette: edition dated 22nd June 1972

Willie Frazer manufactured and erected two wooden cubicles to serve as dry toilets at the back of the hall, using matching cedar wood timber. There was still no running water or electricity at the site. Gas lighting and heating were once again installed.

For many years the Sunday School children performed a drama each year to a packed hall, based on a bible story. One such drama, still remembered by some, was based on the story of the prodigal son, and another on the Christmas nativity (see photograph in colour section).

Rodney Wilson (son of David and Doreen Wilson) remembers participating in those plays and shares his memories of these, as well as other events:

"I remember the Christmas plays at Mountain Lodge, probably because as a young lad in my teenage years, I enjoyed being asked to perform the role of Master of Ceremonies on at least a couple of occasions!

I vividly remember Clyde Shields and the Filipino Choir singing the song *'I know, I know, I surely do know that I've been born again.'* I still recall one of them sharing how as a child he had been raised in a shoe box!

I also recall how Jim Clarke always greeted everyone at the door, with an infectious smile and a big bear hug.

I remember well the night I got saved – Harry Creighton preached on the Second Coming of Christ with a vivid illustration using something like a glass bowl representing the world, and the church (Christians) being taken up out of it. That was in 1973 when I was seven years old.

Mum and Dad attended the Prayer Meeting every Tuesday night, while my aunt Yvonne cared for my sister Esther and me. I remember Brian Smithyman staying in our home one time, while he ministered in Mountain Lodge. He dedicated my sister Esther to the Lord. I remember lots of courting going on, with young lads driving suped-up cars like Escorts and Avengers in the 'seventies."

To facilitate believers seeking to follow the Lord in obedience through the waters of baptism, a galvanised steel water storage tank was installed in the ground behind the hall. Very few of today's modern conveniences existed back then. No indoor baptisteries! Many believers were baptised in this out-door tank over the years, and experienced much blessing as a result.

'I'm Hungry, Lord'

During 1972 and again in 1973, Pastor Fred Dunn and a team of fourteen travelled from Sheffield, England, to minister in various churches in Northern Ireland for about a week. Their itinerary included meetings in Mountain Lodge, where there were great times of blessing in the new hall, still fondly remembered by some in the fellowship today.

You can imagine the surprise, when in August 2012 - forty years later - some of the team who came at that time, turned up at the Sunday morning meeting! What a joy to meet John and Helen Simms and Wendy Connerton after all those years. In December 2012, they wrote to Pastor David, giving an account of what they remember of the meetings back in 1972-73.

John writes: "In the autumn of 1972, my wife Helen and I had the privilege of providing transport and accompanying our late minister, Pastor Fred Dunn and his wife Edith, to visit a number of churches in Northern Ireland. The contacts were made by Brother David Greenow, and so we were made welcome to minister and fellowship with God's people night after night, enjoying the rich blessing of God, and the generous hospitality and company of His people in this lovely area.

Yes, it was in a time of trouble, and some places were like a war zone, but the Christians we met were zealous for God and confident in Him, stating in one place on a wayside pulpit, '*The terrorist cannot kill a Christian: they can only give him a swift passage to Heaven.*' On the 2nd October 1972, we arrived in good time, on a lonely hilltop near Keady, to find a simple wooden church building on an open site, with some trees, but not so many as to close the view of the beautiful locality, but where were the people to come from we wondered?

But come they did, as the time of the meeting drew near. That Monday night we were surprised to see so many people come. They sang with the enthusiasm of Pentecostal people, and the meeting was warm and open for the moving of the Holy Spirit. I was asked to give a word, although my ministry was with the organ, and really I was only the chauffeur for God's servant. Helen and Edith also gave a word of testimony briefly. Mr Dunn then preached under a powerful anointing from Revelations 13:7-9, on the state of the world, and the power of the work of the Lord in this conflict and tribulation of the latter days, to keep His people unto salvation.

Six men responded to an invitation to come forward for God to bless them. God met us in Church, and we also enjoyed rich fellowship, when we were welcomed by Pastor Bain and his wife to have supper with the family at their home. We still carry the lovely memory of this precious servant of God being respectfully served by his dear wife and five daughters in that Godly home."

After the 1972 trip, Edith (Pastor Dunn's wife) wrote, "Writing about the few days we recently spent in Ireland, the first thought is an appreciation of the hospitality given by the people over there. Everywhere, we were welcomed very warmly. But even more thrilling was the response to the ministry, both from pastors and congregation. There was no doubt that God was with us, from going out to coming back.

Times are very hard for the people of Ireland, and one can feel the spirit of fear that is abroad in the country, but the atmosphere we experienced in every meeting we had was one of love for God and the brethren. The Christians we met surprised us, with their ardent hunger for God and fellowship with His people, and we all were richly blessed with the unity and love we could feel in their presence.

Most of you heard Fred testify before we went, that he was not looking forward to the sea crossing, and I am pleased to say we saw God's hand in this, for the water was very still and calm, and we crossed both ways more comfortably than most train journeys. We thank you for your prayers and your support, making this journey possible."

Edith Dunn.

John's wife Helen had also kept a record of those meetings in 1972: "The overall picture of Northern Ireland was grim, but we found the Christians warm towards us and, more important, towards the Lord. It strengthened me in the Lord, sharing the same truths with people we have never met before, confirming and convincing me that the Spirit of Truth leads us into truth. Organisations seem to bind and blind people, but those with an open heart who seek God themselves, receive much from Him. Praise His name.

I think I can speak for us all when I say we gained more than we took to Ireland, and I can appreciate with Mr Dunn, his pleasure at being accepted as a man of God. The crossings were smooth, the weather was good. We stayed by the sea but it was far more than a holiday. God is good to us."

Helen Sims.

John continues: "In September 1973 we visited Mountain Lodge again with Mr Dunn, but this time there were fourteen of us, including our first baby aged three months. Again we stayed by the sea at Whitehaven, but joined fellowship at Mountain Lodge on the Friday and Saturday night, and Sunday morning and evening. Many sang and testified of the goodness of the Lord, and Brother Dunn preached under an anointing time and again. I can see him now, full of life and joy and the wonderful word of God, as he moved about the platform as if he was a young man, although he would have been then about fifty years old.

We carried a cabinet Wurlitzer organ with us, as well as our new baby boy, and so I was able to play and share the songs and choruses that we were being blessed with.

On 19th August 2012 Helen, Wendy Connerton and myself were in the area for the first time since then, and we found ourselves with a Sunday morning to choose where to go for worship, so we headed in the direction of Keady, to find Mountain Lodge

Pentecostal Assembly. What a joy and thrill to find that same wonderful blessing on the music, the singing and the worship, but in such a beautiful building. The welcome of those in the church, and the pleasure of sitting in the meeting with Mrs Bain again, touched us immensely.

The instant welcome of Pastor David Bell and his wife, and their hospitality, was so much appreciated. The fact that Mrs Bell remembered our coming, all those years before, and even remembered a chorus that we left with the church at that time, 'I'm hungry Lord, my soul cries out for Thee,' moved us, and confirmed the work of God. In the short time of fellowship, so many truths were agreed, and it confirmed as Helen wrote, that the Spirit of truth leads us into all truth. Wendy recalls during the 1973 visit, Pastor Bain with a very large tambourine, and she remembers the blessing and certainly appreciated finding it again when we visited in 2012."

I'm hungry Lord, I'm hungry Lord:
My soul cries out for Thee.
The Living Bread, the Wine of Life;
The One who quickens me.

Chapter 11

The 50 Mile Coach Ride
:: Coffee and Cream ::

In 1975 Gary Anderson, then the church secretary of Mountain Lodge, found himself seated on a coach next to a young man called David Bell, as they travelled from Aughnacloy to Belfast to hear a preacher called John Haggai. David was just eighteen years old and, as a young Christian, was seeking for all that God had for him. They were both travelling to some special meetings held in the Presbyterian Buildings; the transport had been organised by David's minister, the Rev. George Dickson, then in charge of Aughnacloy and Ballymagrane Presbyterian Churches in Co Tyrone.

As they travelled together, Gary introduced himself to David and they talked of things pertaining to the Holy Spirit for the entire duration of the journey! Such was the blessing that they enjoyed in fellowship that their conversation continued throughout the worship time, until someone in the row behind 'encouraged' them to cease talking!

Gary would prove to be instrumental in introducing this young man to Mountain Lodge Pentecostal Church. David, being from a Presbyterian background had become a Christian some ten years previously and, in his quest for all that the Lord had for him, sought every opportunity to fellowship with believers everywhere. Initially, he didn't even possess a driving license but that would not deter him from finding a way to travel to wherever the Lord would lead him, to meet with others in prayer and fellowship! He tells his own story:

"The Bible began to come alive to me, and I had an appetite

for the Scriptures and loved the fellowship of God's people. I soon found myself attending three prayer meetings a week, one in my local family church, and two in local Prayer Unions attached to the Faith Mission. One of these in particular became a real blessing to me. It was held each Wednesday night in the home of a Mr and Mrs Andrews, a godly Baptist couple who really loved the Lord. Maybe it was the boiled egg for supper each night after the meeting but the fellowship was sweet. By now I was in my mid teens and had finally acquired some wheels - only two though - and so Willie Reid and I cycled to the meeting and back each Wednesday evening, a round trip of about seven miles. Willie was an elder in my local church, another godly man who made a great impact on my young life, and what blessed fellowship we enjoyed together as we travelled to the meeting each week.

While at a youth meeting in school one evening, during my final years of secondary education a speaker from Belfast, Graeme Hall, challenged young people to follow Jesus and live for Him. About thirty young people committed their lives to the Lord that night, and so a Thursday night youth prayer meeting was started in a local home. Graeme began to show us from the scriptures that the Holy Spirit was given to us as Christians, not only to guide us but also to empower us for service. These were truly amazing meetings, spent each week in bible study and prayer. As my spiritual appetite increased for the presence and purpose of God in my life, I began to seek out other opportunities to meet with like-minded people.

For a period of time, I travelled by bicycle regularly to Markethill Elim Church, a round journey of forty miles each Sunday evening. I made some wonderful friends, and really benefited from the teaching of the Word of God. One conversation in Pastor Cottor's home stands out in particular. A young visiting student pastor was present, who was having difficulty grasping the concept of tithing our income to God. I clearly remember Pastor Cottor describing how he personally tithed of all that he owned.

The student couldn't grasp how the pastor donated part of a chair, for example, to God. Of course the explanation seemed so simple - he gave a tenth of his income to God before he bought the chair!

Then I was asked to go to a youth meeting one night to share my testimony, an opportunity I never turned down! My friend Gary (whom I had just recently met) collected me in his car, and we seemed to travel forever along minor country roads, until at last we arrived at the church. I immediately noticed the name over the door, a place I had already heard of - Mountain Lodge Pentecostal Assembly! For me, that was an incredible meeting, and one that was to change the path of my life. In particular, I recall a young man, Victor Cunningham, coming over to me after the meeting, welcoming me, and really encouraging me in the things of God. I will always remember Victor for his exuberance and encouragement. He was a perfect example of how we as Christians should live our lives. That night was a turning point for me – I could never be satisfied any longer with less than the full purpose of God for my life.

Over the coming months I began to attend Mountain Lodge, at first occasionally, and then more regularly. I was by this time involved in open air preaching and tract distribution in the local villages. Although I had no aspirations for any leadership position, I knew God was calling me into fellowship at Mountain Lodge. I began to be challenged and encouraged by the teaching I received in the meetings, and appreciated the openness and warmth of these new friends.

One family in particular, the Wilsons, took me under their wing, having me to their home for lunch each Sunday between the meetings. This meant I no longer had to make the forty mile round trip back home between the services, and so I began to attend both Sunday meetings on a regular basis. I particularly remember Doreen serving dessert, and then making coffee afterwards. Up until then I did not care for the taste of coffee. (I can remember attending a business meeting in a hotel a short time before, and being handed a cup of black coffee, with neither sugar nor milk in sight! I literally sought for a rubber plant and promptly gave it a good dose of caffeine!) However Doreen's coffee was different – a big dollop of left-over fresh whipped cream from the dessert was stirred into the cup! Scrumptious! From that moment I was addicted to coffee made with cream. Oh, and I must mention her home baking - such hospitality must surely have played a big part in my being drawn into the fellowship. David Wilson (who later became an elder in the church) quickly became a spiritual father to me and my 'best friend.'

I then followed the Lord through the waters of baptism by full immersion. I was baptised in a large inflatable swimming pool at Keith Gerner's house in Holywood, Co Down, and I also sought and received the Baptism of the Holy Spirit while at a house meeting in the village of Hamiltonsbawn one evening. I remember that evening well; I was determined not to leave until God had baptized me with His Holy Spirit!

My absence from the Sunday morning service at Ballymagrane Presbyterian Church was now becoming noticeable. Eventually one day my minister (and good friend) the Revd George Dickson called to visit me. I explained that I felt that the Lord was leading me into fellowship in Mountain Lodge Pentecostal Church, and that I had been baptised by immersion in water, and also had received the Baptism in the Holy Spirit. If I was concerned as to what his reaction would be I shouldn't have been. If I have ever seen grace at work I saw it that day. He prayed with me, said that "the Pentecostals are good people" and encouraged me to follow the leading of the Lord, although I would be missed in Ballymagrane. I have never forgotten his gracious words of encouragement as he released me into the plan and purpose of God for my life. He and I remained good friends, and during the few months prior to his home call, we enjoyed some wonderful times of fellowship together.

In June of 1983, David Wilson asked me to accompany him

to a Morris Cerrullo crusade in Glasgow, Scotland. During the crusade that week-end I experienced a wonderful miracle of healing when deteriorating vision was restored to my right eye. I immediately abandoned my spectacles, and a short time later had an eye test which indicated that my sight was normal in both eyes. From that moment I was assured of God's will to heal.

I certainly had no aspirations for leadership, and like the one whom I would eventually succeed, I had no formal training for the ministry, but the Lord already had a plan mapped out for my life."

(Pastor David Bell has served as minister of Mountain Lodge Pentecostal Church from 1990, until the present time).

Chapter 12

All in a Cuppa
:: The River of life ::

*"For whosoever shall give you a cup of water
to drink in My name, because ye belong to Christ,
verily I say unto you, he shall not lose his reward."*
St Mark 9:41.

During the seventies and eighties, several new faces came into Mountain Lodge, many of whom are still in the fellowship today. Robert Weir is one such person. Robert (Bobby) first entered the doors of Mountain Lodge Pentecostal Church in 1979, and has remained part of the fellowship ever since.

He recalls how he first met Pastor Bob Bain: "It was in 1979 when I first met Bob Bain. I was delivering a lorry load of meal. I had been to his farm a few times and each time he would come out and talk to me. Bob Bain showed me the love of God through his words and his hospitality. He always invited me in, and while his wife would make a cup of tea he talked to me about the Lord Jesus. Pastor Bob would tell of the things the Lord had done through prayer, how people had got healed and saved. He invited me up to the church, so I brought my family with me and we started to go to the evening meetings.

One year later I gave my life to the Lord. There was a drawing to the church. We enjoyed the lively singing and you could feel the power of the Lord around the place. One of my outstanding memories is getting baptised outside in a big tank and coming out of the water to the sound of people singing and praising God. It was a memory I'll never forget.

The church went from strength to strength. The presence of the Lord has still remained on the hilltop. Through the years I have been a witness to many signs of God's faithfulness. God has always been true to His word and, through many trials, we are called to be faithful also (2 Tim. 1:12).

For many years we raised money for the building fund, through selling refreshments on some of the marching days here in Northern Ireland. I have learned that if you are faithful in the little things, God will provide a bumper crop. One 12th July I witnessed crowds for what seemed to be miles long, waiting on us to provide food, while other tents were empty! We ran out of food, went and bought more, and sold it to a tent full of hungry men, women and children. I believe if God brings you to it, He will bring you through it. The hand of God has been on Mountain Lodge through many trials. We are a close family working together for the glory of God.

As I sit and reflect on my journey, I can say with assurance that I am truly blessed to be a part of Mountain Lodge Church."

Around the same time, Liz Brown (now Liz Gordon) from Brookeborough, also began attending the evening meetings. For those of you who think an eighty mile round trip a long journey to church, Liz - like so many young people attending the meetings - had an ulterior motive for travelling so far. She had become friendly with a young man, who was a native of Keady. Liz remembers the atmosphere in those early meetings:

"The first time I came to Mountain Lodge was in the autumn of 1979. I was invited along to an evening service. I can still remember feeling a real sense of God's presence in the meeting.

Then in the summer of 1988, after our marriage, Hugh and I felt God would have us worship at Mountain Lodge Church. Since then we have been blessed and encouraged in the fellowship, and under the leadership of Pastor David."

Her husband Hugh, on the other hand, recalls attending the evening meetings since childhood, as his parents brought their family along each Sunday evening to listen to the visiting speakers: "I have been attending Mountain Lodge since a boy. I always enjoyed the meetings especially the youth meeting. They were good. Our children have all been dedicated to the Lord in this church and they also enjoy worshipping at Mountain Lodge".

Hugh's brother Kenny also draws on his own recollections of his earliest visits to Mountain Lodge:

"Mountain Lodge holds a special place in my heart and life. I thank and praise God for all the teaching and ministry I have received over the years, for all those who have been faithful in sharing the Word, and for the prayers of God's people, and for God's healing hand upon my life.

Belonging to the local Presbyterian Church, we did not have an evening service on Sunday, so my earliest memories of attending Mountain Lodge were being sent along by my mother as a child, and we were really well looked after. I remember walking (sometimes hitching a ride) to the church for the Saturday night meetings and the conferences at Easter and Christmas (now the Camp). I particularly liked hearing the different speakers, the testimonies and the singers.

My late mother attended, as did the whole family, and she often remarked that even the singing seemed to lift you if you were feeling down. Bob Bain, the previous pastor (now deceased), was a very humble and gracious man and would have visited and prayed for our family. He played his tambourine with great gusto and had great singing ability, and often repeated the singing of choruses. Indeed, many would have phoned Bob for prayer for healing for themselves, and other family members. I even heard of him praying for sick animals! This was all done in Jesus' Name.

I recall the Sunday night in November 1983 when, as a student in Belfast, I heard the news of the terrible shooting, and wondered if any of our family were present. Thankfully, they were not. I shed tears and prayed for the families of those murdered and those injured.

The church is warm, welcoming and inviting. The people are friendly, caring and resilient. They reach out to the needy and hurting in the community, and show Christian love and forgiveness. They have been through the fire in more ways than one, yet many still attend the church from far and near. Pastor David Bell continues to lead the meetings today, and he also spoke at my mother's funeral service. She was a great believer in the power of prayer and enjoyed attending the meetings in Mountain Lodge.

Jesus is still the Saviour, Healer, Baptiser and Coming King today. I truly have been blessed and challenged, and continue to be ministered to, by attending the services. I pray God's richest blessing upon the church, and wish Pastor David well as he shepherds the flock. Yes, miracles still happen today. What a wonderful God we serve."

Strange as it may seem, the longer one walks with the Lord, the more one is astonished afresh at the 'little miracles' God does in and through our lives on a regular basis. Raymond and Kathryn Thompson still remember one such instance when the Lord met a very real need on their part. Kathryn takes up the story:

"We first came upon Mountain Lodge in the mid 1980s, when Raymond ministered on several occasions for Pastor Bob Bain. At that time Tommy Bain was the treasurer, and we remember on one specific occasion, Tommy handed Raymond an envelope after the Sunday morning meeting. Raymond was reluctant to take the envelope, and placed it in the glove compartment of the car.

Later that day we went for a drive, and the car began to

overheat. We drove the car to a mechanic on the Armagh Road and left it there. The next day the car was repaired (a new water pump was fitted), at the cost of £30. Later, when Raymond opened the envelope that Tommy had given him, it contained exactly £30!

In 2005 we felt the Lord calling us back to Northern Ireland, and after much prayer, we returned to South Armagh. On Sunday mornings, we began to visit a church that Raymond's mother had attended for over twenty years, and we went to Mountain Lodge on Sunday evenings. We were still praying and seeking the Lord, as to where our spiritual home was to be. One Sunday morning, the church's pastor announced that there would be no more morning meetings as the attendance was too low. We knew immediately that God was closing that door, and that Mountain Lodge was to be our spiritual home."

Many people have somehow found their way to Mountain Lodge over the years, mainly as a result of seeking the blessing of God. John and Doreen Greenaway's story is similar to most:

"Our experience of Mountain Lodge Church began in the summer of 1986. After we gave our hearts to the Lord, we had a hunger for more of God. We had heard of Mountain Lodge Church but didn't know where it was, so one Sunday afternoon we set off as a family to Keady. We drove around for over an hour, trying to find the church. Eventually we found it, arriving as the people were coming out!

The following Sunday we went back to the church, and found what we were seeking – a warm welcome, the presence of the Lord, and a love we had not experienced before. Pastor Bob Bain was such an encouragement to us. He had such a depth of faith in God that it touched our very beings. Once he said, 'Keep under the spout where the Power runs out!' We never forgot that. The times we have spent at Mountain Lodge have been life changing."

John and Doreen Greenaway came into Mountain Lodge and

discovered the things of the Spirit. They were from a Methodist background. For several years they continued to visit the meetings in Mountain Lodge regularly, while still attending their local Methodist church.

Some time later however, after being baptised in the Holy Spirit, they felt the Lord speaking to them, and began to hold some meetings in their home. This step eventually led to the creation of the 'River of Life Fellowship', which has evolved throughout the years and today consists of a sanctuary, complete with bedroom accommodation and conference facilities frequently used for Christian camps etc. For many years, the 'River of Life Fellowship' has also maintained a Charity Shop, and an integral part of their ministry has been to minister to those less fortunate than themselves.

John, Doreen and the members of the 'River of Life' continue to attend various special events at Mountain Lodge church throughout the course of the year, and a close bond exists between the two fellowships.

Chapter 13

Vision and Purpose
:: The Lighthouse ::

When a man's ways please the Lord,
He maketh even his enemies to be at peace with him.
Proverbs 16:7.

'Vision and Purpose'

Lexie Johnston, a member of Ballymena Elim Church, has been preaching in Mountain Lodge for many years, and still recalls the first time he came to preach:

"My first visit to Mountain Lodge Pentecostal Church was in the seventies, at the invitation of Pastor Bob Bain, and quite possibly through the recommendation of Brother David Greenow.

I remember well the long wooden building with the corrugated iron roof, and coming in through the small porch and up through the main hall to the prayer room behind the pulpit, for a time of prayer. I remember meeting Bob for the first time, and the extremely warm welcome he gave me.

I had envisaged in my mind a stone or brick built building on the top of a mountain, and although not stone or brick, it certainly was on the hill top, and the name always intrigued me. I remember like yesterday what I spoke on: *'Be ye not unequally yoked together with unbelievers'*, 2 Cor. 6:14. This message was burning in my heart!

At that time in my church, I was responsible for the 13-18 year old Bible Class, and we were discussing at length all the areas of relationships, and looking to the word of God for answers and the truth that we could with confidence build our lives upon, and by God's grace keep our relationships pure.

I spoke on the many ways that seem right and look right, and how our flesh yields to them, but they aren't right, and how we need to build on much more than our feelings.

In my mind I can still see the expressions on the faces of the people and families that were in the congregation. I remember Pastor Bob leading the hymn, *'Have you been to Jesus for the cleansing power, Are you washed in the blood of the Lamb?'*, and singing it over and over again with great fervour, *'Are you fully trusting in His grace this hour, Are you washed in the blood of the Lamb?'* Bob meant what he sang, and lived what he believed and preached.

Because he was a farmer, like myself, he had many answers to prayer with livestock, and it enthralled me and inspired me to pray for my own animals. I thank God for the input Brother Bob had in my life and walk with God.

I have been to Mountain Lodge many times since that Sunday evening and have always been blessed and refreshed, and my prayer to God for Mountain Lodge is that the sense of vision and purpose that inspired Bob Bain - a heart for the lost and broken, and those needing healing both physically and otherwise - will continue to be passed on from generation to generation. And now to all the brothers and sisters and young people in Mountain Lodge I, like Paul, salute you for your faithfulness to God and His Word, right up to this day. Please be encouraged and like the song Marty Tharp sings: *'You're of a special kind, for when He was on the cross you were on his mind.'"*

Indeed, it would be Lexie who would eventually introduce the Tharps, an American family, to Mountain Lodge ... but more about that later.

'The Lighthouse'

Like Lexie Johnston, Dr. Cecil Stewart OBE has been a regular speaker at Mountain Lodge for many years, and he likens the church to a lighthouse: "When I think of Mountain Lodge, it reminds me of a lighthouse sending beams out over the whole community, and giving hope to the hopeless, faith to the fearful, and healing to the broken, who have lost their purpose in life. From the earliest days when I visited Mountain Lodge, I can still remember the passion expressed in the singing of Gospel hymns that impacted so many of us. And who could forget Pastor Bob Bain's unique way of playing the tambourine?

The prayers of those who lifted their voices with such strong desire had a personal impact on me, and I'm sure the key to the success of Mountain Lodge has been largely due to the wholehearted and united prayer, that has been so evident from the beginning. For me it has been a great privilege to minister there over many years, and I've found the hearts of the people so open and responsive to the Word of God.

One of the most outstanding testimonies of the Mountain Lodge Church has been the amazing way they coped with the tragedy, when several precious people were shot dead by terrorists in a Sunday evening service. It would have been easy for the leadership to have closed the Church for fear of further attacks, especially following the overwhelming grief they must have experienced. But they showed outstanding courage as they dealt with such a major loss, and not only continued the work but built a new Church with increased influence for the Kingdom of God. Rarely has a Church manifested such steadfastness, and strong faith, in the midst of such suffering and loss.

Those of us who have had the privilege of being associated with Mountain Lodge for such a long time, have been filled with gratitude by the grace of God, revealed in such a powerful way by the leadership and congregation. We've learned so much more about the meaning of steadfastness, faithfulness and commitment.

The leadership of Pastor David Bell has had a great personal impact on me. Pastor Bell has stayed at the helm through the worst kind of storm anyone could imagine. His quiet, strong leadership has spoken louder than any words could say."

Chapter 14

Minutes, Missions and Ministry
:: 1976-1983 ::

Mountain Lodge Pentecostal Assembly has always been a missionary minded church. Many missionaries and mission organisations have been (and still are) supported by the church. Some records were destroyed in a later fire, (more about that later) and the earliest record available is therefore the first minute in a 1976 Minute Book.

The church minutes dated 11th December 1976 indicate that *'present were Robert Bain, Jimmy Gibson, Jim Clarke, Albert Warmington, Gary Anderson, Tommy Bain'*. No apologies were recorded so obviously these men formed the 'oversight' (or leadership) of the church at that time.

Item 11 recorded in the above minute states: *'proposed by T. Bain and seconded by R. Bain that David Greenow be approached to chair the ordaining of new Elders on the first Saturday he is available in January 1977. Carried unanimously'*. David Greenow had an apostolic ministry and provided a much needed spiritual covering to many independent churches and fellowships over the years. Tommy Bain remembers Jim Clarke, Bob Flanagan and Jimmy Gibson being installed as Elders at that time.

The minute referred to above goes on to record that *'the will of God in the matter of continuing the mission after Christmas be sought by the assembly, and a decision by Sunday 19th December be arrived at'*. The mission referred to was conducted in 1976 by two evangelists, Graham Sanderson and Espie Young. This mission was well attended as the two men stayed on site in a caravan and visited the homes in the area, praying with people and encouraging them to attend the meetings. Many people came in for the first time, some of whom were saved later as a result of the mission, and still frequently attend the meetings today. The gifts of the Spirit were in much evidence during these meetings. The leadership felt that God was at work and so they decided to continue after Christmas.

During August 2012, after not having been in contact for many years, Graham Sanderson and his wife Margaret walked into the service one Sunday morning! It was great to renew fellowship again after so long. They had chanced upon the details of the church services through the church's website. Modern technical innovations had eventually reached this bleak mountainside and now Mountain Lodge was reaching out to the world through the internet!

The minutes of 11th December 1976 also record that a decision was taken to forward a gift of £60 to missionaries Alie and Stella (Miracle Bible College, Philippine Islands). This would have been a substantial gift from a small fellowship at that time, considering that the same minute records a decision that £5 towards travelling expenses be given to part time preachers! This was probably more than adequate if you remember that petrol cost five shillings and six pence per gallon – about 33 pence in today's British currency!

The 1976 church minutes also records that 'estimates for thermostatically controlled electric central heating be obtained from Bobby Herron'. Electricity had by now obviously reached this backward area! It would however still be some years before a mains water supply would be available.

A further church minute states that other missionaries such as John and Sandra Levy, working with 'Christians in Action' received £30 (later increased to £40) per month and Wilf O'Brennan (evangelising in the Republic of Ireland) received £40 per month, later increased to £50 per month. £100 was also sent to Underground Evangelism.

The minutes dated Monday 5th June 1978 appear to indicate that a new committee had previously been appointed and, on the evening stated, the following were present at the committee: Gary Anderson, Alex Frazer, Robert (Bob) Flanagan, Harold Browne, Victor Cunningham and Jim Clarke. Robert Bain and James Gibson were obviously still members of the committee but appear to have been absent at the meeting outlined above. Their names however appear in the subsequent monthly minutes of the church.

The minutes of 3rd July 1978 state that it was *proposed by R. Flanagan and seconded by R. Bain that the morning meeting be left open for a trial period of one month*. This would provide opportunity for believers in the meeting to share any thought or scripture they felt the Lord had given them, as an encouragement to others. It was during meetings such as these, that many young people became accustomed to public speaking in the meetings, thus providing a valuable training ground for various forms of ministry throughout their lives.

A church minute dated 4th September 1978 states: *'that £150 be given to Miss Neville at the end of the mission'*. Miss Neville, who had previously conducted a very successful mission back in 1959, conducted a further evangelistic mission at Mountain Lodge during 1978, this time accompanied by Miss Vera Kelly.

A further minute dated 6th November 1978 indicated that it was *'decided to send £200 to Stanley Mawhinney and £100 to World Christian Ministries'*. At the following committee meeting on 4th December 1978 *'it was proposed by Alex. Frazer and seconded by Jim Clarke that £100 be sent to Mr and Mrs Wilf O'Brennan'*.

The minutes of 13th August 1979 indicate that a decision was taken to sell one hundred folding chairs, Jimmy Burney having been approached to obtain new upholstered seating for the hall. The decision was taken that he *'be given £150 as a token of appreciation for the work involved in the seating'*. It is also on record that 228 carpet tiles were purchased at that time to cover the floor of the hall. These would be more comfortable than the original wooden floor.

According to the minutes dated 6th October 1980, £27.20 was

the amount of the quarterly electricity bill, and the minutes dated 4th May 1981 state that £38.26 was paid to Mc Cullagh's Bakery for pastry; obviously the Easter Convention had just taken place! As Pastor Bob used to say, "... nothing left but bun papers the day after".

The minutes also show that Jimmy Burney provided minibuses at that time which transported people (mainly children) in from the surrounding villages and housing estates, to the Sunday evening meetings. The records show that the church paid for the fuel and the road tax for the buses.

The minutes indicate that the meetings continued to be advertised each week in the Armagh Gazette, a local weekly newspaper. Monthly support payments continued to be made to designated missionaries.

At a committee meeting held on 8th July 1983 it was *'proposed that a tape recorder and tapes be purchased by D. Bell for taping of meetings. Unanimous'*. From this point forward the Sunday morning and Sunday evening meetings would be recorded and copies made available to those who requested them.

The last recorded minute in this book is dated 4th November 1983, at which Gary Anderson, Jimmy Gibson, Robert Bain, Victor Cunningham and Alex Frazer were present. The record indicates that, after all cheques were accounted for, there was a bank balance of £264 and cash on hand of £42.61 making a balance of £306.61. No other business appears to have been transacted on the evening of that committee meeting.

Those present could never have known it then, but that would be the last committee meeting for at least three years. When the church committee would eventually re-convene, its composition would be very different from that of November 1983. In just a little over two weeks' time, an event would take place which would shake both the world and the 'church-at-large'. It would plunge this little fellowship of God's people into some very dark days and, as a result, place it on the world's map.

Chapter 15

A Dark Day
:: 1983 ::

Sunday 20th November 1983 began just like most other Sunday mornings for many of those who normally attended the Breaking of Bread (Communion) service at Mountain Lodge. For some, there were the necessary farming chores to be completed; for others, children had to be fed, washed and dressed for church. Those who had just worked the night shift in the local factory would prepare to attend the meeting before finally catching up on a few hours of much needed sleep. For those who travelled a distance, there were no customary Sunday morning lie-ins; the service started at eleven o'clock and most folks tended to arrive early. All had a great sense of anticipation of what God would do in their midst.

David Bell set off from his home at Aughnacloy (where he lived with his parents) around 10 am. It was only a thirty minute drive but he always liked to be early. His task was to record the services on cassette tape so that those who wished to hear the service again could obtain a copy later. Everyone agreed, as they fellowshipped together at the conclusion of the service, that it had been a good meeting that morning.

As the congregation dispersed around 12.30pm, David Bell made his way along the winding country roads to David and Doreen Wilson's house on the other side of Keady, about four miles away. Since he had begun to attend Mountain Lodge on a regular basis, David and Doreen had invited him back to their home for dinner each Sunday afternoon. He was keen for the fellowship and enjoyed spending time with the Wilsons and their two children

Rodney and Esther, discussing the things of God. He had grown particularly close to David Wilson, who had become a mentor and a spiritual father to him. The author relates some of the events that unfolded that day, in his own words, as he remembers them:

"Sundays were special to me. I looked forward each week with anticipation to the following weekend, when I would travel the twenty miles or so to Mountain Lodge Pentecostal Church where I would fellowship on Sunday morning with my brothers and sisters in Christ around the Lord's Table in the little wooden church situated on the top of the South Armagh hillside. One of our number would be asked to speak from the scriptures as we gathered together. On that morning I set off from home as usual with an air of spiritual expectation in my heart.

You see, at ten years of age I had responded to a talk given by a servant of God called Mervyn Moffatt (CEF worker) during some children's meetings held in Rehaghey Orange Hall, which was situated close to my home. I realised for the first time on that May evening in 1968 that I could never have any certainty of Heaven unless I repented of my sin, accepted God's offer of mercy and forgiveness, and invited the Lord Jesus to be Saviour and Lord of my life. So I did just that. From that moment I realised that my sinful past was forgiven, and I wanted more than anything else to serve the Lord whom I loved and who had given Himself for me!

As I travelled along those county roads that morning of the 20th November 1983, I sang songs and talked to the Lord in prayer. I prayed in tongues and worshipped Him. Eventually, I arrived at the church, having stopped along the way at a remote spot on the road. There I had parked up and spent a half hour or so reading the Scriptures and praying unto the Lord in preparation for the meeting, as was my usual custom. Such times were blessed moments and occur in our lives all too infrequently.

I had just recently begun dating a young woman who also attended the meetings. Since we both wanted to be sure that it was God's will for us to be together, we had agreed previously that we would not see each other for six weeks or so, instead we would pray individually seeking God's assurances that we were meant for each other. One previous Sunday morning as I walked towards my car, something within me propelled me to approach Pastor Bain's car, where his daughter Sally was already seated. As we chatted together Sally told me that she had asked the Lord to give her a sign that very morning that we were meant to be together. I had just confirmed the answer to her question as we chatted together! Herein lies an important truth for all those seeking the mind of the Lord concerning the choice of a spouse. Take time to pray, seek the will and mind of God and then, having determined it, have the courage to test it with a period of separation. That time apart will either release you from each other or it will bind you even closer together.

Sally and I decided we would keep our relationship quiet for just a little longer.

On the morning of 20th November I sat by a window on the left hand side of the hall, beside the recording equipment with which I recorded the entire morning and evening services. It was another good meeting that morning, and afterwards I chatted to many of the friends I had made since beginning to attend the morning services at Mountain Lodge.

I then followed behind David and Doreen Wilson as usual, to their home on the farm at 'The Temple', just a few miles from the church, for lunch. I had always enjoyed Doreen's cooking and this Sunday was no different. Dinner, a dessert and then the usual mug of coffee with its spoonful of left-over cream stirred in for good measure!

Lunch over, we settled back into the well padded sofa in the living room for our Sunday afternoon siesta. How I loved being around this family – our conversation always centred around the things of Zion, plus David had also come from a Presbyterian background and I could therefore easily identify with him on many matters. We watched the Sunday afternoon farming programme on television. Although I was raised on a farm, I never had much of an interest in farming, however the Sunday TV programme always seemed enjoyable to me, simply because I was in the company of this family whom I loved so much. Once the farming programme concluded, David would don his farming boots and set off to the yard to check the livestock and ensure all was well with the herd before preparing once more for church.

By this time our routine followed a similar pattern each Sunday afternoon – David would check the livestock, dress for church, and then he and I would set off together in my car (a little blue Daihatsu Charade) for the meeting. David and I always travelled to the Sunday evening meeting together in my car in order to arrive early so that I had time to set up the recording system and so that he was in time to join Victor and Harold in the porch to greet visitors. Doreen and the children would follow behind a little later in their car, arriving in time for the beginning of the service.

And so on Sunday evening, 20th November 1983, David Wilson and I arrived at Mountain Lodge at approximately 5.40pm, about twenty minutes before the service was due to start. I proceeded to set up the cassette recorder, while David joined the others in the porch.

Pastor Bain's son, Bobby, stepped onto the platform and led a time of worship as the congregation gathered. Bobby's wife Barbara was playing the organ, while his sister Minnie was at the keyboard. A congregation of approximately seventy people had gathered, about fifty adults and twenty children. The singing was in full flow, for Mountain Lodge was well known for its lively singing to the beat of Pastor Bob's tambourine!

The service that evening began by singing the choruses below in the following order (this information was taken from the tape recording of that evening's service). Each one was sung two or three times in succession –

My feet are on the Rock, the oil is on my head,
I'm drinking at the Fountain, feasting on the Bread,
My soul is filled with music; my heart is filled with song -
I'll praise my Saviour all day long.

***

Learning to lean, Learning to lean,
I'm learning to lean on Jesus.
Finding more power than I've ever dreamed;
I'm learning to lean on Jesus.

***

I am the Way, the Truth and the Life,
That's what Jesus said.
I am the Way, the Truth and the Life,
That's what Jesus said.
Without the Way there is no going,
Without the Truth there is no knowing.
Without the Life, there is no living,
I am the Way, the Truth and the Life,
That's what Jesus said.

***

He is worthy to be praised, who lifted me,
He is worthy to be praised, who set me free,
He is worthy to be praised, who opened heaven onto me,
He is worthy to be praised.

***

Mine! Mine! Mine! I know Thou art mine;
Saviour, dear Saviour, I know Thou art mine.

Following the singing of these choruses, Pastor Bob came to the front of the platform and led the congregation in the opening hymn, the words of which were-

Have you been to Jesus for the cleansing power,
Are you washed in the blood of the Lamb?
Are you fully trusting in His grace this hour,
Are you washed in the blood of the Lamb?

Are you washed in the blood,
In the soul cleansing blood of the Lamb?
Are your garments spotless? Are they white as snow?
Are you washed in the blood of the Lamb?

Are you walking daily by the Saviour's side?
Are you washed in the blood of the Lamb?
Do you rest each moment in the Crucified?
Are you washed in the blood of the Lamb?

When the Bridegroom cometh will your robes be white?
Are you washed in the blood of the Lamb?
Will your soul be ready for the mansions bright,
And be washed in the blood of the Lamb?

Lay aside the garments that are stained by sin,
And be washed in the blood of the Lamb;
There's a fountain flowing for the soul unclean,
O be washed in the blood of the Lamb!

The congregation had just begun to sing the final verse, *'Lay aside the garments that are stained by sin.'* And then it happened.

For a moment, we all thought someone was throwing pebbles against the outside of the window panes, on that wintry

November evening. It sounded just like the rattle of small stones on a tin roof. After all, very few of us had ever heard the sound of gun fire before! It took a few minutes for the reality of what was happening to sink in. Falling to the floor for cover, we realised all too quickly what was taking place – somehow our church had become the latest target in the Northern Ireland 'Troubles'.

David Wilson entered the main sanctuary and ran up the aisle, blood streaming from his face, shouting at everyone to take cover under the seats. A few moments later he fell to the ground, just outside the emergency exit door.

All instinctively obeyed his command and dived for cover beneath the long seats, lying there for what seemed an eternity. Eventually, the sound of the gun fire ceased. Miraculously, the automatic machine gun the terrorists were using had jammed. This action most certainly saved additional lives, although by now a number of people were dead and several others had suffered serious injuries.

How the words of the final verse of the hymn must have rung in the terrorist's ears as they began to open fire – *'Lay aside the garments that are stained by sin.'*

Only a few minutes had passed, but it seemed like it was for ever. People slowly began to rise from the floor. It became very evident that a number of people had been injured, mostly as a result of bullets penetrating the wooden walls of the building. Two gun men had entered the outer porch and had shot the three elders at point blank range. They had then re-loaded their rifles and proceeded to circle the outside of the building, firing through the external timber walls. Harold Browne and Victor Cunningham died instantly in the porch while David Wilson had exerted sufficient energy to run through the building, warning people to fall to the floor, before also dying from the fatal wounds he had received.

The eerie silence was almost as fearful as the gunfire. Violet

Clarke and I were amongst the first to rise from the floor. We set off for Clarke's house, approximately a half a mile away, where I phoned for an ambulance and police assistance. Mobile phones did not exist in those days.

After making the necessary telephone calls, we returned by car to the church where we found that the local doctor, Dr. Richard Dorman, was already on the scene and attending to the wounded. A number of ambulances arrived a short time later and the paramedics offered what assistance they could, before removing all the injured to Craigavon Area Hospital. Seven people in total were injured and three church elders were killed on that fateful evening."

William Whyte had five bullets embedded in his stomach. He was bleeding profusely when Pastor Bob came down to the back of the hall to pray for him. As he prayed the prayer of faith, the bleeding ceased immediately. However, the local doctor was of the opinion that so extensive were his wounds that it was unlikely that William would still be alive by the time he reached the hospital. It is a testimony to God's healing power that William is still alive today. William's wife's spine was grazed by another bullet; just millimetres separated her from being paralysed. Miraculously, a bullet passed through the trouser leg of their young son of just 18 months, without even grazing his flesh.

Bobby Herron and his wife Muriel had been attending the meetings for some time and enjoyed the fellowship each Sunday evening. They entered the building and sat in their usual place that night, about half way up the aisle on the right hand side. They fell to the floor seeking shelter, like everyone else. Moments later, as bullets whizzed through the air just inches above the floor, they were both hit in the leg. The gunmen had by now moved outside the porch and were circling around the wooden building, firing through the walls. Bobby would endure the physical pain of that wound for the rest of his life.

Sally Bain had also joined the others on the floor, like them thinking that this position would afford her some protection. By now bullets were flying in all directions. One passed through her elbow joint, totally demolishing it, and lodged in her thigh. She also was rushed by ambulance to Craigavon Area Hospital that night, where surgeons talked of amputating her right arm at the elbow as the joint that connected the bones above and below the elbow no longer existed! Thankfully they decided to defer that decision for a few days as it appeared that she still had feeling and movement in her fingers. That deferred decision was to prove crucial. In the coming months, Sally was fitted out with a brace at Musgrave Park Hospital which gave her some mechanical control over the movement and use of her right arm. This was a plastic and stainless steel hinged contraption that was strapped around her upper and lower arm. It had a hinged joint fitted with a ratchet type fitting which allowed her to raise and lower her right arm by lifting it with her left one. It was a dark day when she was advised that this was going to be her lot for life.

For almost two years she fitted it on each morning and removed it each evening before retiring to bed and was thankful for the help it provided. However, Sally was trusting God to fulfil His promise to her. He had told the Israelite children during their exodus from Egypt to Caanan in the Old Testament book of Exodus: *"I am the Lord that healeth thee"*. Sally knew that if God was true to His Word, then what He could do for them He could do for her. And so one morning she arose as usual, and found that she could raise her arm slightly. Only one thing was different – she hadn't fitted her brace – yet she had partially raised her arm. This was something that the consultant at Musgrave Park Hospital had said she would never do! And so the journey to recovery began. In the coming months she amazed the staff at the hospital as she continued to raise her arm more and more. Finally, they discharged her, concluding that a 'Greater Power' obviously had been at work.

Another family had travelled the fifty five miles from

Enniskillen that evening to be at the service. Ronnie Kenny, his wife Edith and their family had been booked to preach and sing. It was their first visit to Mountain Lodge. Before Edith could fall to the floor a bullet grazed her cheek, a scar she still carries to this day. Over the years that followed, the Kenny family became good friends of all at Mountain Lodge, and Edith still returns from time to time to fellowship with her brothers and sisters in the Lord.

Nigel Whyte and his girlfriend Cathy were seated close to the front of the hall. Nigel sustained a bullet wound in his leg, while the bridge of Cathy's nose was damaged and required bone restructuring and plastic surgery.

The police interviewed those present, but few could give any meaningful information as the gunmen had not entered the main building. By the time Pastor Bob and his family finally reached their home, the telephone was ringing red-hot. Families were anxious for news of relatives who might have been in the service. Well-wishers were keen to express their support and sympathy, having heard scant details on the recent news bulletin. Newspaper and television reporters were phoning for further information. Camera crews from local television stations began arriving at the house, while all the time the Bain family were anxious for news of their daughter Sally's welfare. Some time later that evening, when the dust settled a little, Pastor Bob and some of the family, together with David Bell set off for Craigavon Area Hospital to visit the injured, including Sally.

The Bullet-ridden Hall

The Aftermath inside the Hall

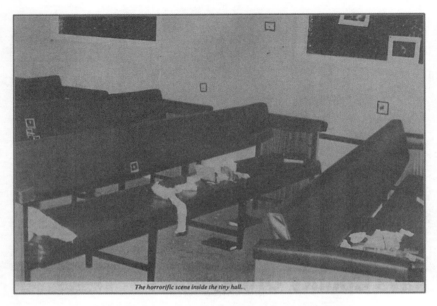

The horrorific scene inside the tiny hall..

The RUC 'Scenes of Crime Unit' marked the bullet holes

Chapter 16

Heaven's Triple Gain

As Christians, we are assured of the fact that our loss is Heaven's gain. The scriptures remind us that for the believer, to be absent from the body is to be present with the Lord. The Christian does not fear death because for him death is not final, it is just the gate-way to a greater and better life.

And so the three funeral services that followed during the next few days were a testimony to the fact that, in the words of scripture 'we sorrow, but not as those who have no hope'.

The following report on Victor Cunningham's funeral, the first of the three, was printed in the Armagh Gazette on 24th November 1983:

The singing of gospel hymns at the funeral of the first of the three massacre victims to be buried was only interrupted by the surges of an army helicopter and rooks in the tall copper beeches of the country church yard. At Tuesday afternoon's funeral of 39 year old Mr Victor Cunningham, it brought back memories of those who had been in the church on Sunday night. Mr Cunningham, like the other two victims Harold Browne and David Wilson, was an elder in the church.

And the pastor who was to conduct Sunday night's service, Mr Robert Bain, and who helped to carry the coffin, told the several hundred mourners at the graveside of the murdered man's great love for his place of worship. "Victor's better off than his killers, he's in the presence of his Lord whom he loved and had in his heart; we sorrow but we know that in the morning we'll meet again," he said.

In the home, which had earlier been visited by the four main church leaders, there was a service in which Pastor Bain, Pastor Jackie Ritchie from the north of Scotland, evangelist Harvey Shaw, and Pastor David Greenow and Pastor R A McMullan, both from Portadown took part. Pastor David Greenow, of IGO (International Gospel Outreach), who gave the address in the home, said he was praying for the killers of these innocent victims and he encouraged the mourners to pray for the government, for those in authority, for the bereaved and suffering relatives.

Mourners at the graveside were assured by Pastor Jackie Ritchie, who often preached at the Mountain Lodge, that the gunman does not kill the Christian; he only promotes him to Glory. He said everything was alright, "because some of us see the face of the Captain." "I met brother Victor, a man who knew his God. He had met the Master and knew the experience of the transforming power of the blood. This stood him in good stead for today," said Pastor Ritchie. "Victor Cunningham confessed God with his lips and in his life. He loved the Lord with all his heart and the lost souls of so many men and women. He prayed for many of you gathered around this grave." "The enemy may think he has got us on the run but NO! This is a day of victory for the people of God," said the pastor. "What a glorious way to die, welcoming people to the Mountain Lodge church. I can say, Victor, bless God, I'll meet you in the morning," he added.

Pastor Greenow prayed for "miracles of divine grace again, again and again" among the terrorists and murderers. The funeral services ended with the singing of the hymn 'Because He Lives' led by Pastor Bain.

The Irish Times reported on the funeral services of Harold Browne and David Wilson:

'Farmers, politicians and clergymen of several denominations walked in the funerals yesterday of the two Pentecostal elders, Mr Harold Browne and Mr David Wilson, shot during their service last Sunday at Darkley.

There was a strong sense in the crowded country churchyards of Armaghbreague and the Temple, both near Keady, of an evangelical community facing death as "the sweet bye and bye." ... The dominant note, however, at the funeral which started in the Browne farmhouse with a short service with strong singing and which ended in Armaghbreague churchyard with Pastor Robert Bain of Darkley leading the hymn, was of holy joy.

Pastor Bain brought cheers of "Hallelujah," "Praise God" and "Amen" for his insistence that God was working to change the tragedy in the Mountain Lodge gospel hall into a miracle of grace. "I never had such a burden on my heart like that I had on Sunday night, and I never felt such a great flow of the Spirit as after it – out of this tragedy people are coming to know God," he told a crowd, who said "Amen" softly between sentences.

"In a home last night I heard from a young woman that, when the tape of our hymn-singing was played on the radio, with that burst of gunfire that riddled the place in the middle of the last verse, as people listened, five young persons fell down on their knees and accepted Jesus Christ as their own personal Saviour."

The same minister officiated at both funerals. The Rev. Hazlett Lynch, of Armaghbreague and the Temple (First Keady) Presbyterian churches, invited Pastor Bain to his side in Armaghbreague to "lead us in worship". In the Temple, Rev. Lynch led the service and gave an address, dealing both with the triumph of a saved soul over death and a failure of the Government to protect the people in the Armagh countryside. "It was a time of despair", the minister said, "but there was another reality: a far more wonderful reality than that of terrorism – God. He was present in the most remarkable way over the past few days."

Among the crowds were the SDLP deputy leader, Mr Seamus Mallon; the DUP leader, the Rev. Ian Paisley; the Official Unionist Assemblyman for the area Mr Jim Nicholson and Mr Jim Kilfedder, the Assembly Speaker. A number of priests attended both funerals.

A group of men shook hands and swapped comments on the size of the crowd and the latest shooting: "a terrible state of affairs, a tragic thing. It's all over the world now. I heard the President of America sent his sympathy." They joined vigorously in singing 'In the Sweet Bye and Bye.' "I suppose they'll not be the last to go," said a man walking slowly away from the churchyard. His friend said nothing.'

The local newspaper, the 'Ulster Gazette' carried the following report in its edition dated 1st December 1983:

'Have you been to Jesus for the cleansing power?' Words which were sung in a lonely churchyard in South Armagh, and which rang out across the wide open prairie-style countryside and beyond, to the other side of the world. For those same words, sung as gunmen burst in and shot dead three elders in the Mountain Lodge Pentecostal Church near Darkley last Sunday week, and recorded by a worshipper taping the service on that horrific evening, had been heard through the media, in Australia.

And as Pastor Bob Bain, who was to conduct the service and who survived the attack, told upwards of 1000 mourners at the funeral of 59-year-old Mr Harold Browne, many listening to these recorded words amid the icy interjection of bullets had accepted Christ, touched by this tragic happening. The coffin of Mr Browne, a farmer and an elder in the church, was carried from his hillside home under the bright sun of a bitterly cold, but crisp and clear November morning to Armaghbreague Presbyterian Church.

The narrow laneway and minor roads were crammed with cars three abreast in places — abandoned. Everything was at a standstill as mourners exchanged handshakes and visited the farmhouse.

Many who witnessed the attack were there joined by all denominations from as far away as Dublin. Ulster politicians and churchmen turned out too.

In the home, the service was conducted by Pastor David Greenow of International Gospel Outreach, assisted by Pastor Eric McComb, Superintendent of Irish Pentecostal Churches; Rev. S. Allen, Methodist minister, Richhill; evangelist David Irvine, Rathfriland, who sang and Pastor David Duncan. Mourners waited; the aged kept back the tears, so did the young.

At the graveside, the countryside undulating for miles in all directions, and the singing of gospel-hymns giving a clear note of challenge, Pastor Robert McMullan of the Elim Pentecostal Church in Portadown denounced those responsible for the murders as a "satanic force" who had assaulted the church of Christ, but nothing, the gun included, "can separate us from the love of God." – "They had made the wrong move," he said. "Some would not even have done it to an animal but here were men coming into the house of God and taking it upon themselves to put three of our brothers into eternity," he said.

Many standing at the open grave broke down and wept. Assuring mourners that Christ was a Conqueror and that the three elders were with God, Pastor McMullan prayed that out of the tragedy, there would come a great Christian revival.

Pastor Bob Bain, who was on the platform when the gunmen burst in, helped to carry the coffins of all three victims. At the Browne graveside he said that while he had suffered personal tragedy before, nothing had hit him like this. "I'll never forget it," he said, remarking that out of the tragedy of those murdered, would flow the love of God. Five young people on hearing the tape on radio, had fallen down and accepted Christ, and he had even been contacted by people in Australia who had heard the tape and wanted to find out more. "The devil thought this was the end when our three elders, the cream of our Assembly were mown down, but it's not the end. We're going up and on. God is with us. I'm going to go on preaching the gospel, inviting people in, praying for the sick," said Pastor Bain who led mourners in the hymn, 'Have you been to Jesus for the cleansing power?' The Rev Hazlett Lynch, minister of First Keady and Armaghbreague Presbyterian Churches who had earlier taken part, committed the body to the ground. Meanwhile, dispersing mourners asked directions to the Wilson home from where the last victim of the massacre was to be buried.

A mile long queue of cars wound its way through Keady and around the border countryside to the home of father of two Mr David Wilson (44) from Killreavy. There was a service in the two storey farm house on top of the hill overlooking the church half a mile away, where interment followed. Taking part were Rev Hazlett Lynch, Pastor Eric McComb and Pastor John Nabi from Bangor.

Among the politicians present were the Assembly's Speaker, Mr Jim Kilfedder; Official Unionist MP for Newry/Armagh Mr. Jim Nicholson; Assembly members for Armagh, councillors Jim Speers, Alderman Mrs Mary Simpson (DUP) and deputy leader of the SDLP councillor Seamus Mallon. Mingling with the mourners were several local priests and nuns, and Protestants of all denominations from both sides of the border.

Conducting the service in the church was the minister, Rev Lynch, while Mr. David Hamilton, General secretary of the Belfast City Mission, a close friend of the Wilson family for over 30 years, prayed for the bereaved and those injured, and for the young that they would not suffer from ill effect, for peace and for those in authority. Neighbouring minister, Rev. W. R. Lindsay, read portions of scripture.

Mr. Lynch described the deaths of the three men as a "colossal loss". The whole land, including people in the United Kingdom, had been sickened and numbed by this attack he said, pointing out that his telephone had hardly stopped ringing with callers telling him of their horror and revulsion that people were compelled to live under such terrible conditions.

"They have confined us to the prison house of terror and frustration," he said. Over the past four years, Mr Lynch continued, they had witnessed atrocity after atrocity but never in their history, until this massacre, had they encountered depraved maniacs murdering people in the worship of God. No one imagined this could have taken place. "The terrifying consequences of this are that decent people are left living in a sense of fear, and wonder whose place of worship is going to be next. Every congregation is vulnerably open to attack."

Mr Lynch stressed the existence of a far more wonderful reality - God, real and in control, but sadly for many just a religious symbol. "There had been a wonderful sense of God's presence in the Wilson home, and the others, and it was God's faithfulness to His redeemed people that counted. The minister in this troubled part of South Armagh said it was easy to be a Christian when all was well but more difficult when murderous violence comes into churches. "There's a danger we could find ourselves doubting God and that would be a tragedy," said the preacher.

Urging the crammed-full church of mourners, many fighting back tears, to get right with God and warning of the end of non-Christians, Mr Lynch said David Wilson had had a place prepared for him by God — those remaining had been spared, but the desire of the Wilson family would be that the people of Ulster would become the children of God.

He had this concluding warning for the mourners. Pointing to the coffin with the single wreath of red roses on top he asked: "Who knows when you'll be lying there?"

The service ended and the coffin was borne out of the church to the graveside. It was now almost dark. With hands raised towards heaven, Mrs Wilson joined in the singing of 'There's a land that is fairer than day.'

Chapter 17

Death Produces New Life

Life in the Cunningham household felt complete; the anxious but exciting months that any young couple go through whilst awaiting the birth of their first child had been no different for them but finally in October 1971, Wendy, a beautiful baby girl arrived.

Wendy's birth wasn't the only important occurrence during October 1971, for during that month another birth also occurred. It was at that time that the young mother Edna, realising her need of a Saviour, invited the Lord Jesus into her heart and was "born again" of His Spirit.

The months that followed proved difficult, for Edna suffered from post-natal depression following the birth of their first child. However someone had told her that Pastor Bob Bain prayed for the sick, and Edna and her parents therefore set off to Corkley Orange Hall, where Mountain Lodge was temporally meeting following the fire that demolished their church building.

These meetings were quite unlike any other that Edna had attended before. They consisted of lively singing and exciting testimonies, but above all, a simple straightforward explanation of the scriptures and an awareness that the risen Christ was the Saviour, Healer, Baptiser and Coming King. Edna sought prayer for healing, realised her need of salvation, and subsequently in her own house invited Jesus into her life! During the weeks that followed she continued to frequent the meetings on a Sunday night at Mountain Lodge and on one such visit received the Baptism of the Holy Spirit under Brian Smithyman's ministry.

Meanwhile Victor couldn't understand her obsession with

church, and as a result he began to drink heavily! Eventually however, at Edna's insistence, he agreed to go with her one night to hear Brian Smithyman from England. As Brian opened the accordion out to its full potential, and the congregation raised their hands and voices in exuberant praise to the Lord, Victor had both seen and heard enough. He had come with a sore stomach but left with a sore head, saying he would never be back.

However, a few nights later, Victor was back! Something about that meeting had made an impression on him: the expressive worship had remained with him; the words of the songs flooded his mind; the presence of the Lord captivated him and the inspired preaching convicted him of his spiritual need.

A short time later, Victor, under conviction of sin, sought the help of Edna's brother Joe, who led him in the sinner's prayer. From that time Victor was always heard to quote Romans 10:9, *'If thou shalt confess with thy mouth the Lord Jesus, and believe in thine heart that God has raised Him from the dead, thou shalt be saved.'* Victor was a new man!

He and Edna began to attend the special meetings arranged by Mountain Lodge in Corkley Hall sharing their new found faith together, while at the same time continuing to regularly attend 1ˢᵗ Armagh Presbyterian Church in the local town, on Sunday mornings.

One Sunday following breakfast, the Cunningham family prepared for church as usual. Victor loaded their young daughter Wendy into the back of the car, and then he and Edna set off.

Edna recalls that morning as clearly as if it were yesterday. They had just travelled the half mile or so towards the crossroads junction at 'Beech Hill.' Victor should have indicated to turn right by now, but a quizzical momentary indecisive look on his face quickly gave way to the firm determined expression of one who had clearly made up his mind. Turning to Edna, he said, "We're going up to Mountain Lodge this morning," and swinging left at the crossroads, he headed in the direction of Keady. This would prove to be a decision that would alter the course of Victor and Edna Cunningham's life.

From that moment these two young converts began to attend the meetings in Mountain Lodge regularly, being some of the first to attend the new building. A short time later, during a Saturday night ministry meeting in the new church, Victor also was baptised in the Holy Spirit. Victor was a new man - a new creation - and one who could face each new day in the knowledge that his Saviour lived and dwelt within his heart!

When Pastor Bob would ask for a favourite chorus, Victor was always heard to request, "Because He lives."

Because He lives, I can face tomorrow;
Because He lives all fear is gone.
Because I know who holds the future,
And life is worth a-living just because He lives.

During the years that followed, Victor and Edna became an integral part of the Mountain Lodge family, their own little family expanding with the arrival of a son Jeremy. Always keen to seek fellowship with others of like mind, Victor and Edna attended the "Spiritual Feast" camp meetings at Portrush, Co. Antrim, where they met Robert and Elsie Caldwell and their son Trevor, from Omagh, with whom they formed a close friendship.

Learning that Gary Anderson, another member of Mountain Lodge, was in hospital Victor and Edna set off to visit him on the afternoon of 20th November 1983. They had a good time of fellowship with Gary before setting off again on their fifty mile journey home. It was ten to six when they arrived back at the Cunningham home, too late by all accounts to attend the six o'clock evening service at Mountain Lodge.

However, they had just entered the house, when Victor said,

"I can still make it; I'm going to the meeting!" Edna recalls telling him to drive carefully as he had just bought a more powerful car a short time before. Edna did not know it then, but the car would not be the thing to fear.

Some time later that evening, Doctor Richard Dorman rang Edna's door bell with the most unthinkable news – terrorists had entered Mountain Lodge Pentecostal Church during the evening service. Three men, including Victor, were dead and a number of others were injured! The words appeared to numb her mind for a moment. Victor was dead – taken in an instant. No opportunity to say goodbye – no time to prepare to meet God.

But then Victor did not need to prepare to meet his Maker – he had already done that some years ago, like one setting off on a long journey, knowing the commencement of the journey is inevitable, but unsure of how long it would take to reach the destination, and therefore sensing the need to make adequate preparation in advance.

In the midst of her pain and distress Edna knew that Victor was "present with the Lord". Victor was in Heaven. In her words, "Victor died in the place he loved."

Late that night, when the commotion had died down, Edna finally attempted to put her children to bed. It was then that Wendy turned to her mum and said, "I want to get saved, and I want to do it now, I want to meet Daddy in Heaven." Edna knelt by the bedside, and led her young daughter in the sinner's prayer that night, a decision that Wendy has held fast to all her life.

On Sunday 20th November 1983, the night that Victor Cunningham's natural life ended, his daughter Wendy's spiritual life had just begun.

Chapter 18

The Letter
:: I Found Faith ::

"The Letter"

There are incidents and events that, even if just for a moment, either directly or indirectly touch our lives in such a way as to serve as reminders of the past. Very often it is these somewhat unrelated happenings that spring-board us into memories for so long locked in the sub-conscious area of our mind and, thereby, bring release and freedom, a freedom that is only found through our faith in Jesus. One such event in the life of David Wilson's daughter Esther involved a fifteen year old letter. Esther recalls the story:

"It was the 16th February 2009. The news report was brief but graphic. A four year old boy had just witnessed his mother being shot dead at the wheel of their car in Surrey. In an instant, his life was changed. Nothing could have prepared him for this real life trauma.

For me, it was a poignant flashback. The years rolled back, the memories still fresh from a night in November 1983.

I was born into the home of farming family in Northern Ireland in the early 1970s. My dad and mum both worked on the farm, and my older brother and I enjoyed all the adventures and hard work that come with farming life.

Yet, already the scene had been set in Ireland for the violent years that became known as "the Troubles" – years which claimed over 3000 lives and maimed and injured thousands of others. Riots, gunfire and explosions, unrest and fear were part of life in Northern Ireland, as communities were split apart in bitter division over religion.

My dad was not involved with the security forces, and therefore we didn't need to take extra measures to ensure safety, as so many others did at that time. We didn't need to look under the car for booby traps before we set out on a journey, or keep looking behind our backs to make sure we were not being targeted. Safety was not an issue for us.

As a family, we attended a small church at Mountain Lodge, where my dad was an elder. My parents had brought us up to respect both Catholics and Protestants in our border town community, and at a young age I followed their example in developing a simple faith in Jesus. It was a faith that was to be severely tested during a church service, the year I turned twelve.

That evening, there was only enough strength for my dad to run up the centre aisle of the church, only breath enough for him to shout out to us to get down and take cover. There was only time enough for him, with the blood pouring from his head, to save the lives of those gathered in the small wooden church. No time for goodbyes.

There was time enough for him to save us, but no time to say goodbye. He breathed his last breath at the front of the church, on that vivid night of November 20th, 1983.

Just moments before, Dad had been welcoming people at the door. Suddenly, masked men had walked in and opened fire, killing two men instantly and mortally injuring my dad.

Gunfire halted worship that night. As the sounds of gunfire faded, the reality of what had just happened became clear. Three men lay dead. Many more were injured. This was not supposed to happen; this was not part of the plan! The days that followed were a blur, as our quiet farm became a haven for people coming from far and near to pay their respects and mourn the loss of a husband, father, son, brother and friend.

Grieving the loss of my father, friend and mentor did not come easily. As a family, our way of processing grief was to not talk about it. It wasn't until 15 years later that a long deep process of healing and grieving would begin. This process was the key that would unlock that empty dark place in my heart that I'd put the lid on so many years earlier, watching my dad being buried.

At this time, I began to envisage my dad's death from a different perspective, seeing it as the same process that births an oak tree. A small acorn, planted in the ground, has to be broken and die in order for new life to emerge. In the dark, its roots are being formed and are making their way deep into the soil – roots that will be needed to make the resulting tree stand tall and strong.

Armed with this new perspective, I found a framed picture in a drawer of our home, with an inscription which read "*A tree has been planted in Israel in memory of David Wilson, who died 20th November 1983.*" I went back to re-read newspapers from the time of the event, as well as the large number of sympathy cards we'd received. There was a letter with my name on it. It was a letter from a friend of my dad's that I did not recall having ever received. In the letter, that friend told me what my dad had been like and why I should be proud to be his daughter. The process of healing continued and took root in my heart.

When Jesus hung on the cross, He said "*Father forgive them, for they know not what they do.*" (Luke 23:34). Through his pain He still had time for the thief hanging beside Him. Even on the cross, He still heard the cry of the broken. Darkness covered the earth that day, just as the darkness hung over the earth the night of November 20th 1983, when my dad laid down his life to save us.

Whatever those gunmen had come to accomplish, their plans had been thwarted. I learned to sing, '*You give and take away, but my heart will choose to say, Lord blessed be Your Name.*' Now, as a worship leader, those words are very real to me, and a source of great comfort. God continues to give me many father figures in my life.

Healing does not happen in isolation. I have learned by

experience that real healing takes time. It occurs only in a place where God's presence, God's peace and God's people are. God promises in Jeremiah 29:11, *"I know the plans I have for you . . . plans to prosper and not to harm you, plans to give you hope and a future."* Although there will be times in our life when these words seem impossible to reconcile with our grief, God does have a plan for us, and we do indeed have a future and a hope."

(Esther Wilson is now married and living in Canada where she is a worship director of a local church).

"I Found Faith"

Rodney Wilson, Esther's brother, who now pioneers a Pentecostal work in Monaghan, in the Republic of Ireland, was a teenager when his father, David, was killed in the Darkley massacre. His memories of that night are vivid and the following is an extract from an article he wrote for a local newspaper where he pays a touching tribute to the man whom he knows died trying to protect others:

"It was a normal Sunday evening in November. After we had done the usual chores on the farm, Mum, Dad, my sister Esther and I set off for the meeting at Mountain Lodge.

We had a habit of being late and this particular Sunday was no exception. It was about ten past six when we walked into the porch and those present were already singing the opening hymn, *'Have you been to Jesus for the cleansing power, Are you washed in the blood of the Lamb?'*

We were welcomed by Dad's friends, Harold Browne and Victor Cunningham. Dad remained in the porch chatting with them, as the rest of us made our way in. We found a seat and joined in the singing.

Suddenly I was startled by a strange loud noise, the doors

behind us burst open, and the next thing I saw was Dad running up the aisle shouting 'Get down, get down!' He ran to the front of the hall and out through a door at the side of the pulpit into the kitchen. I then realised we were being attacked by gunmen. The gunfire continued for what seemed like an eternity.

When all the noise had stopped there was an eerie silence before everyone started to get up and move around in a daze. I went to look for Dad. I found him on the kitchen floor where he lay motionless. I couldn't believe that he had been shot. Someone confirmed my worse fears and told me he was dead. I thought that as I had just seen him run up the hall, he was ok. Sadly this was not the case and I couldn't believe what had just happened. Was it for real?

I soon realised that Dad was not the only person shot dead that evening, as his friends Harold and Victor had been killed too. The whole scene was unbelievable and unimaginable and it was hard for me to comprehend that it was really happening.

The terrorists were not expecting to encounter anyone on the porch. Their believed intentions were to open fire on a whole congregation from the rear. It was the presence of Dad, Harold and Victor that startled them and saved many lives including my own.

They opened fire on the three men and even though Dad had been shot and wounded, he found strength to run up the hall to warn us and also ensure the front outside door was closed to prevent them from entering the hall and causing more deaths.

The next few days were somewhat of a blur as Dad's funeral preparations got under way. Many people came to offer us support and help. Dad's funeral was well attended like the others but apart from that, I can't really remember much more about it and I put that down to the immense grief and loss I was feeling at the time. In the days that followed, Dad was sorely missed. We had grown very close as he and I worked on the family farm together.

I have many happy memories of my short time with Dad. I am forever grateful for the Godly example he set me and the role model he was. It was during this time that I witnessed the Christian values and Godly character in his life which I have tried to emulate.

As a young boy I learned that the gospel of Jesus Christ was able to save people from a lost eternity in Hell and at the age of seven fearing death without Christ as Saviour, I asked Jesus into my heart and life. From that moment the fear of dying without knowing that I would be in Heaven was gone, and I knew peace with God and the hope of eternal life with Christ. Ten years later that hope was to be the anchor in the severe and unexpected storm of loss and separation. Today I can truly thank God for keeping His hand upon our lives. We have experienced the power of the Gospel through forgiveness, healing and restoration which we believe is a true miracle of God's grace and love for all."

A group of fellow Christians from Dublin planted three trees in Israel in memory of Victor Cunningham, Harold Browne and David Wilson.

Chapter 19

The Dawn Chorus

The Browne family farm was similar to most others. There were cattle to feed, fences to fix, hedges to mend. The three boys had jobs to go to, so Harold would attend the weekly livestock sale-yard, where the local news would be exchanged with other neighbouring farmers.

A kindly hearted man, he had a great love for animals. He was a well loved husband and father, a respected member of the local community, and an elder in the local Pentecostal church at Mountain Lodge.

Harold, a hard working farmer, would rise with the dawn each morning, conscious of the long day's work ahead of him. His day always began with the reading of his bible, which usually lay open on the kitchen table, and then he would begin to sing, accompanied by Lassie, his faithful friend.

Harold loved singing, and it almost seemed Lassie knew every note, as the old sheep dog raised her voice in accompaniment to his! The family recall being woken more than once by the musical duet! Harold had two old favourites –

He poured in the oil and the wine;
The kind that restoreth my soul.
He found me bleeding and dying on the Jericho road,
And He poured in the oil and the wine.

There's a Light at the river,
A Light at the river,
A Light at the river, I can see.
My Lord will stand,
And hold in His hand,
A Light at the river for me.

The Sunday evening of the 20th November 1983 began just like any other. The 'redding up' had to be done; then it would be time to scrub up, and set off for the weekly Sunday evening meeting at the church.

A new family were coming to speak and sing that night, something interesting to look forward to. Harold only lived five minutes from the church, and so he arrived in good time, taking his usual place in the porch to welcome those arriving for the meeting.

He could never have known it, travelling to Mountain Lodge that night, but in just a few moments, as gunmen entered the building under the cover of darkness, a Light would shine at life's river bank for Harold, that would escort him into the immediate presence of his Saviour.

Life itself became a blur for the Browne family as they, like the others, began to prepare for Harold's funeral service. Again, like the others, a massive crowd of mourners attended the service. The family particularly remembers how, on the day of the funeral, local neighbours Catholic and Protestant alike from the village of Darkley and the outlying areas came over to the home, and prepared a three course dinner for one hundred and fifty family members and friends returning from the graveside.

Although, on the one hand, all this happened in a previous millennium, the events of that evening seem like yesterday in the memory of his family. In their words –

Each day that goes by, seems harder to bear,
When we wake in the morning, and you are not there.
We are told so often, 'Be patient, time heals'
But the people who tell us, don't know how it feels
To enter a room, when it's empty and lonely
And say to ourselves, 'If only, if only.'
When asked, how we are, we reply, 'Just fine'
But can anyone tell us, how long is time?

Chapter 20

The House of Commons

On Monday 21ˢᵗ November 1983, the day following the massacre, the events of the previous evening were discussed at length in the House of Commons in the Westminster Parliament. The following is a Hansard transcript of those discussions:

County Armagh: Church Shootings (House of Commons)

21 November 1983 vol 49 cc23-8   3.36 p.m.

§ *The Secretary of State for Northern Ireland (Mr. James Prior)*

I shall, with permission Mr. Speaker, make a statement about the shootings at Darkley in county Armagh yesterday evening.

At approximately 6.15 pm yesterday, at least three men armed with automatic weapons entered the Mountain Lodge Pentecostal gospel hall near the village of Darkley in county Armagh. They opened fire in the entrance hall, killing two church elders and fatally wounding a third, whom they then followed into the gospel hall itself. There the gunmen opened fire on the congregation of between 60 and 70 people, including about 20 children. Seven members of the congregation were injured, two seriously. The gunmen then ran outside, fired another 25 shots at the congregation through the outer walls of the hall, and then fled. None of the congregation had any connection with the security forces. Responsibility for this appalling attack has been claimed by a body calling itself the Catholic Reaction Force. One of the weapons used has previously been used in incidents for which the

Irish National Liberation Army has claimed responsibility.

The whole House will join me in extending our sympathy to the families of those killed and injured. It will also share my horror and disgust at this outrage. Though in the course of the 14 years campaign of terrorism endured by the people of Northern Ireland there have been other incidents involving greater loss of life, none before has involved the cold-blooded murder of people at worship. The shootings show the true nature of terrorism, and the true nature therefore not only of those who perpetrate it but of all those who advocate and support it.

The universal condemnation they have received from all sides of the community, and from all parts of the United Kingdom and Republic of Ireland, shows in full measure the revulsion that this hideous act has aroused.

The Government of the Republic have given the strongest possible assurances of their full co-operation in pursuing those responsible. The RUC, assisted by the Army, is determined to arrest the murderers.

§ Mr. Peter Archer (Warley, West)

Will the right honourable Gentleman accept that the Opposition share fully his feelings of outrage at this heartless and mindless act of wickedness? We strongly associate ourselves with the right honourable Gentleman's expressions of sympathy for the victims and their families.

Does the right honourable Gentleman agree that if the Protestant community reacts by seeking some form of retaliation or by withdrawing from the search for a solution, not only would that be to blame the Catholic community for an act that it has overwhelmingly condemned but it would bring about the objective that the murderers set out to achieve, and it might encourage such murders by those who wish to widen the divisions?

Will he further agree that while he will, understandably, receive calls to take further action against terrorists, any action relating to the processes of the criminal courts, taken in advance of the report by Sir George Baker, is unlikely to reduce terrorism or to increase protection of the public, as terrorism is not discouraged by increasing the risk of convicting the wrong people?

§ Mr. Prior

I am grateful for what the right honourable and learned Gentleman has said and I agree with all of it. I urge the people affected by this horrific situation, about which they feel extremely deeply, to leave security to the security forces. However hard or desperate people may feel, they must not take the law into their own hands. Under no circumstances will the Government permit that to happen.

§ Rev. Ian Paisley (Antrim, North)

I am sure that the right honourable Gentleman will be aware of the feelings on both sides of the House of those who represent Northern Ireland constituencies. I associate myself with the Secretary of State's expressions of sympathy.

When gunmen appear in a congregation of worshippers on a sabbath evening, slay three of the church elders and spray the congregation with bullets in an attempt to murder them as well, I assume that the right honourable Gentleman is aware that this is a new departure in republican terrorist strategy.

As the RUC had intelligence to the effect that there would be an attack on a place of worship yesterday, why was there no security for that very isolated Protestant building? After the incident, why were orders given to the RUC that it should appear in strength in Protestant areas in case of a severe backlash, with the result that men were unable to go into the areas to which those who had committed the outrage had, perhaps, fled? Why was it that although the police visited Protestant ministers and congregations in the same area and warned them that similar atrocities might take place, they could not assure them that there would be a continual presence during church services because of manpower shortages and difficulties resulting from a cut in overtime?

Will the Secretary of State give the House an assurance that isolated congregations will be protected so that they will not have to defend themselves? Will the Secretary of State accept that a person has a duty to defend himself if there is no possibility of him being legally defended by the security forces? Does not the Secretary of State agree that in those circumstances people are entitled to defend themselves against murderous thugs?

§ Mr. Prior

Of course, I understand the strong feelings that exist throughout the House and, not least, among Northern Ireland Members.

It is true that the police had some information that led them to believe that there might be an attack on a policeman, or policemen, at worship somewhere in the Province. That is a very wide indication. Of course, it would be quite impossible for the police to guard every congregation. However, after the attack, every effort was made to tell congregations near the scene of the attack what had happened. I should have thought that that was a wise precaution. The honourable Member for Antrim, North (Rev. Ian Paisley) mentioned the concern about a backlash in Protestant areas, which had led to a shortage in the numbers of police available to round up the murderers. I cannot comment on that without further notice, other than to say that there would have been no question of any curtailment of overtime on operational duties. I can assure the House about that. The Chief Constable knows that he has any amount of overtime available, when requested.

Of course, there is a right to use a weapon, but only in self-defence, when an attack has been made. Some people are issued with weapons for that purpose. Concern about a backlash, sectarian killings and the Protestant Action Force—which has since made a statement—would seem to suggest that everyone in Northern Ireland has a duty to ensure that the police are given every possible support.

§ Mr. J. Enoch Powell (Down, South)

I should like to ask the Secretary of State two questions. First, the Government say that they are determined to arrest the murderers. How can they do that if the murderers are in another jurisdiction; or have the Government received an assurance from the Irish Republic that those wanted for the murders will be extradited? Secondly, bearing in mind that no area can be saturated indefinitely by the security forces, will the right honourable Gentleman do his best to ensure that where—as in the case of county Armagh—there is an indication that a definite set is being made upon a sector of the frontier, that part of it is so saturated by the security forces that terrorist movements become virtually impossible?

§ Mr. Prior

With regard to the right honourable Gentleman's second point. I am, of course, in close touch with the General Officer Commanding and the Chief Constable. Obviously, we shall have to see what else can be done in that area of county Armagh, and in the Dundalk corridor, which is now causing us so much trouble. I had a long talk with the GOC and the Chief Constable on such matters only yesterday. I cannot answer for the Government in the South, but the North will do all that it can to catch the murderers. If they are caught in the South, we very much hope that they will be extradited. Indeed, there are grounds for thinking that the Government of the Republic take the same view on this issue.

§ Sir Humphrey Atkins (Spelthorne)

Will my right honourable Friend do everything that he can to persuade the Official Unionist party to reconsider the decision that it is reported to have made to withdraw from the assembly? Does my right honourable Friend agree that that is precisely what the terrorists want? Does he further agree that if terrorists can get what they want by violence, it will only make them increase the level of violence?

§ Mr. Prior

I am grateful to my right honourable Friend for those views. It is much easier to destroy than to find a solution in Northern Ireland. I would very much regret any decision by the Official Unionist party that helped, even in a small way, to make Northern Ireland's institutions more difficult to run and less effective. I greatly hope that in its understandable anger and concern about what has happened, it will recognise that it is only by building democratic institutions slowly and methodically that we shall overcome the problems.

§ Mr. Merlyn Rees (Morley and Leeds, South)

Does not the Secretary of State agree that these latest murders by the so-called Catholic Reaction Force, like the actions recently taken by the Protestant Action Force—as I think it calls itself— clearly illustrate to all those who want to see that the murders in Northern Ireland are pure criminal murders, and that those who invoke politics—whatever organisation or side they may come from—are deceiving the world about the sort of pure criminal murders that occurred last night? Will the right honourable Gentleman confirm that in Armagh and on either side of the border there are no more than 20 or 25 such men who move from one organisation to another? Does not he accept that to swamp the area with soldiers would be to fail to understand that a small number of guns move around within the group? Will the Secretary of State take up the response in the South? Perhaps he or one of his Ministers could meet a Minister from Southern Ireland on the border. We all know the names of those whom the police want. Someone knows where those men are. That is what the police need to know. We do not want any talk about soldiers swamping the area as if a John Wayne sort of battle was involved.

§ Mr. Prior

I am grateful to the right honourable Gentleman for his points, and I shall certainly consider his suggestion. I think that we know who the people responsible are, and we want them to be caught. There is a good deal of concern because they have not yet been caught. Anything that we can do by better co-operation with the Republic, along the lines suggested by the right honourable Gentleman would be much appreciated.

§ Mr. Peter Robinson (Belfast, East)

Will the Secretary of State take it from me that this act of genocide will not weaken the resolve of the Protestant community in Northern Ireland to resist Republican terrorism from whatever organisation? Will he also accept from me that the Protestant Community, in particular, in Northern Ireland will study his words today to see what comfort they can get from him? Is he prepared to tell the House that there have been failures under his present security policy? Gallant men in our security forces are sitting ducks for the terrorists. Will he change that security policy to one of resolute initiative against the IRA and its kinsmen?

§ Mr. Prior

I suspect that there are always some failures in security policy. I should be deluding myself and the House if sometimes we did not admit to getting things wrong. I believe that the security forces have done a fantastic job in the past year or two in the frustration of many attacks that could have been devastating. They never receive any credit for frustrating these attacks.

I am in close touch with the security forces. Yesterday, I addressed 200 officers of the Ulster Defence Regiment and gave them a number of assurances about the importance which the Government and the country attach to their role. I am doing all that I can to help Northern Ireland proceed towards peace and the defeat of terrorism. That will require enormous effort by all the people of Northern Ireland if we are to be successful.

§ Mr. Stephen Ross (Isle of Wight)

I assure the Secretary of State that we share his revulsion of that terrible deed, which has hit an all-time low in depravity. We admire greatly the courage shown by many people recently, particularly the former chairman of Armagh council—I think it was—who not only had his council stand in memory of a shot Catholic but who was blown to smithereens within minutes himself. His action showed great courage.

Will the Secretary of State resist any demands for the resignation of the Chief Constable who, I believe, is held in high regard in most circles in Northern Ireland? Certainly all who have met him think a great deal of him. Will the Secretary of State resist any demands for his resignation and impress upon local residents, north and south of the border, that the greatest thing they can do is to expose these people who are, as the right honourable Member for Morley and Leeds, South (Mr. Rees) has said, generally known to the police, so that they can be brought to justice as rapidly as possible?

§ Mr. Prior

I am grateful for what the honourable Gentleman said, particularly about the Chief Constable. I cannot imagine that there is a more difficult job than that of Chief Constable of the Royal Ulster Constabulary in Northern Ireland. He deserves all possible support from everyone in the House and the country. He is a man of great integrity, working under enormous pressure, and carrying out his tasks in the highest tradition of the Royal Ulster Constabulary. I am grateful to him and to the honourable Gentleman.

§ Sir Hugh Rossi (Hornsey and Wood Green)

Will my right honourable Friend accept that the feelings of revulsion expressed in the House today are fully shared by all Catholics throughout the United Kingdom? Does he agree that these acts of horror are perpetrated by evil men—whatever label they may give themselves—who are more intent upon destabilising society in Northern Ireland to further the aims of revolution and more interested in an atheistic philosophy than any aspect of Christianity?

§ Mr. Prior

These are just cold-blooded murderers out to cause all the trouble that they can, and to destabilise the Province. I accept that the whole Catholic population feels as much revulsion about these murders as anyone else.

§ Mr. Martin Flannery (Sheffield, Hillsborough)

Is it not a fact that no matter how horrified we are about these murderous events, our task is to help the legitimate security forces to handle this problem and not to usurp their function by intensifying an already inflammatory position by making speeches calling on new forces to enter this dreadful arena? Must we not try to make it clear that our aim is to lower the tension and to show that sectarian killings invariably result in a mirror image in the other community? We must try to gentle that down and to help the security forces to do the job without further inflaming the position.

§ Mr. Prior

We need the security forces to catch murderers, to prevent terrorism, and to give confidence to the local population. I have to bear those points in mind at the same time as I bear in mind the other point raised by the honourable Gentleman—the need, the whole time, to try to lower tension and to allow people to lead normal lives. It is a difficult balance to keep and the security forces have a difficult job.

§ Rev. William McCrea (Mid-Ulster)

I join the Secretary of State in saluting the gallantry of the Ulster Defence Regiment and all members of Ulster's security forces. Does the Secretary of State agree that ... terrorist thugs have plumbed the depths of depravity with this latest atrocity? Has the Secretary of State any information or evidence that ... any of those who escaped from Long Kesh have been involved?...

§ Mr. Prior

I condemn violence and murder from whatever source, whether Catholic or Protestant. ...

§ Mr. David Winnick (Walsall, North)

As this foul and evil deed was plainly carried out to stir up sectarian warfare, should not anyone with influence in Northern

Ireland exercise restraint so as not to play into the hands of the murderers? May I make the suggestion that I have made previously after such atrocities. Would it not be useful for such crimes to be well publicised in the United States so that people over there understand that this is not political warfare? These are crimes against humanity.

§ Mr. Prior

It does not happen very often that I say thank you to the honourable Gentleman for what he has said, but I thank him very much. Yes, I agree with the honourable Member.

§ Mr. Anthony Beaumont-Dark (Birmingham, Selly Oak)

Does my right honourable Friend agree that in circumstances like these, in fighting a guerilla war where people can hide in the jungle or the mountains, people who harbour these criminals— that is all they are—should be treated as though they had taken part in the offence? All these people cannot flee across the border. If we are to solve this matter, surely the time has come when people, even families, who shelter such people and who know that they possess arms for these deeds, should be treated as mad and criminal, and be deemed to be as guilty as those who take part in the offence.

§ Mr. Prior

I shall have to study the legal position of what my honourable Friend said, but I should be surprised if those who harbour known criminals are not in some contravention of the law. I am not a lawyer and I shall have to study that point.

Chapter 21

The House of Lords

On the day following the massacre, the events of the previous evening were discussed at length in the House of Lords in the Westminster Parliament, at the same time as they were discussed in detail in the House of Commons. The following is a Hansard transcript of those discussions:

Darkley, Armagh: Shootings (House of Lords)

21 November 1983 vol 445 cc20-5 3.45 p.m.

§ *The Minister of State, Northern Ireland Office*
(The Earl of Mansfield)

My Lords, with the leave of the House I shall now repeat a Statement being made in another place by my right honourable friend the Secretary of State for Northern Ireland.

At approximately 6.15 p.m. yesterday, at least three men armed with automatic weapons entered the Mountain Lodge Pentecostal Gospel Hall near the village of Darkley ... (The Minister of State for Northern Ireland continues to read the statement made a few moments previously in the House of Commons by the Secretary of State, as recorded in the previous chapter).

My Lords, that concludes the Statement.

§ *Lord Underhill*

My Lords, I thank the Minister for repeating this Statement. It is a tragic commentary that consideration of an order dealing with the recreation and ordinary life of people in Northern Ireland has to be interrupted by a Statement of this tragic nature. First from these Benches we join in expressing sympathy to the families of all those persons who have been killed and to those who are suffering injury.

We join also in the expression, in the Statement, of horror at this indiscriminate and insensate act. I note in particular in the Statement the emphasis of the universal condemnation which is being given by all sections in the United Kingdom and also in the Republic of Ireland.

No stretch of imagination could justify these acts for any reason whatever. It may be understandable that there are reactions to these horrific acts. From these Benches I would implore that there should be no reprisal activities, and urge also that there should be no protest withdrawal from the Assembly. Either course would play into the hands of the terrorists. I should like to feel that the Government will endorse these two appeals.

Reference is made to steps to be taken by the RUC assisted by the Army. I welcome in the Statement the assurance that the Government of the Republic has promised all cooperation in trying to track the perpetrators of this act. These shootings may bring pressure for additional security measures and changes in legislation.

May I ask the Government, if they should consider such pressure, to await completion of the review now being undertaken by Sir George Baker?

§ *Lord Donaldson of Kingsbridge*

My Lords, we in the Alliance in both parties wish to be

associated with the horror which has been expressed by the Secretary of State, and we thank the noble Earl for repeating the Statement today. Those noble Lords who heard Lord Fitt's maiden speech a few minutes ago will realise that we can say very little to improve upon what he said in his disgust and horror at this intolerable action.

There are two things which are very significant about it. The first is that it was a Nonconformist church. ... It was unquestionably an action motivated by an indirect religious motive. I think that those who did it were probably using religion but were not themselves religious. This feature is particularly disgusting to all of us who believe that people's relationships with their Maker, if any, should be respected by other people as well.

The other significant fact is that one of the weapons used belonged to an organisation which has done great damage already. It is, as it were, the extreme wing of the IRA. I believe it has never been specifically dissociated from the IRA by the IRA, though I may be wrong about that. So far as we are concerned, this is an extreme wing and an even more extreme group which has done something which we all deplore.

In his maiden speech, my noble friend said that he thought that this was a deliberate attempt to induce a religious war. It is the first time that I have heard those words used in this House. I believe he was right to use them. I hope he is wrong in his expectation, but I think it is a great warning to all of us to relax not at all in our fight against terrorism. I am glad that the noble Earl, in repeating the Statement, has made it perfectly clear that we will pursue these scoundrels as hard as we possibly can.

§ *The Earl of Mansfield*

My Lords, I should like to thank the noble Lord, Lord Underhill, and the noble Lord, Lord Donaldson of Kingsbridge, for their welcome to this Statement. It is quite obvious that feelings of disgust and revulsion are universally shared throughout the House.

The noble Lord, Lord Underhill, made an extremely important point about possible reprisal activities. It is true to say that no amount of horror at these shootings could ever be a justification for people taking matters into their own hands. The rule of law can only survive if its enforcement is left to the proper authorities. To do otherwise will merely mean an escalation of violence and will further the objective which the terrorists themselves seek. There can be no question of a religious war; it would merely be an escalation of terrorism.

The noble Lord, Lord Underhill, made another point which is also important. Of course the framework is there in the Assembly at Stormont for the people of the Province to work out their political differences in an atmosphere of democracy and union, and it is for them to take up the opportunity. One hopes that the OUP will determine its attitude with the good of the greater number—indeed, of all people in the Province—in mind.

To reply to the noble Lord, Lord Donaldson of Kingsbridge, very little is known about the Catholic Reaction Force, because no organisation bearing that name has ever claimed responsibility for an incident and therefore nothing is known either about it or about its members.

§ _Lord Rawlinson of Ewell_

My Lords, having regard to what the noble Lord, Lord Donaldson of Kingsbridge, said, which, in certain quarters, may not be fully understood, will my noble friend make perfectly clear the utter horror and degradation which is felt by everybody, and particularly the Catholic community, at this vicious and vile murder which took place last evening?

§ *The Earl of Mansfield*

My Lords, I am grateful to my noble friend. I am sure that all responsible sections of the community in Northern Ireland, and not least the Roman Catholics, will, if they have not already done so, express their revulsion at what has happened."

§ *Baroness Phillips*

"My Lords, I wonder if I may put on record, following what my noble friend and the noble Lord, Lord Donaldson, said, that, as I understood it, the Roman Catholic Archbishop has already stressed his condemnation. It would be most unfair if that were not recorded.

§ *Viscount Brookeborough*

My Lords, may I add my expression of horror at what happened last night? It has increased the danger of retaliation. I can only say that any of us who live in Northern Ireland in areas which are under attack will have to do a lot to try to convey confidence back to the people who suffered this appalling tragedy.

What I think has come out—I should very much like my noble friend to convey it to the Royal Ulster Constabulary—is what a magnificent force it is and how scientifically based, so that, within 24 hours, it can trace the ammunition back to the person who has been using it. That is how efficient the force is, and it deserves our tribute from the whole House.

Will my noble friend represent to the Secretary of State that a certain increase in over-security adds confidence in areas where there is a shortage of confidence? That is the presence; a higher level of profile, I think it is called. Secondly, will my noble friend remember that the rule of law is a very delicate thing when there is an attempt at revolution and that suspension of freedom as given by the emergency legislation is something which has, so far,

deterred retaliation? When the new emergency laws come back
for re-enactment, will he remember that any further weakening
of the forces of law might have a disastrous effect in the present
climate? Therefore there must be no weakening in the new laws
of emergency.

§ The Earl of Mansfield

My Lords, I shall be very happy to pass on everything that
my noble friend has said by way of congratulation. In fact only a
week ago I went to the forensic science laboratory in the suburbs
of Belfast and was extremely impressed with what I saw. I have
no doubt that a word of congratulation should be passed to that
organisation and the scientists there. I also endorse the other
matters which my noble friend mentioned.

§ Lord Fitt

My Lords, will the noble Lord agree that there are a number of
factors attached to this very brutal murder which are not evident in
other murders? First, it was deliberately and overtly, without any
ambiguity or qualification, designed to be a sectarian murder. It
took place in a church hall. What arose from that was deliberately
designed to bring about retaliation from the other community.

Secondly, the word 'Catholic' has been used by those who
claim to be the Catholic Reaction Group. This is only the second
time that the word "Catholic" has been used by those who claim
responsibility for murders. The other occasion was when 10
Protestant workmen were killed in the very same area in January
1976. Again, no one has been apprehended for that. It may well be
that it was the very same bunch of murderers who murdered the
10 Protestant workmen which carried out the atrocious murder
yesterday.

Thirdly, there is a question which frightens me in Northern

Ireland. There are many Northern Ireland politicians on the minority side who talk of the alienation that now exists between the minority community in Northern Ireland and this Government. Such sentiments expressed can only but give succour and support to the murderous thugs of the IRA and the INLA. Alienation from the establishment or from the Government can mean one thing, but it should not mean that one then proceeds to the ballot boxes, as many Catholics did in June this year, to vote for candidates who were openly in support of murderers and thugs. That is most important.

Finally, no matter how many troops you may have in Northern Ireland or how many members of the RUC, the only people who can defeat these murderers are the community which at the moment would appear to be giving them support. These murderers could not operate for a single second were they not given the assurance that people within the community either in Northern Ireland or immediately over the border are willing to protect them. It is those people - and particularly the Catholic community in Northern Ireland - who now have it in their own hands to take those people out of circulation by giving information to the security forces. By doing so, they will not only be protecting their own lives but they will be protecting their own community in Northern Ireland and - whether or not it is said by Cardinal O Fiaich - it is in the interests of the Catholic community in Northern Ireland that they should inform on those people, if they know who they are, to the security forces.

§ The Earl of Mansfield

My Lords, I am sure that the whole House agrees that the noble Lord, Lord Fitt, has neatly and succinctly summed up the situation pointing out not only the difficulties and dangers but - perhaps most important of all - that if it were not for the regrettable attitude of some parts of the community, then the men of violence could not exist. This, of course, applies on both sides of the sectarian divide. So I think that it is up to all those who live in the Province - and it is certainly up to the Government – to continue to provide the machinery and the framework which will enable people on each side of the sectarian divide to sink their differences and resort to the ballot box and the debating chamber rather than the bullet.

Chapter 22

In Darkley without a Sat-Nav!

An article printed in the Belfast Newsletter on Thursday 20th November 2008, to mark the 25th anniversary of the massacre at Mountain Lodge, featured former News Letter editor Austin Hunter. Austin was a young BBC journalist, on duty on the night of the massacre. In the article he recounts his harrowing memories of what it was like to report on what he describes as one of the worst nights of the Province's history:

"It was a Sunday evening in November 25 years ago and I was on duty in the BBC news-room in Belfast as the weekend television reporter. The first indication that something terrible had happened came from the RUC Press Office. Details were sketchy but they told us there had been a gun attack on a small church in Co Armagh and there were casualties, possibly fatalities.

We very quickly assembled the standard television crew of the time, a cameraman, sound recordist and lighting engineer, and headed off to south Armagh in three cars, a decision that was to have logistic benefits when the full horror of what happened became clear.

As a television reporter in the 1980s, I had got to know south Armagh fairly well. Unfortunately most of the stories I covered in that area were related to the troubles. I had never been in Darkley but we checked the map on the newsroom wall before we set off and managed to get there fairly quickly - in the 1980s there was no sat-nav to check on directions and no mobile phones to find out the latest developments.

It was dark when we arrived at the small church and police had the area sealed off as they set about their follow-up operation. We knew many of the police who were there and it became clear very quickly from speaking to them that officers who had seen many awful things in their careers were suffering from shock and revulsion. The senior police officer gave us a very moving interview describing the horror of what had happened - but even his words did not prepare us for the scene inside the church. The bodies of the three men brutally killed had been removed by the time we were allowed to the church to film, but the aftermath was all too visible.

Where cold-blooded murder is concerned, there should be no hierarchy of deaths but the scene inside that place of worship seemed to transcend anything we had experienced before. There was blood everywhere, pews were over-turned, there were bullet holes in Bibles and hymn books, and there was an atmosphere of absolute despair. We were only in the church for five minutes but I have never forgotten the scene and I know the rest of the crew felt exactly the same.

But we had a professional job to do and our next task was to get the film back to Belfast for transmission on the BBC national news at 10 pm. There were no satellite links in 1983 - all the film or video had to be driven back to Belfast.

I believe we split up the video cassettes between the cameraman and lighting engineer and they set off in their separate cars to get back to base as quickly as possible. While they were on their way back I drove the short distance to Keady and from a public telephone box I dictated my report to a copytaker in Belfast. I also passed on details of the interviews we had done and explained the pictures obtained by the cameraman.

By this stage my reporter colleague James Robbins had been called into the newsroom and, using the film from the scene, he did what is called a voiceover which led the national news. The interview with the senior police officer was used at length.

I drove back to Belfast to be reunited with the crew and we were then told by the police that the congregation had been recording their Service on an audio tape.

We set off again back to Gough Barracks in Armagh and got a copy of the tape, which is one of the most chilling things I have ever heard in my life. People were obviously singing a hymn when there was the unmistakable crack of gunfire and then total silence.

It was horrible to know that was the moment when people died.

We worked through the night on reporting what happened in Darkley and the next morning the pictures and audio tape was the lead story on all the major BBC outlets on radio and television.

A couple of days later I reported on the funerals of the people who died. I interviewed the pastor and met survivors who were so helpful, dignified and above all Christian in their response to the tragedy.

It was in total contrast to the actions of the depraved people who carried out the attack. I have never been back to Darkley but I intend to go there some day. When I do, I just want to stand quietly at the scene and remember those Christian people who were singing hymns and clutching Bibles when evil walked into their place of worship.

It all happened 25 years ago but we must never forget the victims and survivors of one of the worst nights in Northern Ireland's troubled and blood-stained history."

~~~~~~

We are troubled on every side, yet not distressed; we are perplexed, but not in despair; persecuted, but not forsaken; cast down, but not destroyed.

2 Cor. 4:8-9

~~~~~~

Chapter 23

'Calm amid the Carnage'

As one can imagine, the massacre made front page news on both local and national newspapers, and therefore word of what had happened at Mountain Lodge spread across the world very quickly. These are some extracts from the many media articles that were printed in the following days:

Belfast Telegraph :: Front Page :: 21ˢᵗ Nov 1983

Mrs T. 'shocked beyond words'

As the Government faced a gathering political crisis over its security policies, Mrs Thatcher was reported to be 'Shocked beyond words' at last night's attack at Darkley. ... Mrs Thatcher was said to have found it difficult to find adequate words to express the 'distress and horror' which the shootings provoked.

A Crime before God

'Would you be free from your burden of sin?' sang the congregation of the Mountain Lodge Pentecostal Hall as the killers burst in. Whatever their twisted state of mind and whatever their motives, the sin of what they did last night will haunt them for the rest of their days.

Air of Calm amid Carnage : Doctor

A local doctor who arrived at the gospel hall five minutes after the shooting today described the 'calmness' he encountered at the scene.

"Basically the scene was not a very pleasant one with two men lying dead in the church doorway and another inside. But one couldn't help noticing the calmness that surrounded the tragedy. Everyone was quiet. There was order instead of chaos. No one was hysterical and even the children were calm. People were upset but even in pain some of them kept directing me towards others whom they believed were in greater need of medical attention.

There was some difficulty, I understand, in contacting me because of the absence of a phone, but I think I arrived about five minutes after it all happened. I am only a couple of miles away from the scene. Initially I was the only doctor on the scene but I realised, because of the extent of the shooting, that I would need assistance and a colleague was called in.

Many of the congregation members who had been shot were bleeding from bullet wounds and I had to put one man on a drip for there was a danger that he would collapse before we got him to hospital. Most of the injured were taken off to hospital pretty quickly and I believe that they all arrived there in reasonable condition.

Admittedly when you are called to something like this you don't have too much time to take in the scene. That's not really what you are there for. As I was attending to the injured I couldn't help realising how unreal, how sick the whole thing was. I have seen people shot before but not to this extent. Yet despite it all, those people remained very calm. That is something I will remember."

Belfast Telegraph :: Page 9 :: 21ˢᵗ Nov 1983

'Don't dare to claim the name Catholic'

Cardinal Tomas O'Fiaich has told the killers of the Darkley churchgoers: "Don't dare to call yourselves Catholics. The Catholics of this area abhor your foul deed and never want to hear of you again."

'Attack was all-time low'

Last night's attack has been described as "an all-time low in horror" by the Superintendent of the Elim Pentecostal Churches in Ireland .... Rev Eric McComb said "the sympathy and prayers of every Elim Pentecostal church member is with the relatives of those who died and those who sustained injury."

'Outrage'

The Moderator of the Presbyterian Church, the Rev Dr Tom Simpson said the murder attack was an outrage of fanaticism without precedence and an act of brutality.

'Horrifying slaughter'

The Church of Ireland Primate, the Most Rev John Armstrong, said: "This truly horrifying slaughter is a terrifying example of hate."

'More determined action'

The President of the Methodist Church in Ireland, the Rev Cecil Newell, said he joined with all Christian leaders in condemning the latest act of savage killing and maiming of people at worship. He appealed to those responsible for security to take more determined action to protect life, and expressed his deepest sympathy to the bereaved.

Belfast Newsletter :: Front Page :: 22nd Nov 1983

Sir John rules out new move

The RUC's Chief Constable, Sir John Hermon, is not to take any new initiative as far as security in the Province is concerned. And he has pledged to ignore calls for his resignation, referring to them as "trite niggling aimed at one individual."

Belfast Telegraph :: Front Page :: 22ⁿᵈ Nov 1983

Church leaders united in sorrow

Protestant and Roman Catholic leaders and lay people today joined in a public demonstration of their united horror at the massacre of three church elders at the Mountain lodge Pentecostal Assembly.

SAS deployed to protect churchgoers

Undercover police and SAS are being deployed along the Irish border to protect isolated churches in the wake of the Darkley massacre. ... Security forces fear that it is not just Protestant churches that could be under threat and that loyalist terrorists may consider carrying out reprisal killings.

Belfast Newsletter :: Page 4 :: 24ᵗʰ Nov 1983

Mourners send united message

Mourners rang out a defiant message to the gunmen at yesterday's funerals of two of the victims of the Darkley church hall massacre in South Armagh. They sang the revivalist hymn *"Are you washed in the blood of the Lamb?"* – the hymn the congregation at the Mountain Lodge church had been singing at the moment the terrorists attacked last Sunday night ... The shock of the triple murder at the lonely church has not shaken the firm faith of many of those who attended the funerals.

Ulster Gazette :: Front Page :: 24ᵗʰ Nov 1983

Hymns of victory at graveside

The singing of gospel hymns at the funeral of the first of the three Mountain Lodge massacre victims to be buried was only interrupted by the surges of an overhead army helicopter ...

Ulster Gazette :: Page 8 :: 1ˢᵗ Dec 1983

Millions are touched by Darkley tape

"Have you been to Jesus for the cleansing power", words which were sung in a lonely graveyard in South Armagh and which rang across the wide open prairie-style countryside and beyond ... to the other side of the world. For those same words, sung as gunmen burst in and shot dead three elders in the Mountain Lodge Pentecostal Church near Darkley last Sunday week, and recorded by a worshiper taping the services on that horrific evening, had been heard through the media, in Australia.

Guards for border churches

No service was held on Sunday in the Mountain Lodge Gospel hall near Darkley, scene of a treble shooting on the previous Sunday night. Christians from all over Ireland had planned to gather at the tiny wooden church but the arrangements were cancelled at the request of the Pentecostalists. A memorial service will be held at a later date.

Harold Browne's Funeral Cortege

Victor Cunningham's Funeral Cortege

David Wilson's Funeral Cortege

~~~~~~

God is not ashamed to be called their God: for He hath prepared for them a city.

Hebrews 11:6

~~~~~~

Chapter 24

The Voice of People Everywhere

In the days and weeks that followed the massacre, over eight hundred letters and telegrams from all across the world arrived at Pastor Bob Bain's house expressing solidarity and sympathy from people of all walks of life. Just a few of them are included below:

"Elim Pentecostal Church, Thornbury, Bristol"

Sunday night 20th Nov 1983, 10pm.

Our dear brethren and sisters,

It was with a deep sense of horror that we learned tonight on the national TV news the outrage which you have all undergone. In Paul's letter to the Romans 12:15 he prompts us to 'weep with those who weep'. We can do nothing less; we send you our tears and heartache for your grievous loss ...

Ian McC   (Honourable Sec.)

~~~

"St Joseph's School and Home for the Blind" (Dublin)

21st Nov 1983

Dear Pastor Bain,

On behalf of the community, staff and children of our school for blind children here in Dublin please accept our sincerest sympathy and brotherly solidarity on this occasion of terrible tragedy among your flock ... Have courage, dear brother ...

Fraternally in Jesus,   M O'N (Superior).

"Elim Pentecostal Church, Ballymena"

21st Nov 1983.

Dear Bro. Bain,

Further to my telephone call to you late last night I just wanted to write and assure you, your family and the members of your Assembly of our prayers and sympathy at this time. ... On behalf of the Irish Executive of the Elim Pentecostal Church and our Superintendent, Pastor Eric McComb, I offer you any help we can give at this time. ... We commend you all for the brave stand you have taken for the Gospel of Christ in the face of such adversity ... may you know the gracious leading and wisdom of the Holy Spirit.

Yours because His,   William McCandless

~~~

"Telemessage :: 21st Nov 1983"

Pastor Bain.

Do not desert your church; this is where faith comes in. Open this Sunday God will be with you. J. P.

~~~

Among the eight hundred letters that arrived from every continent of the world, were two dated within two days of each other. Both were personally penned by the hand of Mr George Allen, the auctioneer from Portadown who had been so instrumental in effecting the sale of Mountain Lodge House to Thomas John Hunniford, all those years ago. A committed Christian, George Allen was a close friend of the work at Mountain Lodge and therefore was deeply touched by the events that unfolded on the Sunday evening of 20th November 1983. His first letter addressed personally to Pastor Bain was dated the following day:

Mullintine, Portadown

21st Nov. 1983

Dear Bob,

What can I say to you under such tragic circumstances, only to share with you Sunday's reading - 'When I sit in darkness the Lord shall be a light,' Micah ch 7 v 8 ... Bob, may God fulfil all His promises to you and comfort and encourage your heart to minister blessing to your flock.

Yours very sincerely,   George Allen.

~~~

And then, two days later-

Mullintine, Portadown

23rd Nov. 1983

Dear Bob,

If there is any sense in which I can use the word "proud" it was today as you spoke and shared your feelings and aspirations at the funerals of our beloved brothers Harold and David. In the coming days let quietness and confidence possess your soul, knowing the battle is not yours but the Lord's as you continue to speak the truth in love. I am only one of a great number of men who stand with you and your people at this time.

God bless you,   George Allen.

Indeed George Allen's words would prove to be far from hollow in the coming months and years. Only eternity will reveal the extent to which he 'stood with' the Assembly at Mountain Lodge from that time until his own promotion to glory in 2006. The congregation at Mountain Lodge owes a great debt of gratitude, both to him, and also to his friend and comrade Billy Burke.

"Airmail :: Iglesia Pentecostal, Benidorm & Calpe"

Dear Bro Bain,

Words would fail to express the true feeling we have as we write this letter. I went to school with Victor Cunningham. Others in your assembly I know, or know of. Tonight in Benidorm we have a prayer meeting and will dedicate time to ask the Lord to help our brothers and sisters in Darkley ...

Sincerely yours in Christ,   L. L.

~~~

"The Presbyterian Church in Ireland :: Armagh Presbytery"

Dear Pastor R Bain,

I write to express the sympathy of the Presbytery of Armagh on the recent dreadful happenings ... we are so shocked that we have had a special meeting on the dreadful occurrence ... we have sent a message to the Minister of State ... we are upholding your people in prayer. Please convey to your people our sincere thoughts about them ...

Yours sincerely,   Rev. Dr. A. R. Scott (Clerk of Presbytery)

~~~

"Faculty of Commerce, University College, Dublin"

21st Nov 1983

Dear Brethern,

Yesterday's news of the attack on your church came with a great shock. This note comes to tearfully assure you that other Christians are prayerfully with you in this your moment of difficulty. By the grace of God those who died in the attack were faithful and so their death represents a promotion rather than a tragedy...

Yours in Christ,   Ezemdi Onyenadum

"Telegram :: 22nd Nov 1983"

Dear brothers & sisters receive our sympathy.

Mr & Mrs N. The Netherlands.

~~~

"Brussels, Belgium :: 22nd Nov 1983

Dear brother & sisters in the Lord,

 I feel moved to write to you ... I feel so grieved because I am a member of what the press would call the Catholic and Nationalist community, the same community from which came, presumably, the people who murdered and wounded your congregation last Sunday. But since I met the Lord two years ago I have come to have a particular warmth in my heart for my Pentecostal brothers and sisters ... I pray that the blood of your martyrs may hasten the day when the Spirit of the Lord will flow over Northern Ireland, and indeed the Republic as well ...

 Eamonn Ó R.

~~~

"Democratic Unionist Party"

Dear Friend,

 At the monthly meeting on Monday of the Fermanagh Branch of the DUP, there was a great feeling of distress and dismay at the sorrow and suffering of yourself and your congregation ...

The members wish to express to you all their deepest and sincere sympathy in your time of great trial and to assure you that their thoughts are with you and the prayers of the believing members are going up to the throne of grace on your behalf. May the Lord graciously comfort the hearts of the bereaved and be pleased to place His healing touch upon the bodies of the injured.

 Yours sincerely, Mrs Miriam C. (Sec.)

"Stoke Bishop, Bristol :: 22nd Nov 1983"

Dear Pastor Bain,

As a Roman Catholic who was born and reared in County Donegal I wish to express to you and your congregation, my sorrow and horror at the dreadful event that occurred in your chapel on the evening of Sunday 20th November. ... Please don't give up Sir, but keep on praying and praising God at your chapel, despite Satan and his followers. The thoughts and prayers of many thousands of people are with you at this sorrowful time.

Yours sincerely,   J. M.

~~~

"Fine Gael – Blackrock, Dundalk Branch"

22nd Nov 1983

Dear Revd. Bain,

At our local branch meeting held last evening, the members present unanimously passed the following resolution-

'That our sincere sympathy be conveyed to the relatives and friends of the victims of sectarian outrage at the religious meeting in Darkley, Co Armagh. We deeply resent that the Dundalk area, even by association, has been mentioned in connection with this infamous crime.' We fully realise that our words are totally inadequate in the face of such great loss suffered by your congregation. We pray that God will give you all the strength to bear with your loss ...

Yours sincerely,

Desmond D. (Chairman)

"22nd Nov 1983"

Dear Pastor Bain,

After the heart rending events of Sunday evening you will have had many expressions of sympathy and I can add nothing more which will not have been already said.

But can I, as a Northern Ireland Catholic, ask you to accept this small gift for the needs of your congregation as a token of the shame and distress which so many of us feel,

> *Yours sincerely,*
>
> *John Q.*

~~~

"Fine Gael – Dun Laoghaire, Co Dublin Branch"
22nd Nov 1983

Dear Mr Bain,

The monthly meeting of our local branch of Fine Gael took place yesterday, the day after the vicious and cruel attack on your congregation while at worship. The members of the branch would like to convey to you their sense of outrage at what happened at your service on Sunday evening. They wish to offer all their sympathies to your congregation, especially those whose relatives were killed and those who were injured. No words can make up for the loss which you have suffered, but we would like you to know that ordinary Dublin people like ourselves, are appalled ...

> *Yours sincerely,*
>
> *Hubert M. (Sec.)*

"Templemore Hall Assembly, Belfast :: 23rd Nov 1983"

Dear brethren in Christ,

The Elders and members of the above Assembly wish me to write to you to express our deep sorrow over the recent tragic events in your Assembly and to assure you of our prayers at this time.

Yours affectionately in Christ,

Mr Raymond McKeown.

~~~

"By Airmail :: 25th Nov 1983"

Northern Territory, Australia

Dear Pastor Bain, brothers & sisters in Christ,

... I want to convey our sorrow for what has happened to members of your flock ... Although we are shocked by what has happened, we rejoiced that those who died are now rejoicing with Jesus, they still have the victory, not those who seek to destroy. ... We don't have to ask vengeance; that is the Lord's business, He will repay. ... We live in a small mining town in an Aboriginal reserve ...

May God bless you all,

P. & B. I.

~~~

"Stockport, 27th Nov 1983"

Dear friends, just a wee note to say our prayers are with you at this sad time. ... It was at Mountain Lodge 24 years ago that I had my own personal Pentecost.

In Christian love

Lucy E. B.

"The Corrymeela Community :: Belfast / Ballycastle"

To the Pastor & Congregation,

... We were deeply moved by the dignity with which you bore this cruel blow and we believe your witness will move the hearts of many ... We were deeply impressed by the lack of bitterness shown by you all in such a provocation. If any of the relatives would value a short time of rest at our centre at Ballycastle in the future please contact me.

Yours sincerely,   J. W. M.

~~~

"Airmail :: Maringouin, LA, USA"

Dear Bro. Bob & family,

We share with you in your sorrow. ... I tried to get a plane to come for the funerals but could not get one and be there until after so I didn't come. ... If we can help, let us know.

May God bless you,   Bro. Wayne Romig.

~~~

"Catering Dept., New University of Ulster"

Dear Mr Bain,

We would like you to know how sad and shocked we were when we heard of the Darkley tragedy. I suggested a collection in our kitchens here at the University ... every member of the catering staff, both Roman Catholic and Protestant, contributed willingly. I enclose a cheque ...

Yours sincerely,

D. B. (Catering Manager), Mrs R. W. (Catering Manageress)

"De La Salle Brothers, Student Community, Dublin"

27ᵗʰ Nov 1983

Dear Rev Bob,

On behalf of our student community here, I would like to extend our deepest sympathy to you, your congregation and friends after the tragic happenings of last Sunday. It was with great shock and horror that we heard the news on the television. Following the events of the past week ... I was just taken by the faith that you and your congregation showed. Even at the graveside you were able to pray with arms outstretched. You are a living witness to Christianity. ... I know I see hope for the future. That hope is in the great faith and love which you and your people have shown the people of Ireland during the past week. We remember you all in our prayers every day here. Pray for us too that we may have the same strength of faith and confidence in the Lord that you have.

Sincerely,   Eugene Ó D.

P.S. It's my first time writing to a Protestant Pastor, so I hope I addressed you properly and not said anything out of place.

~~~

"St. Anne's Post Primary School, Co Waterford"

Dear Rev Mr Bain,

As members of the Roman Catholic community in this locality, we wish to express our deepest sympathy for you and your community. You have given us all a wonderful example of Christian forgiveness and fortitude, and you are the only ones to emerge in a brighter light. Please God, all the people on this island who so freely invoke the name of Christ, will soon begin to see as you do.

Sincerely,   (twenty signatures)

"Johnston, Arklow, Co Wicklow"

Dear Pastor Bain,

I know how deeply shocked everybody is by the terrible deed committed in your chapel on Sunday evening. I am a Catholic priest who wishes to add my small voice to the many expressions of sympathy that will be conveyed to you in these sad days. On Sunday next I shall join with our people in praying for you all. We will pray that healing will come to those who have been injured and to those who have lost a loved one... We will pray also that the power of God's love will conquer hatred.

Yours sincerely in Christ,   John D.

~~~

"HMP – Maze Prison, Belfast"

27th Nov 1983

Dear Mr Bain,

Greetings in the precious name of our Lord and Saviour, Jesus Christ. I do hope and pray that these few words which I have penned may bring some comfort to you and the families that have been bereaved. Brother, as you can see, I am a prisoner, but I pray that you will see past me and see none other but Christ. "Blessed are they which mourn, for they shall be comforted."

God bless,   Samuel D.

~~~

"Sunderland, England :: 28th Nov 1983"

Dear Brethern,

Please accept my deepest sympathy in your sad loss – I and all my church mourn with you. We are praying to God that he will comfort you and surround you with His love. We know that God *in His wisdom and mercy will bring good out of this evil act. I bear witness to this and thought you might like to hear of one of the first fruits of good that I pray will only be one of many – so that your sad loss will not have been in vain – as I am sure it will not be. My daughter was sitting in our church after the gospel meeting and was in great confusion and in some despair trying to make a decision to accept Jesus as Lord of her life, when the sad news of your loss was relayed to us.*

We prayed and raised our voices to the Father that He would comfort you all and when we had finished praying my daughter immediately made a decision to accept Jesus as her Saviour. She prayed to God to forgive her sins and prayed that Jesus would be her Lord. The decision was made as a result of the news we had received. God bless you all and keep you in His love.

Yours in Christ Jesus,   Tom E.

~~~

"By Airmail :: 30ᵗʰ Nov 1983"

Secunderabad, India

Dear Pastor and members,

You and the members are surprised to see this letter from an unknown pastor from India writing to you. Myself and our small congregation of twelve members are very much shocked after what took place in your church. We were all worried for the families of the lost lives and the injured. We all prayed in our church and homes for your church and for the members. May our great God comfort each one … We read this news in the leading daily newspaper.

Yours in His blessed Hope,

Josephdas.

"Fife, Scotland :: 2ⁿᵈ Dec 1983"

Dear Bro Bain,

I am the pastor of the Elim Church in Kirkcaldy... I must write and tell you of the joy myself and many others have experienced because of the faithful witness of the dear saints in Ireland. Just today it was reported to me that a group of your flock led 35 souls to Christ in the Maze prison.

I personally was greatly moved by the TV reports of the glorious entry into the kingdom of God of your three elders and the further scenes of the families showing their faith and confidence in God...

Yours in Christ,

K. Crocker.

~~~

"Airmail :: India :: 19ᵗʰ Dec 1983"

Dear Bob,

Warm greetings to you and all Mountain Lodge saints in the precious Names of our Saviour, Jesus Christ! Through BBC I heard a church in S. Armagh had been attacked by terrorists. Later, a special programme described the Mountain Lodge setting. I learned of the three elders who were called higher ... my prayers are very much with the bereaved ones and with you all ...

In His bonds of grace,

Iris McBride

"The Gideons International In Ireland :: Dundalk branch"

19th Feb 1984

Dear Mr Bain,

    I am writing on behalf of the members of the Dundalk Gideon Camp to say that we have felt led to send a gift of £150 to our headquarters to purchase scriptures for distribution in memory of the members of your church who were so tragically killed last year...

    Yours sincerely in Christ,

        Kenneth Allen (Sec)

~~~

"St Patrick's Cathedral, Madison Ave., New York"

2nd April 1984

Dear Friends,

    The 'Fund for Peace and Justice in Ireland', connected with St. Patrick's Cathedral (in New York), is a small fund and unable to make large contributions to worthy enterprises. Nevertheless we hope that the enclosed gift of $1000 will symbolize our concern for the terrible happening at your church...

    Sincerely,

        Monsignor James F. Rigney.

One particularly moving handwritten letter arrived from 'The Religious Society of Friends (Quakers)' in Cork dated 27th November 1983. Included with the letter were a number of hand-drawn Christmas Cards prepared by six year old to ten year old children, on which each child had drawn a picture and had written their own personal message.

Letters and telegrams continued to arrive at Pastor Bain's

home on a daily basis. Virtually every church denomination and political opinion was represented in the views expressed. It is only possible to include a few of those received on headed notepaper. However, two are especially worthy of note, delivered by dispatch rider the following day: the one from the Prime Minister, Margaret Thatcher and the other from the Secretary of State for Northern Ireland, James Prior.

1O DOWNING STREET

THE PRIME MINISTER

21 November, 1983

My dear Pastor Bain,

    I had to write to you straightaway to send you personally my deepest sympathies on last night's horrific outrage.

    I can imagine the sense of shock, grief and anger that must be in all your hearts today. I fully share these feelings. It was a despicable and disgusting act perpetrated by people without humanity and without conscience. We shall do everything in our power to bring them to justice.

    I deeply mourn the deaths of your elders and pray for their families and the families of all those who were so wickedly injured. I profoundly hope that Sally will soon be restored to health and that all of you will in the fullness of time be able to rebuild your lives together.

With all kind thoughts
Yours sincerely
Margaret Thatcher

Pastor Robert Bain

NORTHERN IRELAND OFFICE
WHITEHALL
LONDON SW1A 2AZ

SECRETARY OF STATE
FOR
NORTHERN IRELAND

Pastor Robert Bain
92 Annvale Road
Tassagh
Keady
Co Armagh

2 November 1983

Dear Mr Bain,

I am writing to offer you my deepest sympathy at the callous and inhuman murders of the three Elders of your Gospel Hall. I would also like to send my personal wishes for your daughter's speedy recovery, and for the recovery of all the members of your congregation who were injured.

I am sure that you feel - as I do - a deep sense of outrage and disgust at these senseless crimes. Nothing could ever justify such atrocities, which are made all the worse by the fact that they took place while the victims were at worship. You can be assured that every possible step will be taken to arrest and bring to justice those responsible.

No words can assuage the pain and grief you now must feel. But our thoughts and prayers are with the victims of these horrific acts and with their families at this terrible time.

Our prayers and hopes are with that overwhelming majority of decent people in N. Ireland who seek an end to violence and a path to peace

Yours very sincerely,

Apg. 2.

PFINGSTEN ERWECKUNGS-BEWEGUNG
Postfach 72
8133 FELDAFING
WEST DEUTSCHLAND

den 21.November,1983.

MOUNTAIN VALLEY PENTECOSTAL CHURCH.
DARKEY.
NORD IRLAND/NORTH IRELAND.

DEAR BRETHREN,

Herzliche Grüße im Namen unseres Herrn Jesus Christus!

Greetings in the Name of our Precious Saviour and Lord Jesus Christ.

Our Assemblies here in Germany send this letter to express our sincere and heart-felt sympathy for you during this time of great trial.

Please convey our love to all those who have suffered from this direct attack of satan's; that we are praying for you and keeping you before our God in supplication.

In der Liebe des Herrn,

Scott Williams.

Apg. 2. 38 — „Tut Buße und lasse sich ein jeglicher taufen auf den Namen Jesu Christi
zur Vergebung Eurer Sünden, so werdet Ihr empfangen die Gabe des heiligen Geistes!"

BLF1684 BEY2482 PAB0316 P01 6185ARMA

British TELECOM

22 NOV 1983/1331

Lisbreen
73 Somerton Rd
Belfast

22 November 1983

TELEMESSAGE   CONDOLENCE
PASTOR ROBERT BAIN
ELIM PENTICOSTAL CHURCH
DARKLEY
KEADY
ARMAGH

HORRIFIED AT MURDEROUS DESECRATION OF
YOUR WORSHIPPING COMMUNITY. I OFFER DEEP
SYMPATHY OF THE CATHOLIC PEOPLE OF DOWN AND CONNOR
AND ASSURE PRAYERS FOR DEVINE COMFORTING OF
AFFLICTED AND FOR THE COMING OF CHRISTS KINGDOM OF
PEACE, FORGIVENESS AND LOVE.

BISHOP CAHAL B DALY BELFAST

All Saints' Childwall

Parish Worker: Miss Jane Hindle
80 Green Lane North, Liverpool L16 8HN
Tel: (051-)722 4885

Tuesday, 22nd November, 1983

Dear Pastor,

I would like to extend to you, and through you, my own sympathy,
prayers and love, at what has happened to you and members
of your congregation over these last days. The shock will
undoubtedly have lasting results on your lives and memories,
not least at the sudden and brutal end of some of your
trusted friends.

We are all shocked at what has happened. We realise that
it could happed to any of us, and so we pray that we will
always be ready; living as if this day were our last; living
it to the full and to God's glory.

I personally would like to extend to you and to any of the
families involved in the incident on Sunday, an invitation
here, to this home or to others perhaps in the Parish,
for somewhere, where you or they could recover, and have
opportunity for healing. . There seems little else I, or
we can do practically for you all; but this may be a means
by which we can enter in support and love, so that you can
at   least have some opportunity to return to what normality
might be for you, as normal human beings, in society to-day.

I extend to you all as a congregation and community my prayers.
I enclose for those bereaved, the cards"Come and I will give you
rest   and trust they will be a help.

In Christ, and with prayer, yours sincerely,

Childwall Parish Church

Bardas Chorcai Cork Corporation

CITY HALL
CORK
Tel. 021-966222/966017   Ref

Pastor Robert Bain,   5th December, 1983
Mountain Lodge Church,
Darkley,
CO. ARMAGH.

Dear Pastor Bain,

Cork County Borough Council at its meeting held on 28th
November, 1983 decided that the sympathy of the Council should
be conveyed to you in connection with the recent killings at
the Mountain Lodge Pentecostal Church.

In condemning those responsible for these killings the
members expressed particular regret that these deaths should
occur when people were engaged in an act of Sunday worship.

On my own behalf and on behalf of the staff of Cork
Corporation I wish to be associated with the expressions of
sympathy.

                         Yours faithfully,

                         T. J. McHUGH,
                    CITY MANAGER & TOWN CLERK.

Whitefield College of The Bible

117 BANBRIDGE ROAD, GILFORD, CRAIGAVON BT63 6DL

Telephone: (08206) 24232

14 December 1983

Pastor Robert Bain
92 Annvale Road
Tassagh
KEADY Co Armagh

Dear Mr Bain

I have just returned from abroad from a lengthy period of work as
a Lecturer in a Christian College and now on my return am anxious
to convey to you and all the families among God's people, who
are in deep mourning at this Christmas Season, our heartfelt and
prayerful sympathy. The tragic news reached me overseas and I
requested God's people there to hold all of you up before God
earnestly in prayer and this they did unanimously.

You are all still being remembered fervently in prayer by the
saints in our own congregations and certainly in our Lisburn
congregation where I minister. May the Lord who is ever "our
refuge and strength be a very present help in trouble".

The dark days of winter have been made unspeakably darker and
only the Lord can fill the vacuum that has been left in the hearts
of those who sorrow in each stricken family circle.

Our prayers centre on the children, for they must have been
terrorized by the deeds of these wicked men, who perpetrated this
dastardly crime.

May the Lord be pleased to grant to these murderers a repentance
unto life and grant to the children, who have had to come through
this horrifying trauma, the rich experience in grace of staying
themselves upon Jehovah who can and will keep them in perfect
peace.

                                              / .....

| *President:* | *Principal:* | *Registrar:* | *Matron:* |
| Dr. IAN R. K. PAISLEY | Rev. JOHN DOUGLAS | Rev. DAVID McILVEEN | Miss M. E. DENNISON, S.R.N., S.C.M., R.M.N. |

Some seventy people gathered
In their Church last Sunday night,
Feeling free to meet for worship
Which ought to be every Man's right.

'Twas near the little town of Darkley,
In "MOUNTAIN LODGE" Church Hall,
Where the glorious gospel is faithfully preached
Doors open to one and all.

They had met to worship Almighty God
And to expound His precious Word,
To exalt and extol the lovely Name,
Of Jesus their wonderful Lord.

In the presence of the Risen Saviour
This little company stood,
To sing of the wonderful cleansing power
Of that all-atoning blood.

Having proved its power, their one desire
That others might know it too,
These were the very words they were singing,
When the bullets came whizzing through.

"Have you been to Jesus for the cleansing power?
Are you washed in the blood of the Lamb?
Are you fully trusting in His grace this hour?
Are you washed in the blood of the Lamb?"

This verse was not quite finished
When three elders were shot dead at the door,
Seven others inside were wounded
Children lying screaming on the floor.

What a change of scene to what it had been
A very few minutes before,
The blood of the dead and the wounded,
Flowed over hymn books, seats and floor.

Not content with bloodshed and havoc inside
They sprayed the outside walls as well,
Merely carrying out the orders
Of their master — the hound of Hell.

Having sold their souls over to Satan
So incensed by the evil one,
When he issues his despicable orders,
His business just has to be done.

But Christ was there in the midst of all
With His people as promised to be,
I hope He said to these wicked men
"Ye have done it unto Me".

In the Book of the Revelation
We read of those who were slain.
For the Word of God and their testimony
With the Lamb, they eternally reign.

To their widows and children who deeply mourn
Loss of husbands and fathers so dear,
May the presence of a loving, comforting God
Be now and forever near.

Our deepest sympathy, prayers and love,
To these dear ones in their great loss,
May they know the covering of the precious blood
That stained the old rugged cross.

Chapter 25

'A Stinging Sensation'

By November 1983, Gary Anderson had relocated to Enniskillen, due to work commitments, but he and his family still continued to worship at Mountain Lodge, travelling the one hundred mile round trip each week. While living in Enniskillen, he made many new friends, among them the Kenny family.

An American group, the Tharps, had been booked to minister at Mountain Lodge on Sunday 20th November 1983. However, discovering that they were supposed to speak and sing at a Scottish school on the following Monday morning, they had to cancel the booking at the Darkley church. And so, at relatively short notice, Gary booked the Kennys to speak and sing at the evening meeting in Mountain Lodge, thus filling the void left by the Tharps' cancellation! This would be their very first visit to Mountain Lodge Pentecostal Church, and it would prove to be a memorable one. Edith Kenny, still living in Enniskillen, Co Fermanagh, recounts the events of that evening in vivid detail:

"My husband Ronnie Kenny and family were invited by our friend Gary Anderson to minister at the evening service at Mountain Lodge Pentecostal Church on 20th November 1983. However, it so happened at the time, that Gary was confined to the Erne Hospital and although due for release, took an infection and could not be at the meeting that particular evening. Although we had four children, only three could attend that night: one of our daughters, Rachel, a nurse in Belfast City Hospital, was on duty there.

As we had not been to this church before, arrangements were made for someone from the church to meet us in Keady village. The family had been invited along to sing, accompanied by my husband Ronnie on the accordion. Ronnie would then preach the gospel.

Our family, consisting of Ronnie, myself Edith, and our three children, Stephen aged 21, Ronnie (Junior) aged 17 and our daughter Janet aged 14, arrived at the church in good time and took our seats in the fourth row from the front, on the left hand side. Pastor Bob Bain and his son Bobby were on the platform at the front of the church leading the meeting.

The first hymn, number 171 in the hymn book, had just started when shooting broke out at the church entrance! One of the elders, David Wilson, ran from the entrance of the church, shouting to us all to get down on the floor! He was quite obviously wounded, with blood flowing from his face, which he was holding in his hands.

Following this, shooting began again, this time raking along the outside of the church walls. I was a little slow to react to David's call, so my son Stephen pulled me down to the floor. As I fell, I felt a stinging sensation on the right side of my face. I landed on top of my husband Ronnie, with blood coming from my cheek. Janet had already been pulled to the floor by my husband. Later, we found the hymn book she had been singing from with a bullet hole in it. She was quite shocked, upset and tearful.

We moved forward after the shooting stopped, and found David Wilson had died. His wife and two children were by his side, his young son saying to my husband, "That's my daddy." People were obviously shocked. Many were crying, some were praying. Victor Cunningham and Harold Browne had both been shot dead by the gunmen and were lying side by side in the front porch of the church, where they had been welcoming people. Seven of the congregation had been injured by gunfire. Three had been killed. We can only thank God that the gunmen did not kill the entire congregation.

As the years passed by, we supported Pastor Bain, until my husband went to be with the Lord in 2003. In 2008, I finally attended the Mountain Lodge Church again, after turning down several invitations to the Easter Camp Meetings.

Whilst there, I met Ian Howarth from Blackpool, England, who was there for his third 'Easter Camp' weekend. Ian had been introduced to Mountain Lodge by Mervyn and Lucy France from Lancaster. The atmosphere at 'Camp' was a jovial one, and Ian and I were introduced to each other by some of those attending the meetings! I being a widow, and Ian being a widower, we eventually decided to get married in the church that I attended, the Elim Church, at Brookeborough, Co. Fermanagh, on 16th April 2009.

Pastor David, his wife Sally, their daughter Esther and her boyfriend Andrew, together with Mervyn and Lucy, all attended the wedding. They all were instrumental together, with friends and guests at 'Mountain Lodge Camp Meeting 2008,' in bringing Ian and I together.

We love and have a high regard for all our friends at Mountain Lodge, and pray that God will continue to bless the work."

Edith Kenny-Howarth.

L-R: Ronnie jun; Ronnie & Edith (with dressing on bullet wound); Janet holding the bullet-ridden hymnbook

Chapter 26

The all Singing, all Dancing Band from America

The Tharp Family, from the USA, have been coming to Northern Ireland since 1980, speaking and singing in churches and conducting school assemblies. It was Lexie Johnston who introduced the Tharps to Mountain Lodge. Marty Tharp vividly recalls the unfolding events of the 20th November 1983 and the ensuing years that followed:

"In 1983 we received an invitation to come to a place called Mountain Lodge Pentecostal Church in an area that was referred to as 'bandit country'. Lexie Johnston, whom we had met in Norwich, England, was arranging our itinerary for the school assemblies at the time and he received a call from Pastor Bob Bain inviting us to come down to Mountain Lodge for a Sunday night service.

A mutual friend of ours heard that we were planning to come to Mountain Lodge and asked me if I had forgotten that we were supposed to be in Paisley, Scotland, on Monday morning for one such High School assembly. "No," I responded, "but they tell me that Mountain Lodge is less than a hundred miles from Larne, where we are to catch the eleven o'clock ferry."

He assured us that since we were supposed to check in and board the ferry at least 45 minutes prior to sailing, that it would be impossible for us to make it after the evening service at Mountain Lodge! When that opinion was reinforced by two others, I called Pastor Bain and cancelled, assuring him that when we returned to Ireland the following year, we would be available.

On Monday morning after the assembly at the High School in Paisley, as I stopped to pick up a newspaper on our way to a late breakfast, I was stunned by the myriad of headlines on practically every paper on the news-stand!

"Massacre at Mountain Lodge Pentecostal Church!"

"Tragedy at Mountain Lodge Pentecostal Church!"

Headlines like these were emblazoned across the front page of every paper!

My first thought was, "Oh my God, we were supposed to be there!"

Then, with great sadness I thought, "What a tragedy! That will surely be the death knell of the Mountain Lodge Church!"

The following year however, I was pleasantly surprised when I got a call from Pastor Bain requesting us to pay Mountain Lodge a visit at our earliest opportunity!

When I agreed to come, he informed me that instead of the usual 6.00pm Sunday service, the meeting would be at 3.30pm on Sunday afternoon, for the Government had suggested that they should no longer have an evening service after the tragic events of the previous year.

We were preaching and singing in a Church at Armagh that Sunday morning and they related to us how the I.R.A. had lobbed grenades over the top of their Church building in an attempt to kill policemen at the adjacent police station, with no regard whatsoever for the danger to their congregation!

We were joined that morning by Jackie Ritchie, an old friend and evangelist from John O'Groat's, Scotland, who was also a lifelong friend of Pastor Bob Bain. Jackie had heard that we were to be at Mountain Lodge and offered to guide us there in the afternoon.

On our way, Jackie began to relate some recent events which had taken place in the area. Just as we topped a rise in the road, Jackie pointed out that some terrorists had fired a grenade launcher into an army vehicle, killing all occupants on that spot!

A couple of miles further down the road, we crossed a railroad track and Jackie related how the driver of a school bus full of children had stopped and opened the door to look down the tracks for safety reasons, when a terrorist laying in the tall grass arose with a double barreled, sawn off shotgun and nearly decapitated the driver right in front of the children as a means of striking fear of the I.R.A. into their hearts at an early age!

Knowing the events of the previous year along with the horrendous stories he had related to us, by the time we reached the Mountain Lodge Church, he had us all very wary to say the least!

Since we had never actually met Pastor Bain, he greeted us at the door of the Church and made the following request:

"Brother Tharp, I don't know whether you preach or not, but we have heard about your singing and your school ministry. If you do preach, please don't be offended, but we would like for you and your family to sing to us for about an hour and a half and let our people just relax and worship with you! If you wish to give some testimony between your songs, that will also be fine with us."

Expecting a meager turn out, we were actually stunned that the building was literally packed to the doors by the time we were set up and ready to go! The resilience of those people has never ceased to amaze us!

There is a song which we had just begun singing in the schools called; 'I love Jesus better than ice cream,' which we rarely ever sang in Church and especially when there were hardly any young people present, but for some reason that is what I felt we should start with.

Much to my surprise, the older ladies in the congregation responded much like the kids in the schools where we generally used that song and when we stopped, they carried on for at least three more times through it!

We had progressed about half way through the allotted time when I saw shadowy figures pass by the opaque glass windows on the right side of the Church! I must admit my heart skipped a few beats as I realised that if a terrorist stepped through the back door as they had done the previous year, we literally had no place to go!

We had our backs against the railing in front of the platform and people were packed in so tight that I knew that if a terrorist came through that back door, we would be sitting ducks.

A few minutes later, I breathed a huge sigh of relief when I saw those same shadowy figures pass by the windows on the left side of the building going in the other direction!

After praying for people with various needs at the close of the service, I stepped through the rear door of the Church where our coach was parked, in order to open the boot (trunk / luggage compartment) to begin loading our equipment. I quickly discovered a means of getting your heart racing, for as I opened the door, the first thing I saw were two hands holding an automatic weapon pointed into the air!

I figured that there was no way I could outrun a bullet, so I shoved the door all the way open to see who was there and, much to my relief, there were three young British soldiers with black streaks on their faces, weeds sticking out of their helmets and camouflaged uniforms!

They had grenades strapped one direction across their shoulders and ammunition clips for their automatic weapons across in the other direction! I must admit that I found myself nearly tongue-tied as I tried to open the conversation;

"Uh, uh, did you get in on any of the singing?" I managed to mumble and the one right in front of me never hesitated, but shocked me with this response:

"Aye, I really like your song about ice cream!"

Without hesitation I asked;

"Would you like a cassette with that song on it?"

Instantly, four more soldiers came around the corner of the building who obviously heard my offer of cassettes, each with a big grin and holding their hand out. Much to my surprise, those seven soldiers acted as if I had given them a wedge of gold, they were so pleased! Out of curiosity, I asked their reason for being there. I was shocked by their response!

"We were sent by the government to protect you!"

I have always wondered how in the world the Government even knew that we were there. If they sent soldiers to protect us, I thought it would have also been a nice gesture if they had bothered to tell us!

I learned a valuable lesson that day, which is still with me some thirty years afterwards. We had sung a number of very powerful southern gospel songs that night, all of which had a forceful, clear-cut message, but I soon realized that regardless of how theological we think we must be in order to reach people with the Gospel, there are times when simplicity rules the day!

For several years afterwards we had very little contact with Mountain Lodge, simply because we placed our dependence on Lexie Johnston to do all our booking while we were in Northern Ireland, and probably because we were and are in such demand in the schools in the central and northern portions of the province, he kept all our time fully occupied.

In 2008, David Bell who now serves as the Pastor of Mountain Lodge (becoming the Pastor after Bob Bain, his father-in-law, died) contacted us and made a request that in the next year upon our return, he would like to have a week of our time to do schools in his area, which I was happy to agree to.

In 2009, we discovered that Pastor David Bell, his wife Sally and their daughter Esther are some of the nicest, hardest working people we have ever met and David is the most organized individual I have ever known!

David not only booked us for a full week of schools, it was at least two assemblies each day and some days one of the schools would be double assemblies back-to-back. Although it is always hard work packing equipment in and out of the schools, David with Esther and her fiancée Andrew took the responsibility of not just helping, but shouldering a good portion of the work every day.

After the schools, we were treated to what I refer to as Sally's five-star restaurant! David took us to lunch every day between assemblies, but when the day was done, Sally treated us like royalty every night with a gourmet dinner at their home!

That first year we did three days of schools performing in eight assemblies. But in 2010 we extended our stay for an additional two and a half days, doing 11 schools, with a total of 13 assemblies.

In 2011 we further extended our stay for a total of one and a half weeks, doing 15 schools, with a total of 17 assemblies.

During 2012 we visited Mountain Lodge again and undertook another hectic schedule, with two schools every day. As usual, David Bell was there leading the pack, loading and unloading the mountain of equipment every morning and afternoon as we engaged in assemblies in both primary schools and high schools; Catholic, Protestant and Integrated schools alike, within a forty mile radius of Keady where they reside.

Looking back over the thirty two years of school ministry in the British Isles, I am still amazed at the tenacity and resilience of the Pastors as well as the congregation of Mountain Lodge Pentecostal Church! Not only have they survived and endured such a horrendous event which took the lives of some of the members of their congregation, they have also suffered through arson by terrorists.

Not only were they targeted by terrorists in 1983, but after building a new sanctuary in 1990, it was burned to the ground! Yet under the dynamic leadership of Pastor David Bell and his wife Sally, the congregation has never wavered in their resolve to remain a relevant force in their community and to the glory of God, in spite of the tragic events of the past, they built once again!"

Dr. Martin Tharp has authored 36 books and produced 27 music albums to date, and spends three months each autumn conducting school concerts in Protestant, Roman Catholic and Integrated schools in Northern Ireland.

Chapter 27

'Picking up the Pieces'

The weeks and months that followed that dark night of Sunday 20th November 1983 were indeed difficult ones. For many weeks after the atrocity, television crews, camera men and reporters would arrive at Pastor Bain's home or at the church, seeking yet another story, a new take on events, a fresh spin on what had happened and the possible reasoning behind it. And yet there was no reasoning, no explanation. Some of the Nationalist terror groups described it as 'a mistake'. There is no question that for them it indeed was a mistake, for every right thinking Catholic and Protestant alike utterly condemned the attack. It proved to be the worst publicity effort of all time on their part.

Many of the injured were confined to hospital for several weeks and were comforted by church members, friends and preachers who visited them regularly, among them David and Emily Greenow.

The three funerals were arranged to take place during the days that followed and well in excess of one thousand mourners attended each funeral. A variety of preachers ministered at each service, all of them long standing friends with the families and of the Mountain Lodge Assembly.

A church morning service was arranged for the following week. No one could face the prospect of returning to the church just yet, so the offer of a local, disused school at Corkley was gratefully accepted. Members set to, tidying the old school and preparing it for service. Just like all those years before, when the previous hall was burned to the ground, the congregation once more found themselves worshipping in loaned premises, for which again they were extremely thankful.

By now, Christmas was just around the corner, and so the question arose as to whether the believers should hold the Convention on Boxing Day and the day after, as was usually the custom, or whether these special meetings should be cancelled. It was decided to proceed and the power of God was much evidenced by those who came. One young man, whose father had been one of those who died in the massacre, received the Baptism in the Holy Spirit during that Convention, speaking with other tongues as the Spirit gave utterance! Some of the fellowship attended the Christmas morning service in the nearby Armaghbreague Presbyterian Church.

No evening meetings were held, but the fellowship was just grateful to be able to meet together for worship during daylight hours. The police and army provided a security presence at each meeting; this would continue for the next five or six years! The church would meet under armed guard, the building being checked beforehand for bombs or booby traps.

After Christmas 1983, the remaining men in leadership began to consider returning to the church. After much prayerful consideration, it was decided to reopen the church in the new year. There had been considerable pressure from various sources to reopen the week following the shooting, but Pastor Bob was resolute in his stance that he would only return to the building when he felt the people were good and ready to follow him.

Everyone felt encouraged by the sense of the Holy Spirit's presence in those Christmas convention meetings and plans were therefore made to return to the church in January. The members began the unenviable task of repairing the building, the police having already performed a basic 'clean-up'.

On Sunday morning 22nd January 1984 at 11am the fellowship returned to Mountain Lodge for the first service in the church since the shooting. Several members of the press were there to witness the event and their reports appeared the following morning:

The Irish Press :: Front Page 23rd Jan 1984

Poignant re-opening of massacre church

Sally Bain, her arm still in a sling, took her place among the congregation yesterday for the first service in the hall since three gunmen burst in two months ago and sprayed the worshippers with bullets, killing three church elders. There was little exterior evidence in the wooden-slatted hall of the seventeen bullet holes that had been left in the building. Only the presence of two policemen and troops keeping guard in the surrounding fields would have alerted a stranger to that horrific event.

Then television crews, cameramen and reporters arrived to witness the opening of the church. The local pastor, Mr Bob Bain, with his customary courtesy and firmness had only one request – that those with cameras complete their task with the minimum of fuss to allow the service to go ahead with dignity.

Pastor Bob Bain took his place on the podium ... his daughter Minnie Bain took her place at the electronic organ and in the front seat sat Pastor David Greenow (whose father-in-law founded the church in 1953). If there was any feeling of apprehension, it did not show and the congregation's fervent responses and spirited singing of the hymns displayed that their strength of faith was undiminished.

Pastor Bain reflected the spirit of forgiveness that was evident less than twenty-four hours after the attack when he said, "There is repentance for these men if they come and repent at the foot of the Cross; God will forgive them."

Inside the hall an attempt had been made to patch up the bullet holes but the red hymn books that had been stained with the blood of those injured were not there. They had already been taken away ...

The Irish Times :: Front Page 23rd Jan 1984

Darkley church still prays for sinners

Last November 20th INLA gunmen burst into a Pentecostal meeting near Darkley, on the Armagh - Monaghan border, killed three church elders in the hallway and sprayed the congregation with bullets. The congregation has now come back to the hall. The Mountain Lodge Pentecostal Assembly is in any case not God-forsaken, or so the congregation testified over and over yesterday morning. "I feel God in the service this morning. God is here, I believe the devil has no part here", said Pastor Bob Bain, in his strong farmer's voice, to cries and moans and whispers of 'Jesus, Jesus'. The devil's work only got the briefest of passing mentions. Pastor Bain commended the hymn, *"Are you washed in the blood of the Lamb?"*, though he did not suggest singing it.

In the plywood door to the porch, a thin layer of white paint covers without hiding a circle of seven bullet holes. Two young RUC men with Ruger rifles slung across their chests guard the little hall until the last worshipper leaves. There seemed no point in asking why they chose this hall to worship in. In almost two hours of singing, sighing, swaying, silent with bent heads and joyful hallelujahs, Mountain Lodge's Pentecostalists clearly forgot the bullet holes beside them.

Not that those who died were neglected in the service. "I stand amazed in the presence of Jesus," said Pastor Bain, pacing up and down, his coat off, his sleeves rolled up. "I wonder how He could love me, a sinner. What about you? Are you outside on such a day of uncertainty? Just think of our brothers taken off so suddenly. Now they are praising Him up there. They've met the Saviour. If they had not been saved, they would have been lost. They were saved. Praise the Lord. I believe these men today are rejoicing in the presence of the great King of Glory, King of Kings and Lord of Lords."

From the congregation came shouts of "Hallelujah, praise the Lord." "Mountain Lodge would go forward one step at a time", said Pastor Bain.

Notably absent from that first service in the church, were the three widows whose husbands had been so cruelly murdered, but some of their families were present. Few, if any, could have expected the wives of those who died so tragically to attend on that bleak January morning of 1984. The coming weeks proved equally difficult for the widows and their children (although they had previously been attending the meetings in the old school). Gary Anderson, Alex Frazer and a few others therefore began holding meetings in Alex Frazer's home, primarily for the benefit of these families. This would later form the basis for a new work, to eventually become known as Lisnadill Full Gospel Church, which Gary would pastor.

All evening services were cancelled, but quickly resumed at the earlier time of 3.30pm each Sunday afternoon, so that people could arrive and leave during daylight hours. It would be many years before the Gospel Service would return to the usual time of six o'clock.

Pastor Bob relocated the weekly prayer meeting to his home where, for a number of years, folk would gather for prayer and fellowship on a Tuesday evening followed by supper.

After January, folk began to look forward to brighter evenings and the prospect of the Easter Convention, which was always a special time of ministry (interspersed of course with tea!)

The Old Corkley School.

Chapter 28

A Piper's Lament

The moment was Sunday 25th November 1984 at 2.30 pm, to be exact. A lonely piper dressed in a kilt stood by the door at the entrance to Mountain Lodge Pentecostal Church, on a cold November afternoon. The strains of *'Amazing Grace'* carried across the open countryside on the gentle but icy breeze.

Although armed police patrolled the grounds and surrounding area, security was discreet at the church, which stands by the roadside just half a mile from the border with the Irish Republic.

Over the next few minutes in excess of three hundred people would pack the tiny building, many unable to find a seat. Among those who gathered were Mr Jim Nicholson, M.P. for Newry & Armagh, and Mr Nicholas Scott, M.P., described as Northern Ireland's second highest ranking Government Minister at the time, who attended with his wife Cecilia and their son Patrick.

The occasion; to honour the three elders Harold Browne (59), David Wilson (44) and Victor Cunningham (39), who had died in the massacre just one year earlier while in the outer porch welcoming late comers to the evening service, and to unveil and dedicate a plaque to their memory. Pastor Bain announced the opening hymn, *"Stand up, stand up for Jesus"*.

The polished granite memorial tablet was then unveiled by Mrs Elizabeth Browne, whose husband Harold had been a founder member of the church. After Mrs Browne had pulled back the blue velvet drapes, the piper played a gospel hymn in tribute. Other family members of those who had died looked on.

One local newspaper reported:

There were many tear-stained faces in the gathering at yesterday's service as Mr Bain recalled the night of the massacre. Several people had been in the church that night and several still showed signs of their wounds. However, there were others who still found the memories of the incident too painful to let them return.

In his opening remarks Mr Bain reminded the congregation that they were not there by chance but in memory of 'these lovely men who had died.' Recalling the incident he said the blood of the innocent cried out. He prayed that those who carried out the atrocity would be brought to justice, but that they would also repent and seek the forgiveness of God.

Describing the three men as born again Christians who had been cut down, Evangelist Mr David Greenow said, "The worst a gunman could do to a Christian was to send him to Heaven. They had been ready to cross the great divide because they had put their trust in Christ."

The media also stated that responsibility for the attack was claimed by an unknown organisation calling itself the 'Catholic Reaction Force', believed to be a renegade group from the INLA.

Inscribed in gold lettering the memorial plaque reads:

IN LOVING MEMORY OF
OUR THREE ELDERS
**WILLIAM HAROLD BROWNE
JOHN VICTOR CUNNINGHAM
RICHARD SAMUEL DAVID WILSON**
WHO WERE KILLED BY TERRORISTS
IN THIS CHURCH ON SUNDAY 20TH NOV. 1983
DURING OUR EVENING CHURCH SERVICE
SADLY MISSED BY ALL
WHO SHALL SEPARATE US
FROM THE LOVE OF CHRIST (ROM 8 V 23)
**ERECTED BY MOUNTAIN LODGE
PENTECOSTAL CHURCH, DARKLEY**

The Unveiling of the Memorial Plaque :: 25ᵗʰ Nov 1984

(L-R: James Gibson, elder; Pastor Bob Bain; William Wilson, David Wilson's father; Mrs Elizabeth Browne, Harold Browne's wife: Mrs Elizabeth Lowey, David Wilson's sister).

Chapter 29

Glory Avenue

During the intervening period between November 1983 and December 1986, the fellowship continued to meet twice on a Sunday, holding a Breaking of Bread Service at the usual time of 11am and a Gospel Service at the new earlier time of 3.30pm, when various visiting speakers would preach and sing each Sunday afternoon.

The Tuesday night prayer meeting continued in Pastor Bain's large living room, about two miles from the church. As one can imagine, these were not easy days for the fellowship. Three elders had suddenly been promoted to glory and a few other senior leaders were now involved with the work that had been established at Alex Frazer's home some seven or eight miles away. No form of structured leadership had been organised to replace those who had died; the fellowship simply existed from week to week.

The church members were thankful for the many local people, as well as those from further afield, who turned up on a regular basis to provide solidarity and support.

One person in particular is most definitely worthy of mention. Billy McCracken, from Portadown Elim Church, was no stranger to Mountain Lodge as Pastor Bob would have booked him regularly to sing at the Sunday evening services and Conventions.

However, the Sunday morning after the congregation moved back into the church in January 1984, Billy turned up at the service, and Pastor Bob asked him to sing and share from the Scriptures.

Without being asked, Billy returned the following Sunday,

and then the next, and the next, and the next... For one full year he came each Sunday morning, leading, singing and speaking, as the need arose.

He proved to be such a blessing and inspiration at that time to all who came. Billy's smile was infectious, his Christianity challenging, his presence in the meeting inspiring.

And then, after one year he began to return to his own church again, frequenting Mountain Lodge less often. He felt he had been obedient to what God has asked of him. And so he was.

Two songs in particular which Billy would sing, accompanied by his guitar were 'Crooked Street' and 'Full up, No vacancy'.

Crooked Street

Well, once my residence
Was down on Crooked Street.
Old formality was the Cop
That occupied my beat.
The devil was my landlord
And he fixed high the rent:
'Twas due that very morning
And I didn't have a cent

He said I'd have to go to jail
To pay the penalty.
Then a knock sounded on my door
And a voice said unto me,
He said, 'You're in an awful fix,
I'll tell you what to do:
Just move right out of Crooked Street
To Glory Avenue'.

I'm glad I moved from Crooked Street
To Glory Avenue
No mortgage on the property
No tax will ever come due
The sun is always shining there
And Monday's never blue
I'm glad I moved from Crooked Street
To Glory Avenue.

A woman once resided,
Down on that Crooked Street.
The devil had her doubled up
'Till her nose was at her feet.
For eighteen years she'd been that way;
A child of unbelief.
Her crooked master told her that -
Only death would bring relief.

Then one day Jesus came along,
And cast the devil out.
Her crooked back now straightened up -
She praised Him with a shout!
The ruler of the synagogue
With anger did turn blue
When he heard about his member's move
To Glory Avenue.

Chorus

Full Up No Vacancy

Chorus:
I've got a brand new sign with bright red letters
Hanging on the door of my heart.
The Lord moved in I've never felt better;
My life has changed, I've made a new start!
So I let the devil know he isn't wanted any more
When he comes a calling on me,
Oh how mad he's gonna be
When he begins to read 'Full up, no vacancy'.

Verse: 1
I've travelled down the road of disappointments,
And faced each new day idle and blue,
But I opened up my heart and the light of the Lord came shinin';
The whole world changed the night that I prayed through.

Verse: 2
The devil said the world was a rainbow,
And I would find my fortune around the bend,
But all I ever found was heartache and trouble,
Until the day I let the Lord come in.

So with the Lord's grace, and Billy's faithfulness, slowly but surely, life began to return to some form of normality for the fellowship at Mountain Lodge.

A number of weddings were also conducted in the church during the next few years, among them the marriage of Sally Bain, the Pastor's daughter, to David Bell on 6th June 1986.

Chapter 30

A Broken Leg
:: and a Radio Station ::

Of all those who have found their way to Mountain Lodge over the years, each one's story is unique and David Robinson's introduction to the church is no different. David paints a picture in his own words of his first visit to Mountain Lodge in 1985:

"I arrived on time and yet the meeting was in full swing, the small wooden building full to overflowing but thankfully a seat was found at the back for this one week old Christian.

It was my first meeting since that wonderful day when, in Portadown Town Hall, I finally stopped fighting God and received His gift of salvation. It all started a week earlier when I was seriously injured in an accident and the doctors told me it would be 12 months before I would be able to get back to work. Thankfully, my son Glenn and the Lord had other ideas and soon I found myself sitting in Pastor Bob Bain's home where his family prayed for me. In all my life I never felt such love for a stranger and instead of twelve months, it took three to four minutes of earnest prayer and I was on my feet. God worked a miracle that evening and the following morning at the same hospital it was confirmed by the doctor who had previously given me a twelve month sentence.

It was a week later as I sat under conviction with tears running down my face that I wept my way to freedom by inviting Christ into my heart.

All around me were people unashamedly praising God with their hands up in the air, some spoke in tongues and I sat thinking these people are weird. Then I heard someone interpreting the message and my heart settled as I just knew this was God. The message was both simple and profound to me as it was; *'I have no hands but your hands, no mouth but yours and no feet but yours'* and I determined and prayed 'Alright, Lord - here are my hands, my mouth and my feet, all yours.' The year was 1985. Little did I realize where this simple act of faith would take me.

Thanks to the people of Mountain Lodge, the encouragement of Pastor Bob Bain and many others, within weeks I was thrown in at the deep end and found myself praying for the sick. I suppose my own miracle made it easy for me to believe in healing for others and soon the work spread out week on week.

A few months later we began developing a radio ministry which started with one radio station and ended up with fourteen stations across Ireland in one year. The following year we commenced healing meetings across the country and thousands of people were saved and healed. Again the family at Mountain Lodge were behind us in prayer and at every meeting urging us on.

Africa called the following year and soon I was part of a team from IGO (supported by the Mountain Lodge family) who visited Kenya. The results were staggering, life changing as thousands came to Christ and healings were a daily occurrence. I remember one night asking the Lord why He would bless me in such a way and He revealed that I had asked Him as an eight year old to make me a missionary and send me to Africa.

During October 1993 the Lord had prompted me to start re-broadcasting UCB in Ireland and we began broadcasting on January 1st 1994 on a small AM transmitter. In two years we had twenty-eight transmitters reaching out to 98% of the population of Ireland and all without a license. Over a period of thirteen years we established a service covering over twenty-five million people in Ireland and Great Britain, again all with the encouragement of the family of Mountain Lodge church.

In 1995 we bought Radio Star Country and turned it into a Country radio station with the gospel going out across the airwaves.

In 1998 my son Glenn heard God's call to China, and so it was a case of packing bags again and heading off, this time with Sally (the wife of Pastor David) and a few others. It was a journey with memories so God-inspired, that they are as real today as they were back then.

Glenn and his wife were very much part of the Mountain Lodge family for years and indeed were married in the church, and like many reaped from the rich heritage of the saints who left such a great legacy to their generation. They established a ministry which touched over a million lives inside China during a period of twelve years and Mountain Lodge was very much part of their work as faithful prayer partners and supporters.

Today we produce radio programs weekly for in excess of 490 radio stations worldwide, our website has an average of one and a half million visitors and up to twenty-five Gigabytes of material downloaded per month. We produce and give away approximately 14,000 CDs each year and send these free of charge to people worldwide. During 2010-2012 we helped to establish seven radio stations in Africa reaching millions of lost souls, using equipment previously used here in Ireland. Also, we have recently started an Internet radio station called 'YES RADIO' and have attracted a weekly audience of up to 12,000 people.

I realize with grateful thanks the Christian heritage which formed the foundation of this ministry. Mountain Lodge and its family past and present are and always will be the real backbone behind the work. Men and women of God sowed for years and today we merely reap what they gave their lives and prayers to see. We are forever indebted and humbled by such a cloud of witnesses."

As a church, Mountain Lodge has always had a heart for missions and outreach, so it was only natural that the fellowship would support David to the hilt, when he felt the Lord lead him in the decision to buy Radio Star Country.

On Wednesday 23rd October 1996, a meeting was therefore held in Pastor David Bell's home to seek the Lord as to how the church might be a help to those involved in Christian radio ministry generally. The minutes indicate that David Robinson, Clifford Hopper, Jackie and Jennifer McNeill, Iris Walker, Liz Gordon, and David and Sally Bell were present that evening.

David Robinson revealed that approximately £2000 - £2500 was required each month to run the station. This covered wages, electricity etc. On top of this, a further burden was the cost of the ongoing repairs to the somewhat dated equipment.

After seeking the Lord, it was decided to formalise the gathering that evening into a committee, and so 'Christian Broadcast Ministries' (or CBM) was born. Pastor David was appointed as chairperson, and Iris Walker and Liz Gordon were appointed to share the role of secretary.

The business recorded that night included the planning of various fund-raising activities and the need to open a bank account. The group also arranged a special Prayer Meeting for the work of the radio ministry to be held on Thursday 7th November.

At the next meeting, held on Thursday 9th January 1997, Elizabeth Hopper and Roy Mitchell joined the committee. The minutes show that a bank account had already been opened with the Keady branch of the Northern Bank and already a balance of £177.50 was held in credit. It was therefore necessary to appoint a treasurer. Jackie and Jennifer McNeill volunteered for the task and were duly elected. It was also noted that a Sale of Work held in the old church the previous November had raised a total of £450. It was decided to lodge £225 in the CBM account and donate the other £250 to the David Chaudhary Children's Home in India. It was also decided to produce a regular newsletter, to which local Christian radio presenters would be asked to contribute. This would help promote awareness of the various programmes on air and also raise much needed funds for the work.

The record of the following meeting, held in February, indicates that 400 newsletters had been circulated, and funds were beginning to come in. The minutes for the following months show further effort by the committee to raise awareness of the work through the production of regular newsletters, bible markers and calendars etc. Some of the meetings were now held in the 'studio' at David Robinson's house: a transformed caravan!

The minutes for Thursday 22nd May 1997 show a balance of £958 in the bank account. One thousand newsletters had been printed and distributed at a cost of £120. David Robinson told the committee that he had an opportunity to buy air-time from Radio Navan for a half hour radio programme each Sunday for a period of one month. CBM decided to pay for the air-time, a cost of £100. Those present were advised that, owing to other commitments, the McNeills had resigned as treasurers, so after bringing the matter to the Lord, Mrs Iris Walker was elected as treasurer.

At the September meeting the records show a bank balance of £1176. Newsletters were now being circulated on a regular basis, with contributions included from various presenters. David Robinson gave an update on how UCB had come on air in Britain and all present were encouraged by this news. The production of a professionally produced demo cassette tape was approved, which would feature many of the Christian presenters currently on Radio Star. A gospel concert was arranged to raise funds in aid of the work of CBM, to be held during October in Mountain Lodge. A decision was taken to send a Christmas card to all those supporters who contributed on a regular basis.

At a further meeting, held on 15th January 1998 final preparations were made for the launch of the new demo tape which featured various Christian programmes on radio. Five hundred C90 professionally produced cassettes had been purchased at a cost of £400. To launch the tape, a special High Tea and Musical Evening was arranged to be held in Mountain Lodge on Saturday 31st January 1998. This would be the first of many very successful such evenings which still continue to be held on the last Saturday of January each year.

The minutes of the CBM meeting held on 14th May 1998

indicate that Helen Gracey, now a well-known presenter on 'Zion's Way', was welcomed as a new member of the committee. David Robinson informed those present that he had just purchased another transmitter for Radio Star. CBM decided to donate £1000 towards this venture. During the meeting held on 17th September 1998, Ivan Rutherford was also welcomed as a new member of CBM.

The November meeting of CBM was held in the home of Helen Gracey, as David Robinson, Sally Bell and several others were away on a missions trip to Hong Kong and China. A 'Lifeline' programme was launched on several radio stations, the air time being purchased by CBM.

At the February 1999 meeting, David Robinson told the committee that arrangements were being made for Albert Chambers to take over Radio Star. Later during 1999, David Robinson shared the vision God had given him which consisted of raising an 'umbrella' of Christian radio transmitters all over Ireland, North and South, a task which he eventually accomplished in full!

By September 1999, Roy and Helen had been appointed by the committee as co-researchers and co-presenters of the 'Lifeline' programme, which mainly consisted of testimonies of people from different walks of life who had come to faith in Christ. At the meeting held on 23rd September 1999, Roy read a letter he had received from Transworld Radio, requesting more details of the 'Lifeline' programmes available for air. The following month, a letter was received from Derek Bingham offering to supply CBM with some of the material he had recorded, and which he felt could be used on the radio.

A promotional calendar was produced for the year 2000 as a fund-raiser, with space for advertisers to contribute on each page. The minutes for 17th February 2000 indicate that a good number attended the Annual High Tea on the last Saturday of January. A special guest, Gareth Littler from UCB, also attended with a team and presented a report on the evening. The work of CBM continues to the present day.

Chapter 31

Moving Forward

It was eventually felt that the time had come to restore leadership within the church, following the death of three of its elders, and a meeting was therefore arranged to take place on Tuesday 9th December 1986 in Pastor Bob's living room, following the Prayer Meeting. All those brethren having an interest in the future of the Assembly were invited to attend, and the minutes of that meeting (the first recorded minutes since the massacre) state that the following were present: Pastor Robert Bain, Thomas Bain, David Bell, Joshua Hewitt, James Gibson, Samuel Gibson, Desmond Martin, David Robinson and Robert Weir. All present were elected to form a committee and David Robinson was elected as chairman, David Bell as secretary and Tommy Bain and Jimmy Gibson as first and second treasurer respectively. Samuel (Sammy) Gibson was appointed as worship leader.

The committee agreed to meet on the first Tuesday of each month, following the Prayer Meeting. At that first meeting designated expenses paid to preachers and singers were updated, and the treasurers were given liberty to provide financially for any visiting preacher in full time ministry as they saw fit.

Arrangements for the forthcoming Christmas Convention were discussed, and a workday was arranged so that members could carry out necessary repairs and maintenance to the building.

Two of those present shared dreams which they felt indicated that the time had come for a more substantial building to be erected on the site. It was agreed unanimously that evening that the existing wooden hall should be replaced with a permanent church building.

Before that evening's business concluded, it was decided to seek the mind of the Lord on the matter for one month. In the meantime, Pastor Bob and his son Tommy were asked to approach the adjoining land owner regarding the possibility of purchasing one acre of land to the rear of the present building in order to expand the site. By now the entire Mountain Lodge estate had passed into the hands of a Mr James Reaney.

It was noted that a balance of £13,593.41 was held in credit by the church.

At the second meeting of the committee, held in January 1987, Robert Weir and Desmond Martin were appointed as Ushers, and it was also decided to open a Membership Book. The faithful work of the two Sunday School teachers, Jeanette Weir and Iris Bain was also acknowledged. (Iris, who faithfully served in this capacity for many years, had previously been appointed as a replacement for Miss Ruth Gibson). Pastor Bob informed those present he had spoken to Mr Rainey, who had indicated that he was unwilling to sell any parcels of land, as he might shortly consider selling the whole Mountain Lodge farm. A number of those present then indicated a willingness to move to a new site, but as the decision was not unanimous, it was held over. Owing to the pressure of business on hand, it was decided that the committee would meet in future on the first Monday of each month, rather than after the Prayer Meeting.

It is evident from the February 1987 minutes that Outreach Meetings were held on a monthly basis in Keady Community Centre.

The minutes for the 4th May 1987 meeting indicates that Mr Reaney, although not prepared to sell the land, would give the church free use of it, with a written agreement to transfer it to the church free of charge when he eventually sold the farm.

The minutes for the 1st June meeting indicate that plans were in hand to hold the usual Open Air Gospel Services on the

12th and 13th July. Those familiar with the 'marching season' in Northern Ireland will know that vast crowds of both marchers and spectators turn up in their thousands at these events. For many years Mountain Lodge preached the gospel, using a lorry as a platform, to an audience of hundreds of people gathered in the open air.

In June 1987, a half night was set aside to seek the face of the Lord in prayer regarding the proposed location of the new church. An alternative location for the church was discussed during the following months and planning permission obtained, but eventually a decision was made to build on the present location, provided that the additional land required could actually be purchased from Mr Reaney.

In the meantime, the African Children's Choir presented a thoroughly enjoyable concert in Keady Community Centre on 13th February 1988, which was attended by many local people from the town.

At the committee meeting held on 9th May 1988, the following new trustees were appointed: Robert Bain, Thomas Bain, David Bell, Joshua Hewitt, David Robinson and Robert Weir.

At the January 1989 committee meeting, the question of appointing new elders arose, but was held over by Pastor Bain. The minutes for this meeting also indicate that Mr Reaney had agreed to sell a portion of land to the church for the princely sum of ten pence! On hearing this news, a unanimous decision was immediately reached with regard to building a new church at the existing site. David Bell was instructed to produce some plans, as he was in that particular line of business.

The March 1989 minutes indicate that two new members, Minnie Bain and Richard Yates, were co-opted unto the committee. In the months that followed, the usual business of the committee included the organisation of Convention meetings at Easter and Christmas, and the regular visitation to the Senior Citizens Home.

On 3rd March 1989, BBC2 television transmitted a film documentary entitled 'Power in the Blood,' featuring Vernon Oxford, an American singer/preacher, interviewing some of the congregation at Mountain Lodge on how the church had recovered from the 1983 tragedy.

For many years Dublin Port Missionary, Billy Jones, visited Mountain Lodge annually, sharing about his work. The congregation presented Billy each autumn with a large box filled with knitted caps and other goodies, to be assembled into Christmas presents for the lonely sailors spending Christmas at the docks.

The last wedding to be conducted in the old cedar wood church, held in 1989, was that of Pastor Bain's daughter Margaret, who married a Mr Trevor Caldwell. They moved away to County Tyrone where at the time Trevor's parents, Robbie and Elsie, were the pastors of an independent Pentecostal fellowship, on the outskirts of the village of Seskinore. Margaret recalls a particular healing Robbie received at one of the Easter Conventions held in Mountain Lodge during those early days:

"I am a daughter of the late Pastor Bob Bain. Between listening to my father at home and attending the church I received all my Christian teaching and upbringing. I was there through the hard times, and as a family we encouraged each other in the Lord. My father, who was the pastor, seemed to carry the burden, but we as a family were always there behind him.

In 1989 I married Trevor Caldwell and moved to Seskinore where we have a Pentecostal Fellowship. Trevor and his parents, Robbie and Elsie Caldwell, attended the Christmas and Easter Conventions in Mountain Lodge. In 1971, in Omagh Town Hall, Robbie was healed of high blood pressure, through the ministry of Ernie Busby. However, during 1996, he had an attack one Saturday evening, when Satan came and made him doubt; he had fallen and hit his head - his blood pressure problem was back.

The next Sunday was the Easter Convention at Mountain Lodge, and Robbie was present. A word of revelation came through a man from Canada, and revealed Robbie's need. Robbie responded, and was completely healed, and never had that problem again. Praise the Lord!

Trevor and I still attend Mountain Lodge as much as possible and still look to it as our home church. It is nice to go up home, as my mother is still there, and then up to the church to hear the different ministries every Sunday evening. I pray that we can all work together, wherever God has placed us, and see great things done for God in these last days."

Margaret and her husband Trevor continue to pastor Seskinore Pentecostal Fellowship, the work Trevor's parents commenced, while at the same time still maintaining their fellowship with Mountain Lodge.

Chapter 32
Believing for a Miracle!
:: Over the Threshold ::

All the plans for the new church were drawn up and approved. It was time to commence work! A 'Cutting of the Sod' ceremony was arranged for Saturday 3rd June 1989. David Greenow, Pastor Robin Hunniford and Pastor Bill Dunn were invited to participate in the outdoor service. It was a lovely summer's afternoon and all present were greatly encouraged as Pastor Bain broke in a new spade, assisted by young Gareth Gibson!

By August 1989 building work was well under way and Saturday 18th August 1990 was set as the date for the opening of the new church building. The minutes of 11th August 1989 state: 'funds stand at approximately £17,000 and that £11,950 had been paid out to date. It was unanimously agreed after discussion that we should continue in faith and that our good and great God would provide our need.' This was a big step of faith financially, greater than any the fellowship had undertaken before.

Many fund raising efforts were planned, to assist with the mammoth step of faith that the assembly had taken, in embarking upon such an ambitious project. The job had been set out to contract, at a cost of £150,000, which was a lot of money for a small fellowship to raise. They would have to put their trust in God, that He would provide. And provide He did! Tommy Bain as treasurer kept writing out cheques in faith, knowing that at times there was no money in the bank. No formal (or informal) arrangement had been made with the bank, yet they never cancelled a single cheque.

The people had a mind to work (Nehemiah 4:6), and work

they did. Families collected their loose change in collection boxes. The men manned car washes. The women baked for cake sales and then offered their merchandise at Portadown Market where they often 'froze to the bone' as they stood in the wintry air on Saturday mornings, pleased that they were able to contribute another £100 or so each time to the building fund. A 'stew night' was planned as a fund-raiser in David Robinson's barn at Portadown, followed by a praise evening. Many others rallied around to help with ideas of their own. Ivan Abraham, a local gospel singer, also organised a gospel concert in Armagh Orange Hall with Crawford Bell and various other artists taking part. An auction was held, when members and friends alike donated items for sale. Of course the auctioneer was none other than George Allen! To this day, some folk still talk of the myriad of stew recipes produced on the evening, especially the 'Worcester Sauce' varieties!

Cutting the First Sod

In addition to holding open-air gospel services, it was also planned to hire a marquee and provide a catering service to those in attendance on the 12th and 13th July at the main marching demonstrations. This would prove to be a useful source of income and a service the church would continue to provide for some time during the years that followed, as a means of raising funds. On occasions, as many as three thousand sandwich teas were prepared and sold during the course of one afternoon!

While the majority of other caterers usually prepared their sandwiches the evening before, Mountain Lodge prepared their sandwiches at the back of the marquee on the day of sale – you simply couldn't get any fresher than that!

Serving hungry customers in the big marquee

As this service expanded, a new provision was introduced previously unheard of at these venues. In addition to providing sandwich teas, the ladies of Mountain Lodge introduced desserts in the form of apple pie and fresh cream, lemon meringue, pavlova etc! It wasn't long before the weary marchers and their families began forming long queues at the Mountain Lodge marquee! Of course we mustn't forget the steak burgers cooked on the large gas barbeque outside at the front of the marquee.

Many friends of the church as well as regular members did their bit to cater for these large functions. Friends like Iris McComb and her daughter Helen, amongst many others. All the men would load up Tommy Bain's lorry the evening before with planks and milk crates; these would form makeshift seating in the marquee. Then they would set off for the 'demonstration field' where they would erect the large two or three pole marquee and fit it out with seating, ready for an early start the following morning. Many a time, they would erect the marquee in the pouring rain, praying for a better day on the morrow and, more often than not, their request was granted. In the meantime, back at the church the ladies set to, washing cups and loading up all the necessary equipment in preparation for the following day.

Special mention must be made of Mollie Wilson, and Peter and Thelma Gorman, three such friends who went beyond the call of duty. Each year saw them rising with the dawn, preparing their aluminium tri-axle trailer, loading up the gas water boilers, tables and other necessary commodities, then hitching up their Range Rover and setting off for the field, like so many others.

As building work continued, church members were not unmindful that their primary calling as Christians is to evangelise and so the various outreach efforts continued on a day to day basis. Open airs and door to door evangelism continued, new amplification equipment having been purchased previously to aid the open air work. A new prayer group was formed at the beginning of 1990 to support the outreach efforts. A Child and Youth Committee was also formed in January 1990, its purpose being to organise children's meetings, barbeques etc. on a regular basis. Also, a book library was opened at the rear of the church that would enable folk to borrow books and then return them the following week.

The minutes of the March 1990 committee meeting indicate that £22,000 was owed to the bank, quite a miracle considering that the building project was well under way at this point! Rev Sam Workman was booked as the Evangelist to speak at a mission arranged to take place immediately after the opening of the new church. It was agreed that the existing seats should be sold off and new similar but longer seats purchased. Hill Engineering in Armagh (who manufactured the entrance gates and the steel frame for the building) agreed to make the steel frames and an upholstery firm in Aughnacloy upholstered the seats, arms and backs. The men in the church spent a couple of nights fitting everything together, saving a few thousand pounds in the process.

The old seats were sold to Lisnadill Full Gospel Church who by now had also constructed a new building of their own. (Some years later, Lisnadill having purchased new seats, these same seats were installed in the River of Life Fellowship where they are still in use today. According to Pastor John Greenaway, a bullet hole is still visible in one of the metal legs.)

By the time the committee met on 30th July 1990, work was well advanced on site with the grand opening just a little over two weeks away! The bank was owed £70,000, yet still no formal agreement had been signed; Tommy the treasurer just continued to write cheques and the bank continued to honour them!

The new church had been built just five feet away from the existing brown cedar wood building, erected in 1972, which now had to be craned over to the side of the site. Therein lay another obstacle: because of its historic significance, no crane operator would undertake to move the building in case it collapsed! One firm eventually agreed to attempt the task for a fee of £5000, but would give no guarantee that the hall would still be in one piece!

Eventually however, Pastor Bob spoke to a firm in Monaghan, who agreed to attempt to move it for a fee of a few hundred pounds. They would do it on a Saturday morning, when the church could provide additional help. The church members borrowed some large steel girders from Arnot Wishart, a local engineering firm at Markethill, and bolted them together to form a cradle under the hall. Gently the hall was swung into its new position. (Now in existence for over forty years it still stands, serving as a youth hall).

The July 1990 minutes also indicate that two buses, one of which had been purchased from the Bible Pattern Church, Portadown (an orange 16 seater Ford Transit) and the other, a 33 seater bus previously owned by Health Services Trust, were used regularly at the time to transport people to and from the meetings. The larger bus was sanded down in Tommy Bain's shed by some of the men, in preparation for a new coat of white paint.

The church was indebted to Wesley Walker (Pastor Bain's son-in-law) who arranged the driver rota and, being a mechanic, carried out all maintenance and MOT work on both buses for many years.

Moving the Cedar-wood Hall

Life was certainly busy, with not a dull moment! Everyone associated with the church turned up each evening with paint brush, paint roller and tray in hand for the mammoth task of painting all the new walls. Mums, dads and children worked alongside professional tradesmen, sound engineers, electricians and plumbers, all with one common aim – to finish this project in time for the grand opening scheduled to take place on Saturday 18th August 1990.

The minutes of the committee meeting held on 30th July 1990

indicate that local evangelist and church apostle David Greenow attended on the evening to advise on the appointment of a new church leadership. Before the evening concluded, Pastor Bain had nominated the following candidates, all of whom were asked to pray about the office offered to them:

Assistant Pastor and Elder:	David Bell
Elder:	Samuel Gibson
Deacon:	Thomas Bain
Deacon:	Robert Weir
Church Evangelist:	David Robinson

In the ensuing days, all those nominated to office confirmed to the pastor that they were prepared to serve the church in the position offered to them, and therefore a central part of the opening weekend celebrations included the installation of church officers.

It was a proud day for the members of Mountain Lodge Pentecostal Church as they put the final preparations in place. It was no longer necessary to bring water in milk churns for making the tea that would inevitably follow the service, as the Water Service had installed a brand new water main to the church, complete with fire hydrant! Baptism services in future would take place within the comfort of the new building, in the purpose built baptismal tank. A sound system had been installed, this time with more modern recording facilities.

A massive crowd gathered outside the building anxiously awaiting the opening ceremony. Meanwhile, anxious tradesmen and engineers were making last minute adjustments to the equipment and others were busy with final hoovering of the carpets and the like.

The main contractor, Trevor D. Bell, together with Pastor Bain, David Bell and other visiting pastors and evangelists gathered on the front steps.

At around 2.45pm on a bright sunny afternoon, David Willows (England) began to lead the assembled congregation in some choruses, accompanied by his accordion and ably assisted by David Robinson and evangelist David Greenow.

Promptly at 3pm the main contractor, Trevor Bell, delivered a short but well prepared speech, congratulating the congregation on their achievement, before officially handing the keys of the building to Pastor Bain.

After addressing the assembled crowd for a few moments, to the applause of onlookers Pastor Bain officially opened the doors to the new Mountain Lodge church building! Approximately six hundred people bustled into the new sanctuary as a team of ushers began finding seats for everyone. Camera crews and media men were in abundance, competing for the best location from which to capture the footage for the next news bulletin!

And so the service began with the capacity crowd singing the hymn 'To God be the Glory.' Pastor Robin Hunniford from Belfast, Thomas John's son, gave a glowing account of how the work progressed over the years from its humble beginnings in the front room of the Big House, to the Gate Lodge days. Then the time when the pony house was knocked through to provide additional space, where folk sat on wooden benches made from the planks of a redundant chicken house! Pastor Hunniford reminded everyone of the first proper hall built on the site by his father. It was burned down, and then replaced with the brown cedar wood building, which had served as the place of worship to the fellowship for the previous 19 years. This latest sanctuary was to be the sixth new, altered or extended building that the Mountain Lodge congregation would worship in!

Pastor Edwin Michael from Portadown Elim Church and Nell Hire from Bangor, Co Down, ministered in song. (Pastor Michael is the current Superintendent of the Elim Churches in Ireland). Pastor Bain's son Bobby operated the new recording equipment. David Greenow and David Willows ministered from the Scriptures. There was a real sense of victory that afternoon.

David Willows, a member of Hollybush Christian Fellowship, and an itinerant preacher (his uncle, Henri Staples was a founder of the Glory Movement), preached at Mountain Lodge on several occasions over the years prior to that special August weekend in 1990. He remembers his first visit as being on the Saturday evening of 15th June 1974. It is very likely that the introduction to Mountain Lodge came through Cecil Stewart or David Greenow.

David returned to Ireland several times during the next few years but did not revisit the Darkley church until 6th July 1989, when he recorded the following information in his diary: "David and Emily Greenow brought me over for the 7.45pm meeting when I preached on *'Speak to the Children of Israel, that they Go Forward.'* There were about thirty five people there. I prayed for those who came out for prayer, under the steel works erected for the new building. It was a good meeting."

David next visited Mountain Lodge on Friday 13th April 1990, just a few months before the new church was due to open. According to his diary he spoke on *'The importance of drinking of the Holy Spirit'*, using John 7.37 and Isaiah 44.3 as his texts. The meeting was followed by a buffet supper. On the following Sunday he spoke on *'Heaven'* during the evening meeting, and again on the Monday evening when he preached on the text *'Isaac digged again'*.

David returned as a special guest speaker at the opening of the new church on the weekend of 18th and 19th August 1990. This is how he remembers the events of that special weekend:

"I preached a short message at the end of the opening ceremony on Salvation. I also had the privilege of encouraging the folk to give a good offering, which amounted to £14,300. On Sunday 19th I preached in the evening from Isaiah 61: *'The Spirit of the Lord'*. I found great liberty to minister. About fifty people came forward to receive from the Lord, including some who came up from Sligo, in the Republic of Ireland. Several of them were baptised in the Holy Spirit. One lady was healed of acute asthma. The time of ministry lasted for over one hour. Many tremendous things happened. To God be all the Glory."

An offering, as previously alluded to, was taken to help defray the £70,000 deficit owing on the building. In addition, George Allen, the auctioneer who had been so instrumental in the formation of the work in the first instance, paid for the full cost of all the carpets and floor covering throughout the entire building! Many others placed substantial gifts in the offering.

The meetings continued on the Sunday as people gathered to worship the Lord. Sandy Thompson, a well known and well loved preacher in Pentecostal circles, ministered unto the congregation. He also assisted David Greenow in the ordination of church officers. There then followed a successful gospel mission, from Sunday 2nd Sept – Wednesday 12th Sept at which Rev Sam Workman, a popular minister, preached each evening.

Local and national newspapers carried the story of the opening of the new Mountain Lodge building. The Belfast Telegraph contained a picture of the assembled congregation in full colour. (See colour section in book).

Local Newspaper Advert for the
Official Opening of the New Church

TO GOD BE THE GLORY

Opening and Dedication

of

Mountain Lodge Pentecostal Church
Darkley, Keady

on Saturday, 18th August, 1990 at 3.00 p.m.

GUEST SPEAKERS
David Greenow, Portadown
Pastor Hunniford, Belfast - David Willows, England

SPECIAL SINGERS
Pastor Edwin Michael, Portadown — Nell Hire, Belfast

Front cover of the Order of Service

You are invited to the

Opening and Dedication

of

Mountain Lodge Pentecostal Church
Darkley, Keady

on Saturday, 18th August, 1990 at 3.00 p.m.

GUEST SPEAKERS:
David Greenow, Portadown
Pastor Hunniford, Belfast – David Willows, England

SPECIAL SINGERS
Pastor Edwin Michael, Portadown – Neil Hire, Belfast

GREAT RALLY / CONVENTION on Sunday, 19th August, 1990 at 3 p.m. & 6 p.m.
Sandy Thompson, David Willows and Re-Union
MINISTRY / HEALING SERVICE
on Monday, 20th August, 1990 at 8.00 p.m. with David Willows and D. Greenow

---

SUNDAY NEWS, 5th August 1990

When border terrorists attacked the Pentecostal church hall at Darkley in 1983, the congregation vowed it would not be deterred. And now, seven years later, Mountain Lodge Pentecostal Church is opening a bright, spacious new hall.

"There is something very special here at Darkley," says Pastor Robert Bain. "God is in this church. In spite of the terrible things that happened here, our congregation had the courage to come back." For seven years the church has met in the same hut that gunmen burst into on the 20th Nov 1983. "The day we open the new church - Aug 18th - will be the greatest day of my life," said Mr Bain.

The new church shares its site with the old hut, near South Armagh's border with Monaghan. On that awful night the three elders, 60 year old Harold Browne, David Wilson (44), and Victor Cunningham (39) were standing outside the hall. INLA gunmen killed them and wounded seven people.

"They were Godless men," said Mr Bain. "As far as bitterness is concerned, I hold none. If these people came back to me and asked for forgiveness, I would be the first one praying with them."

Although £70,000 seemed an insurmountable mountain to climb for a small fellowship, with continued sacrificial giving and dedicated fund raising by the congregation, the church would clear this balance owed to the bank in just over four years.

However, they could not have known it then during that jubilant celebration, but by the time the debt would be paid, the fellowship would no longer have a building to worship in!

Sun shines for opening of new Darkley church

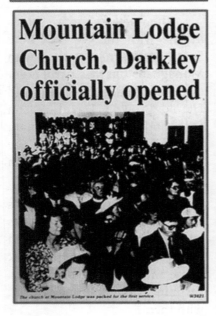

Mountain Lodge Church, Darkley officially opened

TOP LEFT:
Ulster Gazette
23rd Aug 1990, Page 1.

BOTTOM LEFT:
Ulster Gazette
23rd Aug 1990, Page 2.

BELOW:
Newspaper editorial.
(source unknown)

Courage and faith

The tremendous faith of the Pentecostal Church members at Darkley in South Armagh in rebuilding their Mountain Lodge place of worship at a cost of £150,000 is a shining example of how to overcome adversity, even of the sort manifest through the evils of terrorism.

Pastor Bob Bain and his courageous colleagues plan to dedicate the new church building during a service on Saturday, August 18. The service, to be attended by pentecostalists from various parts of Britain and Eire, will be in sharp contrast to that dark Sunday evening in November, 1984 when INLA terrorists broke up a prayer meeting with genocidal intent, murdering three Church leaders and injuring seven other members of the congregation.

The decent, sincere Darkley worshippers will never forget the ravages inflicted upon them six years ago but with their simple evangelical message of "Christ Saves" they can still manage to forgive the terrorists who came to gun them down.

As Pastor Bain says: "There is something very special here at Darkley. God is in this church. In spite of the terrible things that happened here, our congregation had the courage to come back."

He refers to the INLA attackers as "Godless men" but, with admirable Christianity, he adds: "As far as bitterness is concerned, I hold none. If these people came back to me and asked for forgiveness, I would be the first one praying with them."

Such faith must surely be an inspiration in our troubled Province.

Chapter 33

The Work Continues

The new building consisted of a large sanctuary with a platform area at the front and a purpose-built stage at the back, which also housed the water baptismal tank. In other words, the building was designed to be dual purpose. The long, free standing, pew-like seating could be removed, moved to the side or turned back to front so the audience could view either the platform or the stage. The stage was used for various performances, choirs, plays etc. In addition to the main sanctuary, the building also contained a kitchen, pastor's office, two Sunday school rooms and the usual ancillary cloakroom accommodation associated with modern places of worship.

The March 1991 committee minutes indicate that the building fund was £57,000 in the red. In the meantime, fund raising efforts continued, among them annual catering provision for a number of years at the Ballygowan Vintage Rally, some sixty miles away. Everyone would prepare the evening before and load up the lorry complete with marquee, and wooden planks and old milk crates to form makeshift seats. Trailers would be filled with catering equipment and then the whole convoy would set off early on the morning of the rally. This allowed adequate time to erect the large tent and seat it out before beginning to prepare freshly made sandwiches and salad teas for the hungry visitors. Gospel outreach crusades were organised on a regular basis, one of which included a meal in the Carngrove Hotel, Portadown, followed by a ministry meeting.

During 1991 the new church building was registered with the

relevant authorities for the solemnisation of marriages, following the updating of the church constitution. In October of that year, Jeanette Weir stepped down as a Sunday School teacher and, after prayerful consideration, the church oversight appointed Miss Violet McFadden as a replacement, a position which Violet would faithfully and conscientiously fulfil for 19 years. As the Sunday School increased Miss Sharon Wilson and Miss Laura Weir were appointed to teach the younger children.

Violet remembers attending a tent mission organised by Mountain Lodge in the village of Loughgilly near Markethill, some years previous to her appointment as a Sunday School teacher. On the Thursday of the mission, she had burned a large area of her hand with hot gravy from a chip pan, and it was very painful. She had kept her hand in cold water during the day, to ease the pain caused by the burn.

She recalls making the effort to attend the meeting: "When the time came to go to the mission, I managed to dress with some difficulty. On the journey there I kept my hand cool by holding it out through the window of the car. When we were waiting in the tent for the meeting to start, my hand was very painful. I had to go outside to cool it down. I saw one of the preachers outside, so I told him how I had burned my hand that day, and how painful it was.

He prayed for me. God answered prayer and healed my hand! He took away all the pain and I was able to enjoy the rest of the meeting. During the next three or four weeks, while the skin on my hand was healing I felt no pain. What a good and wonderful God we serve. I do praise Him and give Him all the glory."

The minutes of the Committee meetings held on 7th September 1992 indicate that the Building Fund deficit had fallen to just £35,000! This was due in part, it was revealed, to the fact that a number of individual members had between them borrowed £20,000 from a local Credit Union. This they deposited in the Building Fund. They then personally repaid the money loaned them by the Credit Union!

The Committee minutes for the March 1994 meeting indicate that the Building Fund had fallen further to £15,489. Everyone gave the Lord heartfelt thanks for this miracle of faith. The decision was taken at that meeting to forward £1000 to the Minus-to-Plus outreach effort run by Reinhard Bonkke, and a further £400 to 'Vision 828', a local Christian radio ministry.

Around this time, two members of the church, David Robinson and Robert Weir, travelled to Kenya to assist local churches there. On their return home, Mountain Lodge helped raise £7000 to purchase a new jeep for a Kenyan pastor.

The Lord's hand of blessing was surely upon His people; His presence was felt continually in the meetings. In addition to the usual outreach efforts, special convention meetings were planned each Easter and Christmas; two meetings each day, with tea between accompanied by the famous Mountain Lodge spread – a variety of sandwiches, pastries and of course tray bakes! This was made easier as there was no longer any need to haul the water in milk churns now that a new water supply had been provided. A small fellowship of faithful people had proved their God again and again, through times of adversity and distress, loss and pain. God is faithful.

Chapter 34

Finishing the Course . . .

"I have fought a good fight,
I have finished my course,
I have kept the faith."
2 Tim 4:7.

By now Pastor David Bell had begun to assume more and more responsibility. The health of his father-in-law, Pastor Bain, had begun to decline following a stroke. In spite of his own illness, Pastor Bob continued to pray for the sick and to minister to the lost on a daily basis. Many people would telephone his home each day seeking a touch from the Lord and as he prayed over the phone, God answered prayer.

However, he eventually suffered another stroke and was removed to hospital, where he entered the Lord's presence ten days later. A godly giant, a great man, a spiritual leader of over thirty years, Pastor Bob Bain had entered into his reward.

His family were by his bedside, praying and giving thanks to the Lord for His divine favour and blessing upon a man whose chief aim throughout his life was to serve and honour his Master, when on Friday 13th May he quietly met his Saviour face to face.

Bob Bain's life was a life well lived. He had seen more, endured more, believed more than many of his peers. Personal loss in his own family all those years ago had severely tested his faith, but he had passed the test with flying colours. He had carried the responsibility of church leadership on broad shoulders. He had been thrown into the limelight of the world's media following the church massacre back in 1983. With determined grace he offered forgiveness to the perpetrators of such a heinous crime. He extended compassion on a daily basis to those robbed of a soul mate or a father and a challenge to the wider world to prepare for that day when they too would stand before God. He had witnessed the opening and dedication of the new Mountain Lodge sanctuary, one of his proudest days.

But above all, he had prayed for an innumerable number of people who were healed from various sicknesses as a result of his prayers, and many more who became Christians as a result of his testimony and his faithful witness.

Once again, the world's media was focused on this little fellowship of God's people at Mountain Lodge. Television crews, as well as local and national newspapers, reported on his death and the funeral service that followed.

The Ulster Gazette carried the following obituary on page 2 of its edition dated 19th May 1994:

Survivor of Darkley massacre is dead

Three elders of the church, David Wilson, Harold Browne and Victor Cunningham were killed and seven other people were injured when worshippers were riddled with bullets. The building was packed with more than seventy people at the time and the outrage shocked even those hardened to the violence in Ulster.   Several young children including a baby in a carry-cot escaped the carnage.

The attack was later claimed by the so-called Catholic Reaction Force but it is widely believed to have been carried out by the INLA. The killers were never caught.

PASTOR   Bob   Bain, survivor of one of the most horrific massacres of Ulster's troubles, has died. Mr Bain of the Mountain Lodge Pentecostal Church in Darkley near Keady, died peacefully in hospital on Friday.   He had had a stroke about ten days before he died.

Ten years ago, in November 1983, gunmen burst into the tiny prefabricated hut during evening service and opened fire on the congregation.

Bob Bain was born 76 years ago at Aughnagurgan near Keady.   He lived at Annvale Road and went to Aughnagurgan Old School. After school he helped his father in the family business selling feed-stuff and groceries in the shop.

When his brother Thomas inherited the business, Bob

decided to go into farming. Just over 51 years ago he married Margaret Gibson and the couple had seven children, Thomas, Margaret, Sarah, Robert, Iris, Violet and Minnie.

Mr Bain went to Mountain Lodge Pentecostal Church which had been set up and run by Thomas John Hunniford in 1957. In the mid-1960s Bob was installed as Pastor when Mr Hunniford left the area.

In 1958 tragedy struck the Bain household and Bob lost his sister and brother within six months. He continued with the farming and although he devoted much time to the church refused to take any salary for doing so.

In the early 1970s the church, which was a wooden structure, was burned down in a sectarian attack and the congregation went to worship in Corkley Old Hall for almost a year. Soon a new prefabricated building was erected and Pastor Bain brought his congregation back to Darkley.

When the massacre occurred in 1983, Pastor Bain was there, leading the congregation in song. He had been taping the hymns when the terrorists arrived and throughout the world the recording of the music followed by the burst of gunfire shocked millions.

Three years ago Pastor Bain saw his hopes realised and officially opened a new £150,000 church at Darkley - a very proud day for him and his family.

Bob Bain was a very friendly man known throughout the area as a caring and thoughtful character. He travelled around marts as a farmer and according to his son loved chatting and talking to people, and sometimes he forgot that he had cattle to sell!

He was fond of playing the mouth organ and often could be heard at weddings and parties. He had a great love of nature and kept an aviary of peacocks, pigeons and a variety of birds. He also took a great interest in the smaller flowers and spent a great deal of time in the garden.

His son said that despite tragedy that seemed to beset

his life, Bob always bounced back and was a basically jolly character.

A huge gathering came to the funeral on Sunday at Mountain Lodge Pentecostal Church where the service was taken by Pastor David Bell, Pastor Bain's son-in-law, Mr Hunniford, (son of the founder of the church) and Mr David Greenow, son-in-law of the founder.

The following editorial was also carried in another local newspaper under the headline:

Pastor who survived the Darkley massacre is buried

A Gospel preacher who survived the horrific Darkley church massacre ten years ago in which three elders were killed has died.

Pastor Bob Bain, 76, of Annvale Road, Keady, was buried yesterday in Tassagh Presbyterian churchyard following a service in Mountain Lodge Pentecostal Church. Mr Bain died in hospital after being in a coma for ten days as result of a stroke.

His son Thomas said yesterday: "My father practised his faith up to the very last minute. He collapsed just after sitting down, having been on the phone praying with a sick person."

On 20 November 1983 Pastor Bain was leading the isolated Mountain Lodge congregation in the singing of the opening hymn, 'Are You Washed In The Blood of the Lamb,' when republican gunmen burst in.

Three elders, David Wilson and Harold Browne, both from Keady and Victor Cunningham from Armagh, died in the hail of bullets which raked the roadside building close to the South Armagh border. They had been standing in the front porch waiting to show late comers to their seats when the terrorists struck. Seven other worshippers were injured in the shooting.

The attack was claimed by the so called Catholic Reaction Force and a weapon recovered later was identified as having been used by the INLA. The killers have not been caught.

Mr Bain said he was prepared to meet the gunmen responsible if they came to repent before God. He is survived by his wife, Margaret and a grown up family of seven.

SADLY MISSED: Pastor Bob Bain in the Mountain Lodge Pentecostal Church

The Bain family decided to ask those who wished to do so, to donate to the church building fund, rather than provide floral wreaths on the grave. A total of £7000 was contributed to the fund.

Assistant Pastor David Bell was asked by the church leadership a little later to assume full responsibility for the congregation at Mountain Lodge as their pastor, a role which he duly accepted as the call of God.

A period of adjustment was inevitable during the months that followed as the congregation mourned the passing of one who had been a faithful friend to many, and a dedicated shepherd to all, for over thirty years.

By August 1994 the debt on the building had been reduced to less than £5000. It now seemed that the church was on the verge of becoming debt free again, the new facilities were a blessing in every way, God's presence was in the House, and people were being ministered to by the Holy Spirit.

The congregation had settled well into the now four year old building and were embracing the new leadership and vision provided by their young pastor who willingly made the forty mile round trip to each meeting. They were on target to clear the outstanding debt by the end of the year. Surely nothing could go wrong?

Chapter 35

'A Small Fire'

:: Planned for Evil, Meant for Good ::

"But as for you, you meant evil against me;
but God meant it for good."
Gen 50:20 (NKJV)

The twenty mile journey from the village of Gilford in Co Down where Pastor David lived at the time, to the church at Mountain Lodge, usually took the Bell family about forty minutes. By this time they had a young daughter, Esther, the pride and joy of their lives, and so it usually took a little longer to prepare for the journey each Sunday morning.

Pastor David generally collected Violet McFadden en route. Her home was in Markethill, approximately half way between the Bell's home and Mountain Lodge. On the morning of Sunday 4th September 1994, David and Sally Bell were each preoccupied with their own thoughts. Later that evening, Pastor David was due to conduct the opening service of a two week long gospel barn crusade. It would be held in Winston Bell's barn at Rehaghey, Aughnacloy in Co Tyrone.

The previous evening, Winston's nephew, Simon, together with Pastor David, had gone to Mountain Lodge church to collect a spare organ and some other additional items of equipment required for the crusade. It had been a busy Saturday ensuring that all was ready for the following Sunday night and so it was around 10.30pm by the time the two men had everything they required loaded into Simon's van. They locked up the church premises and set off towards Aughnacloy to off-load the equipment at the barn. The hour was late by the time they both returned to their respective homes.

Consequently, on that Sunday morning, the conversation centred upon the forthcoming gospel crusade as the car pulled into Markethill. A few moments later, Violet ascended the steps at the rear of her house and approached the car. They had already given a lift to Doreen Robinson and the two ladies would normally exchange the usual pleasantries. However, this morning Violet had just received a telephone message which she must pass on to the Pastor first of all.

Pastor David's brother-in-law, Tommy Bain, had arrived to open up the building and had just phoned. Would she please tell Pastor David that there was a fire at the church? As Violet relayed the message, she assured everyone that Tommy didn't sound too alarmed; possibly it was just a small fire due to an electrical appliance or something of that nature.

As they completed the journey up the winding hills towards Mountain Lodge, there was some discussion in the car as to what may have happened. Pastor David tried inwardly to reassure himself. It was a relatively new building after all, just four years old. There were ample fire extinguishers on the premises, unlike the time of the last fire in 1971; Tommy would have all under control. And of course there was a mains water supply now as well, and a fire hydrant. What could go wrong?

On approaching the church, they immediately noticed that all was not as it should be. Two or three fire engines occupied the most prominent part of the car park, up close to the front door! Behind them, a couple of police cars were parked. Fire crews were running with hoses, thankful that a fire hydrant had been installed just outside the front wall. Policemen were trying to look busy. Members of the congregation slowly began to arrive for the morning service. The building looked more or less normal from the outside. Why all the commotion? What could be wrong? Where was the fire?

As Pastor David edged towards the door, he was met by the Fire Chief. "Are you the minister?" he asked.

Pastor David answered: "Yes, what's happened?"

"There's been a bad fire, the building is badly damaged. We are just damping everything down. We will have to stay with it in case it re-ignites," was the reply.

"Is it safe to enter?" the pastor asked.

"You can proceed with caution, but be aware of the debris," the Fire Officer answered.

As Pastor David entered the building, he was followed by some of the congregation who had arrived for the service. Tommy Bain was among them. "What happened?" Pastor David asked.

Tommy responded, "I arrived and proceeded to open up the church. I couldn't understand why the inside was so dark, it seemed like someone had blacked out the windows. Then I switched on the lights, just a glimmer from some, others weren't lighting at all. I felt the intense heat, then I saw a fire begin to re-ignite, it seemed that the fresh oxygen supplied by the open door had rekindled the fire."

As Pastor David and a few others entered the building the full scale of what had happened eventually began to dawn on them. The Fire Officer explained that the fire had been started maliciously, the result of an arson attack. The culprits had entered the building by breaking a rear window. They had lit three fires in the main building, one at the back, another in the middle of the aisle and a third at the front under the two inch thick mahogany communion table. There was nothing left to indicate that the heavy table ever existed, other than a small sliver of one of the offering plate rims! The wool carpet under the table had 'vanished' completely. Instead of black or white ash, as you would expect – nothing! Absolutely nothing. A large portion of the floor carpet the size of the communion table had 'gone' revealing only the white concrete below! Such was the intense ferocity of the fire.

Everything else was as black as coal, just dimly visible as one's eyes slowly adjusted to the blackness. The intense heat felt like a sauna. The Fire Officer explained that the perpetrators had, in their opinion, used heating oil to fuel the fires. This was obtained by cutting through the copper oil supply pipe at the oil burner outside. It appeared that they had possibly used three bales of straw to ignite the fires.

Slowly, the magnitude of the destruction caused by the fire began to dawn on those assembled in the middle of what, just a few hours before, had been a beautiful sanctuary. All the seating was absolutely ruined. The piano was burnt to a cinder. The charred remains of the electric organ became slowly visible through the adjusting light. Virtually every pane of glass was cracked. The Fire Officer said it was a miracle the glass hadn't blown out as the fresh flow of oxygen would have refuelled the fire. The thick glass and smaller Georgian window panes had been a saving grace.

One by one the church members began to turn their eyes towards the twenty eight foot high pine ceiling that had been treated to three coats of a special fire retardant varnish. The fire had burned its way right through the ceiling, into the roof space above, and had even charred one or two of the rafters at the very apex of the roof.

What hadn't been destroyed by fire was saturated in water, thanks to the efficiency of the fire crews! The sound system, recording equipment and the like were rendered utterly useless. The mahogany brass rimmed clock, on the other hand, donated as a gift at the opening of the new church, still proudly hung on the wall, admirably ticking away the minutes! Thirty years on, it still hangs in the church, undefeated by the fire or the water! Maybe there's a lesson there for us all: not to let the trials of time wear us down.

What do you do when confronted with such a situation? What is the correct way to respond? Is there a manual that explains how to move forward from such a moment? Apparently not.

Very often, in such devastating circumstances, one almost sub consciously reverts to auto pilot and, as a result, begins to do what comes naturally. And that's what the people of Mountain Lodge did. As they left the fires crews and police personnel to complete their business, the people of Mountain Lodge immediately set about the all too important business of their own. After all, they had come to this hilltop for a purpose that morning and no amount of fire or water was going to prevent them from accomplishing the worship of their God.

So, in one accord, they scrambled an accordion from the back seat of a car and, with just that one solitary piece of musical equipment, set off for the old cedar wood church at the side of the car park. Until now, it had remained largely unused, almost surplus to requirements; indeed away back in 1983, some well-meaning well-wisher had advised that it should be demolished and burnt to dust, rather than serve as a link to that horrific past.

But the people of Mountain Lodge were glad on the morning of Sunday 4th September 1994 that the old hall was still in existence. Everyone gathered into the hall, and having no seats to sit on, and only an accordion for music, they began to worship the Lord. People experienced the presence of God that morning, not to mention the presence of the Police and Fire Chiefs interrupting the service on a number of occasions while seeking the assistance of the pastor!

When an animal is caged or frightened or terrified of its attacker, it will revert to its basic instinct. And that's what Christians do. When they are persecuted or afflicted, tormented or tortured, Christians revert to their first instinct – to worship the One whom they know is already working out a plan on their behalf. What a meeting that was that morning, as folk worshipped the Lord and gave Him their praise!

One thing was already certain in their minds – they would rebuild again! After all, the people of Mountain Lodge were no strangers to the flames of adversity. They had already endured a previous fire and then the bullet but they would arise again like the proverbial phoenix rising from the ashes!

Article printed in the Ulster Gazette the following week

Later that evening, the people of Mountain Lodge set off to support their pastor as he conducted the first night of the mission in Winston Bell's barn at Aughnacloy, resting in the knowledge that God would take charge of His House!

The scriptures teach us that Joseph's life was fraught with disappointment, despair, distrust, danger and difficulty. However he remained determined, definite and resolute as he focused on the plan of God for his life, through which God would save a nation. When one knows the call of God, he or she has a sense of purpose that not even the devil himself can shake.

And so in the weeks that followed, the leadership of Mountain Lodge met once more, to set about a task to which they were no strangers. Perhaps it comes as no surprise that the church has had an abundance of builders, plumbers, electricians, architects and general handymen (and women) over the years in its congregation! Most of them perhaps were raised on diet of 'needs must' when it comes to setting about the Lord's work. Just as Nehemiah of old called the Children of Israel together to build, so in the coming weeks the leadership of Mountain Lodge would call its people once more to put their hand to the plough.

The existing debt was indeed cleared by the end of December that year. It was important to the leadership that the financial 'slate' was wiped clean prior to embarking on another project. The new church had been built by contract in 1990, but this time the congregation would carry out most of the work themselves, thus saving as much money as they could. There was good reason why the church needed to economise on the cost of the reconstruction. When the insurance company was approached, it was found that the church was under-insured and, as a consequence, the underwriters would only contribute about 60% of the cost of reinstatement!

During the years of the 'Troubles' in Northern Ireland, it was customary for the Northern Ireland Office to cover the cost of reinstating buildings which had been bombed or burnt down as a result of terrorist related activity, and so the NIO was the next agency to be approached.

You can imagine the horror, shock and dismay of the Mountain Lodge Church leadership when they were informed a few weeks later, that since the fire had taken place four days into the recently announced terrorist ceasefire, the NIO did not consider the attack to be sectarian related and as a consequence they were rejecting the claim for financial assistance.

However, the leadership took a step of faith and commissioned the re-design of the building. The original sanctuary had been built with an extremely high ceiling, and while at times the new church had been filled to capacity, at other times it was almost too large.

The plans for the restructured church would go well beyond simply reinstating everything as it had been before. Someone said once that when Mountain Lodge was faced with adversity, when their previous buildings were burned down or destroyed, they built bigger and better than before, and this time would be no different.

The meetings were moved back into the old cedar wood hall,

the site of the massacre, for eleven months. During that time, new plans were drawn which detailed the lowering of the ceiling in the main sanctuary to facilitate the inclusion of a new general purpose church hall in the roof void above, and also a balcony which would serve as a smaller meeting room. A second kitchen was incorporated at the upper level together with several other ancillary rooms.

As the plans progressed, it was with a great sense of joy that the leadership were informed that the NIO had had a change of heart and would contribute towards the cost of rebuilding the church after all! This was an answer to prayer.

As the church awaited the necessary approvals to be granted for construction work to begin, members and friends alike set to on evenings and Saturdays stripping out the debris, tearing down partitions and ceilings, and scrubbing the soot stained walls.

Many faithful workers toiled long into the night pulling down that which had only been built just a short time before. It's always risky to mention names for fear of overlooking someone, but mention must be made of Gerry who travelled from Belfast each Saturday, happily doing whatever was asked of him to further the work.

Recently purchased sound systems were scrapped, the remains of musical instruments discarded, wool carpets by the yard were dumped and light fittings by the score cleared to the skip.

Many a soot-stained volunteer wearily made his or her way home after a long evening's work, seeking only a hot bath and a good night's rest, safe in the knowledge it would all have to be done again the following evening!

It almost seemed a familiar routine by now but a 'Reopening Service' was arranged for 18th August 1995, five years exactly to the day since the building was first opened. Externally, a new fire escape and some roof windows were the only tell-tales that the building had undergone a major transformation in its few short years, however internally its layout was vastly different. The main sanctuary had been turned around back to front, and a foyer area had been created close to the entrance, with concertina doors which allowed the sanctuary to be extended. A new sound system had been installed and a new platform created. Another great crowd turned up for the weekend celebrations as the fellowship gave God the glory.

By doing the majority of the work voluntarily, a great saving had been made on the cost of achieving the now greatly improved building, although the cost of the full renovation was still in the region of £160,000. The leadership was thankful to God for the compensation money received from the insurance claim and the Northern Ireland Office but they were once more in debt. This time it was to the tune of approximately £40,000. However, they had faith that God would provide.

The congregation at Mountain Lodge once more had a building to worship in. This time there was the added benefit of a church hall, which would prove to be a very real blessing in the years to come. The floor area now approached double that of the original building.

On one of the following Sunday mornings, George Allen arrived at the meeting, accompanied by his old friend, Billy Burke. Billy approached Pastor David at the end of the meeting, reflecting on how he had noticed that both the organist and the pianist were expecting babies! He was also conscious that they would benefit from more comfortable seating when not playing the instruments. The result? Billy bought six new upholstered chairs for the platform and donated them to the church!

A great debt of gratitude is owed to the church session and members of Second Keady Presbyterian Church, who for many years kindly granted the use of their church hall to the folks at Mountain Lodge for parties etc, when they had no hall of their own.

It is something of a sad reflection on the legacy created by the 'Troubles' in Northern Ireland however, when in the same week that the local newspaper reported on a positive note the re-opening of Mountain Lodge church, it also reported on the arson attack on a Roman Catholic church at Tandragee, in which a stained glass window was badly damaged.

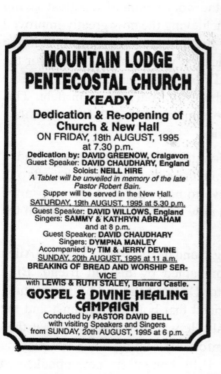

Scenes of destruction inside St Patrick's Roman Catholic Church, Ballyargan, Tandragee, which was attacked last weekend. PW3406

ABOVE LEFT - Newspaper Notice advertising the re-opening of the newly renovated Mountain Lodge Pentecostal Church.

ABOVE RIGHT - Newspaper editorial describing the arson attack on another place of worship, which occurred the same weekend that Mountain Lodge was re-opened.

Chapter 36

The Vision of the Ark
:: *The Ark Begins to Fill* ::

The new design was effectively three storeys high. It wasn't until some time later however, that someone remembered a vision that the Lord had given Tommy Bain several years before, in December 1989. The congregation were still meeting in the brown cedar wood building at the time, while the new church was being built.

Now all these years later, the vision was being implemented, the base was being laid, for God to fulfil His purposes during this next chapter in the life of Mountain Lodge. The 'Ark' would be built!

Tommy shared the vision God had given him one Sunday morning in the church service:

The Vision as told by Tommy Bain during the church service in January 1990

"What I have to say is based around the 6th, 7th and 8th chapter of Genesis. It is based around the story of Noah and Noah's ark.

In the last days of this past year, just before the New Year service, one night I had an inspiration in bed, and it kept me awake for about three hours.

It was concerning the parallel with our church out here, the exact parallel between the situation in the days of Noah and the situation that we are in out here.

The days of Noah were dark days; the days of Noah were days

prior to Judgement; the days of Noah were days when there was apathy among the people of God for the Word of God.

The questions came to me and the answers came with them and I just lay and listened. The sort of questions that are going through the mind of the people at this time is –

Why did you build a church so near the Coming of the Lord, there's only a few years left?

The answer came: Noah built an ark for a few months to do a very important job - just a few months - and it did a very big job, and a very important job - and it's still recorded right down through history as being the saviour of the known world at that time.

And the big question is: How do we fill it with people?

The answer came again: the Spirit of the Lord drew animals out of the woods, and they all came two by two, and they all came drawn of the Spirit of God.

The answer came: nothing but the Spirit of God can bring people, and I saw people coming as married couples, a lot of families two by two coming, again they came from all different parts and they were all drawn by one Spirit, and that ark wasn't built one bit too big or one bit too small. I think it was just exact.

And in that ark there had to be food left up for people that would come in and animals that came in. And I believe the job of the church would be not just mainly to get the people in, but to feed them when they are in, and to keep them prior to the great and final judgement day of the Lord.

Now everyone who starts to come doesn't come. The Spirit of God, as I saw it, would move upon animals; there wasn't much success with people in those days - I saw the Spirit of God moving on the animal world as people - that's the parallel I saw, because the population at that time was very small compared to now, and there were only eight people saved, but the Spirit of God did the impossible thing; Noah could not have brought a lion or an elephant.

We couldn't bring in people, impossible, but the Spirit of God did that, and I saw as the animals started to come towards the ark, there was only two singled out. All these animals did not come in. The scripture for this one was: *"Many are called, but few are chosen."* There will be a chosen people come in.

I saw that the church out here was built, as I believe, for the last day move of God in this part of the country, and I saw that the Spirit of God is what we are depending on to bring in people, and I believe He will bring in people. I believe it is prior to the judgement and there are few years left. I saw Noah's ark was built a very short time before the end time of that known world.

Another thing I saw about it was the expense of this ark. It was never mentioned that it wasn't paid for or couldn't be paid for. The expense never came into it, so I believe that all expenses will be paid for in this new church.

God didn't ask Noah, "Can you afford to build an ark?" All expenses were paid and we believe that the ark was done to perfection, the way it had to be.

I honestly believe that we will see the church flourish with people that God will select, that God will bring in and that God will put His hand on, and that there will be food left in for those people in the church, to feed them until the coming of the Lord. The gifts will be in operation.

This came to me out of the blue and was unfolded to me. It's a message of encouragement that we are on the right track and will inspire us through dark times.

Noah hammered away for one hundred and twenty years, working to the blueprint that God had given to him, and to the exact size and pattern, while people passed by and scoffed, but when the rain came, he and his family were saved."

The test of whether any vision is from God is in its fulfilment - the proof of the pudding is in the eating, so to speak. And so, on occupying the newly renovated building, the congregation of Mountain Lodge waited with bated breath to see if the vision

Tommy claimed to have received from God would be fulfilled. They didn't have long to wait. People began to arrive almost immediately, some for a season, while others are an integral part of the work to this very day. Those who began to attend on a regular basis included Ivan and Valerie Rutherford, Raymond and Kathryn Thompson, Bert and Jean Hadden, Jackie and Jennifer Mc Neill, Alannah Geary, and Andrea McClure. Bert Hadden played accordion on the worship team for many years, while Kathryn Thompson still continues to teach the Sunday school at this present time. These are just some of their stories –

Jackie and Jennifer McNeill

"Back in 1992, when God gloriously healed my wife, we started to get hungry for more of God. We began to attend Mountain Lodge, and experienced things like we never did before - the presence of God was awesome, the praise and worship was mighty. We sat under great preaching, and we both were baptised in water. What an experience that was! Then I was filled with the Holy Spirit during the prayer meeting one night.

I preached my first sermon away back then, and we will never forget Pastor Bob, a great man of God, a real encourager. And for Pastor David, just like Bob, a real man of God, and also a great encourager. These two men really encouraged Jennifer and I over the years, there is so much more we could say!

Really to sum it up, what attracted us was the presence of God in the meetings - you just did not want to go home. Being involved with the church from time to time over the years, it has been a privilege to have fellowship with everyone, and especially to know the presence of The Lord."

Ivan and Valerie Rutherford

"It was in August 1995 that Trevor and Maureen Bell invited us to a mission which was being held to mark the reopening of the church after the fire. We had been attending house meetings in their home in Crilly (near Aughnacloy in Co Tyrone) at the time. We had heard of Mountain Lodge but had never been there before. I can't remember who spoke or anything about that first meeting. We then started going along to the Sunday evening services and to the prayer meeting on Tuesday nights. We also were involved in the formation of the Loft Youth Club which began in November '98. We found the folks very welcoming and the presence of the Lord was very real.

In 2001, after much prayer, we felt led by the Lord to also go along on Sunday mornings. We have made many friends and enjoy the fellowship and teaching each week."

Alannah Geary

"Since first coming to Mountain Lodge, I have met a lot of wonderful people, who are now my friends for life. I first started to attend 'The Lodge' when I was in high school, through the invitation of my friend Gillian. I went to the summer barbeque that year, and thought it was great, and I then started going to the youth club, youth meetings etc. and then to church every Sunday night.

I remember when I was in primary school, I always used to pass the church in the school bus and always thought it was a nice building, and now I go to the church! It's amazing how God works in mysterious ways. Over the years, many wonderful things have happened to me, in Mountain Lodge, because of my friends. I got the assurance of salvation at a theatre production of 'Heaven's Gates Hell's Flames' in Armagh Elim Church, and God didn't stop there! I was baptized in water and I also received the Gift of Speaking in Tongues in Mountain Lodge.

Through life's mysterious journey, God has truly been there, through my attendance at Mountain Lodge. God has a victorious plan for my life. I know He will always be with me, as it's in His will for me to go to the Mountain Lodge. I am now a stronger and more confident person. Praise the Lord!"

Sharon Martin (nee Carrick)

"I began to attend Mountain Lodge in 2007 as it was here that my future husband Andrew attended. The first time I came to the church was at the Annual High Tea at the end of January, in support of Christian radio ministry. The people were so friendly, and there was a lovely Christian atmosphere. We were married in 2010 and it's been here that the Lord has blessed me with a lot of Christian friends, and a family."

Andrea McClure

"In January 2008, a friend of mine invited me along to Easter Camp at Mountain Lodge Pentecostal Church. I distinctly remember the amazing feeling of God's presence the moment I walked in through the door, and I remember thinking that there was something very special about this place. At that stage I had no idea of how God was going to use Mountain Lodge to enrich my walk with Him. Camp was absolutely amazing; it was a place where I met with God, and experienced His presence like I never had before. From then on, I was hooked on the exhilaration of God's strong presence in the place, and I started to attend the church each Sunday night.

At Easter 2012, I felt God leading me into full membership in the church. My experience of Mountain Lodge has been a very special one, as God has used Mountain Lodge to bless me more than I could ever have imagined. In 2008, through prayer at the church, I was healed of irritable bowel syndrome. In 2009, I went through the waters of baptism, and then in 2012, following prayer, I was baptised in the Holy Spirit.

These are only some of the many highlights of my time at Mountain Lodge so far, and they are moments that are very precious and close to my heart. To me Mountain Lodge is a very precious sanctuary of the Lord, one which He delights in, and where He manifests His presence like I have never felt anywhere before."

Chapter 37

A Remarkable Healing

The fact that God uses an individual as a channel or instrument of His choice to convey a message or prophetic word to His people does not make them immune from the usual challenges of life. In the years that followed the fulfilling of the vision that he had shared with the church, Tommy became unwell for a time, but after seeking God, experienced a remarkable healing. This is his account of what happened:

"I am writing this testimony to prove to everyone that Jesus Christ is the same yesterday today and forever. I have always been brought up to believe this. When I had a need, I would bring it to the Lord in prayer. Just after the new church opening, I took a weakness in my body, and it was getting me down every day.

It came to the point when I wasn't able to work with the men. I just opened the doors of the workshop in the morning. I told no one, not even my wife, and definitely not the doctor. I kept doing small runs which did not require much energy, as this way it kept down suspicion that anything was wrong.

I was always brought up to believe the promises of scripture like, *'I am the Lord that healeth thee'*. I decided that I would seek the Lord on this matter. I was a key holder of the church, and had access any time I wanted, so I went to the church every day for weeks, and lay on my face before the altar for hours at a time.

Then one day without knowing it, the miracle started to happen - my strength began to return, and I had more energy, and knew that I was healed! I went back to work as usual for many years without any bother. I just want to praise God for the experience of His healing. To God be all the glory, for in this case man had nothing to do with it.

Many years later, however, I experienced a very different type of attack. I went to bed as usual one night, and about two o'clock in the morning, I was awakened by a power coming over me which I can only describe as demonic. Something came over me and I thought I was going to go mad. I shivered and sweated and jumped out of bed for a minute.

I did not know what to do, so I grabbed my bible, fell on my knees at the side of my bed, calling on the name of Jesus and pleading the blood, doing all I knew to do. In about 20 minutes it passed away, but leaving a mark on me that was to last many years.

The next morning I went to work after a sleepless night but did not feel well. On the Saturday after that, I was in a very bad state of depression, so I went down to Pastor David's house. He was building his new house and he showed me around. I told him I did not feel well, but he not realise I was as bad as I was.

I went straight from David's house to Mountain Lodge church, and went in to pray. I was afraid that I had displeased God and was afraid that He would smite me. I was very serious about all this and prayed that God would forgive me if there was anything in my life that displeased Him. I came out of the church just the same.

In a few days the doctor was called and my family and he insisted that I go into hospital. I was in hospital for two weeks when they discharged me, and I started back to work as best as I could, but I was not the same. One year later, I took a very bad attack, something similar to the one in bed, and again I had to go into hospital this time for four months. I could no longer continue with my business, so my wife closed it down and paid off the men, and I gave my van and all my tools to my brother Bobby, so he could carry on with the maintenance of the poultry business that I was in, and not let my customers down.

I was again discharged from hospital but was not better. I sat in the house and would not go out. Then I started to go to the church every day and prayed very hard, and walked the aisles and knelt at the altar. This went on for years. A nurse came to visit me every week but she could only talk to me of positive things. She said to me, "Tommy, I know you are in agony of mind, but you can only help yourself."

The doctor told me, "You will never come out of this now, you have been ill too long." I was taking panic attacks and they were driving me mad; I thought I was going insane. I had tried all the tablets I could get anywhere, but nothing helped me.

But then one day in 2008, this thing started to lift off me, and my peace began to return. It had to be God. I had tried all the doctors. While I may not be one hundred percent, I am almost there. No more panic attacks.

I started to go out of the house and meet people, even going down to the hospital to see patients I had made friends with, some of them there twenty-five to thirty years, with no hope, and I say Praise God, for that is where I could have been, only for the grace of God. If you have never experienced depression, thank God, for it is the most awful thing you could be suffering with. I am living from day to day, thanking God for taking me from the very edge, and setting me free."

Chapter 38

"I Haven't Forgotten"

Mountain Lodge has been blessed with an array of visiting ministry over the years, one of the many blessings that has flowed from maintaining an 'open platform,' where visiting brothers and sisters in the Lord are encouraged to share and minister that which the Lord has given them. Some have travelled relatively short distances to minister at Mountain Lodge while others have travelled from the furthermost ends of the earth.

Very often such visitors become lifelong friends, returning again and again, while others, like passing ships in the night, may only have travelled this way once but nevertheless left a lasting impression.

One such person was Leila St. Claire-Linaker, a poet, who being moved by the history of the church, penned the following poem in 1999:

The pain's been so piercing-
It went through and through.
You thought never more
Could your plans, you ensue.
But your Father in heaven's
Been standing close by;
And in the expanse of Eternity
Yes He knows the 'Why.'

Those loved ones you lost
Now sit at 'His' feet:
Their sorrow all over,
Their victory complete.
But many down here
Have now heard of His Word;
And many, so many
Have turned to their Lord.

With no rhyme or reason
You'll hear them all say.
It took such a shock
To turn them away;
From the wild lonely road
They were travelling through life:
'Twas in the 'Light of Eternity'
That they saw their light!

So don't be dismayed
My children today.
For I only I,
Your God, knows the way
To touch all the pain
You still hold in your heart.
So bring all the hurt,
And I'll give a 'new start'

As you lay all your burdens
Now down at My feet,
My arms will surround
And I'll lift all the defeat

You've felt through the years
The numbness all gone
If you listen, My children
You'll hear a 'new song.'

Heaven's choir of angels
Sing in triumph sublime,
For they see the seasons
And they know the time.
I've given the signal
And breakthrough is here,
So stand up and worship
Cast away all the fear.

The victory's in sight
As I take you on,
In worship and praise
You'll see the new dawn.
My 'Light' now resplendent
On this spot in the world,
That the God of Creation
Has begun to unfurl.

His love and His beauty
Your eyes can't escape:
The threads on the loom
All now taking shape.
I've chosen to use you
So bend at My Will,
And as you touch others
Their lives then I will fill.

Remember the victory
Now here in your grasp,
Raise up 'My Standard'
And remember to fast.
The darkness will vanish
As forward we go,
New boundaries to take
And the enemy o'er throw.

For this is My land
And I'm taking it back,
From the hands of the 'enemy'
So don't get side tracked.
Keep your eyes on your Saviour
And wait for the 'cry,'
It's when I shout 'forward'
That Jesus is nigh.

The darkness will flee
The victory won,
Then tell others about me
And My Kingdom to come.
One day up in Glory
Then we'll all rejoice.
As the Lord Jesus declares
Yes, you heard My voice.

Poem by Leila St. Claire-Linaker
Sunday 19th December 1999 at 11.00am.

Chapter 39

The 'Minutes' Tick Away

The Mountain Lodge congregation continued to worship in their newly refurbished and extended building. The fire in 1994 may have brought much heartache, but the people on this hilltop are a resilient lot. Their steadfast faith in a faithful God has always enabled them to triumph in spite of tragedy.

The church minutes recording the business of the committee meeting held on 6th September 1995 indicate that Vernon Oxford from the USA had been invited to participate in a Gospel Concert to be held in October. It is also evident from the minutes that the congregation continued to raise funds through various large catering events at a number of venues throughout the country.

Another item of importance was also discussed at that September committee – the need to appoint a new pastor to replace Pastor Bob, following his home-call the previous year. It was acknowledged that Pastor David, the assistant pastor, appeared before the Lord to be the obvious choice. The entire committee without exception placed a vote of confidence in Pastor David.

At the following committee meeting on 5th October 1995, Thomas Bain proposed that the congregation be given an opportunity to make nominations for pastor, and David Robinson as secretary therefore was asked to draft up and issue an appropriate letter to all those in membership.

A Special Meeting of the leadership was called on 5th December 1995, when it was revealed that Pastor David had received 100% of the congregational nominations for the office of Senior Pastor. David was asked if he would accept the office, but the minutes record that he chose to take time to consider prayerfully the Lord's will, before making a decision, and so the matter was held over.

The minutes of a leadership meeting held on 1st March 1996 confirm that David Bell accepted the role of Senior Pastor. Those minutes also record that the amount owed on the new building had fallen to £27,000. Praise the Lord!

A Christian leaders' seminar was arranged for Friday 29th March. This was extremely well attended by ministers and leaders alike from various denominations and consisted of the following speakers ministering on the topics listed:

Dr Cecil Stewart – Divine Healing

Rev Jim Hagan – Spiritual Warfare

David J Greenow – The Anointing & Gifts of the Spirit

David Chaudhary – Full Gospel Ministry.

The minutes dated 1st February 1997 indicate that the debt owed on the building had further dropped to £21,000. It was decided at that meeting that the Forest Service, who by now owned the Mountain Lodge estate, be approached regarding the possibility of acquiring additional land from them.

A new committee was elected at the beginning of 1998 and Tommy Bain, William Martin, Keith Leyburn, Iris Walker, David Robinson, Violet Wilson, and Robert Weir were appointed, with Pastor David as chairman.

Valerie Rutherford was appointed as Leader-in-Charge of the youth work, a position that Valerie has continued to hold to this day and the church is greatly indebted to her for her role not only as Leader-in-Charge but in more recent years also as Treasurer of the youth work.

Owing to the number of young children attending the evening meetings at that time, a crèche was commenced on the new balcony, which the minutes recorded as 'very successful.'

Several items of business were discussed by the new committee at their inaugural meeting on 8th January 1998, including one item which would re-shape the Convention meetings traditionally held at Christmas and Easter for many years, for which Mountain Lodge has been famously known, but more about that later.

In October 1998, David Robinson and Sally Bell travelled out as part of a team to Hong Kong and China, encouraging the churches and providing assistance where needed. The trip was organised by David's son Glenn, and would prove to be a turning point in Glenn and Jeanette's life and ministry. Following this tour they eventually answered God's call, and moved to China to serve as missionaries for twelve years.

The minutes on the meeting held on 15th January 2000 record that gifts were presented to Mrs Minnie Morton and Mrs Liz Gordon for their valued ministry at the organ and piano respectively over many years, a service they still provide to this day.

The record of the committee meeting held on 16th August 2001 indicates that £5000 was raised through a dinner and various other fundraising efforts. The entire amount raised was forwarded to the Robinsons in China, to support a home they had rented as a safe place for young girls who had previously been involved in prostitution.

The acclaimed singer/songwriter Robin Mark and his band played in concert at the church on Friday 23rd November 2001 to a packed audience. The event was organised by Crossfire Trust, a local cross-community residential project in Darkley House, set up by Ian Bothwell in the 1980s, to offer structured emotional and practical support to those in need. Several of the temporary residents at Darkley House have attended Mountain Lodge church over the years.

A young lady in the fellowship, Jill Rutherford, pursued a degree at Belfast Bible College, and a gospel concert was organised in May 2002, the proceeds of which went towards her support.

Due to increased catering efforts an industrial dishwasher was installed in the first floor kitchen. Now a full load of dishes could be washed in three minutes!

In November 2002, Tommy Bain retired as church treasurer, having served in this capacity for sixteen years. He was presented with a watch in recognition of his faithful service. William Martin was elected to serve as treasurer in Tommy's place, a task that William still faithfully continues to fulfil until this present day.

A new committee was elected by the congregation in 2004 and the following members were appointed: William Martin (Treasurer); Valerie Rutherford (Secretary); Ivan Rutherford; Robert Weir; David Robinson; Iris Walker; Liz Gordon; Pastor David (Chairman). Valerie has faithfully continued as secretary to the present day.

The minutes of 3rd November 2004 indicate that the church was once again debt free! Praise the Lord! Not only had the debt in respect of the renovation work that was so necessary following the fire in 1994 been fully cleared, but a new twelve bedroom chalet had also been built in 2002 to provide accommodation at camp time etc. A local window company supplied all the new PVC window frames free of charge, and other local firms donated the carpets.

By 2007, the minutes record that a balance of £14,185 had accumulated in the church savings account. Hallelujah! Time to bless some folks out of the abundance of that with which the Lord has blessed. £2000 was forwarded to Glenn and Jeanette Robinson to assist with a trip home on furlough. A further £1000 was gifted to Seskinore Pentecostal Fellowship when they purchased a new church building.

The minutes of the committee meeting held on 25th April 2007 record an expression of interest in the adjoining farm belonging to the Warmington estate, which it was thought would shortly come up for sale. The minutes also record that 'joy riders' had driven a truck through the gates causing quite a bit of damage, which was duly repaired.

Dr Tony Stone, from England visited with an American singer, Anita Pierce, and during that visit, Dr Stone formed an excellent relationship with many of the young people in the church which he has continued to maintain.

A monthly missionary offering was introduced on the third Sunday of each month, beginning in January 2008, and this has enabled the ongoing support of missionaries and outreach activities over the following years. A gift of £1000 was forwarded to Wendy Cameron, Scotland, in May 2008.

In January 2009, the decision was made to produce a monthly church newsletter, with testimonies and stories, as well as the details of all the planned events for that month.

A gospel concert was held on 12th February 2009 at which George Hamilton IV, from USA was the guest artist, supported by Live Issue, a local band. The building was packed to the rafters, with many local people in from both sides of the community, as the proceeds were donated to the Meningitis Trust, following the support they had given to a local family who had suffered the trauma of a young child being diagnosed with the illness. The church was much in prayer for this young boy and, praise God, he made a full recovery!

In November 2009, Mervyn France and Pastor David visited a children's work in Brazil led by Dindo and his wife Lene, Brazilian missionaries, whom the church have supported for a number of years.

History in Pictures

Mountain Lodge
Pentecostal Church

The New Church, first opened in 1990, as painted by Miss Helen Bell (2013)

The cedarwood Church (erected 1972), the scene of the 1983 massacre

DAVID WILSON

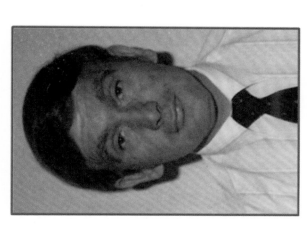

VICTOR CUNNINGHAM

HAROLD BROWNE

The three elders of Mountain Lodge Pentecostal Church who died during the Sunday Evening Service on 20th Nov 1983

Jim and Violet Clarke on a Sunday School Excursion (1970s)

The coming of the Lord draweth nigh

Clyde Shields and the Filipino Choir at Mountain Lodge during the 1970s

A Christmas Play in the old Cedarwood Church (1980s)

David and Emily Greenow with Pastor Bob and Mrs Bain.

Moving the Old Church in 1990.

David Greenow, David Robinson & David Willows at the Official Opening of the New Church (1990).

Gathering for the Official Opening of the New Church on Saturday 18th August 1990

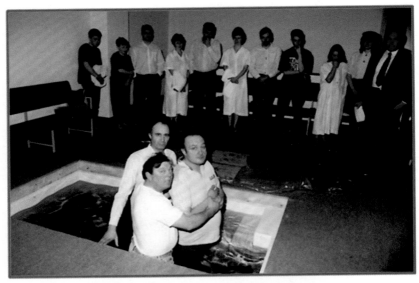

One of the first Baptisms in the New Church

The First Wedding in the new Church (March 1992)

An Open Air Gospel Meeting at Scarva

George Allen auctions off David Robinson's beard for charity!

The Devastation caused by the Fire in the new church (1994)

The Refurbished Church (1995) viewed from Front to Back

The New Church Hall, created during the 1995 Renovations

Ok, how many more for Dinner?

'Pierre the Pirate' Youth Outreach with the NET Team

Billy Jones (SCFS) receiving donated Christmas Gifts for Sailors

A Christmas Play in the newly renovated Church

The 'Paralytic Man' is lowered down through the roof during a children's outreach production

A Drama on Christmas Morning (2001)

'It's OK, I've got him!'

(Andrew Leonard rigged out in a Fireman's uniform during a visit by the Fire Brigade to the August 2010 Annual Fun Day at the church)

One of the church Praise Teams during the 20th Anniversary Celebrations of the New Church, held during 2010

Mrs Bain receiving a Presentation during the 20th Anniversary Celebrations on 13th August 2010

Mr Harte, The Tharps, and the pupils of Darkley Primary School all waving for the camera at the end of school Assembly

Pastor David and his wife Sally

Chapter 40

"The Tumours are Gone!"

In 1998 a young couple, Tony and Libby Hamilton, began attending the meetings at Mountain Lodge regularly for a season, before relocating to a different part of the country. During that time Libby was diagnosed with a number of tumours in her womb. They asked the church to pray. Tony tells the story:

"My wife Libby and I had been attending Mountain Lodge Pentecostal Church for only a matter of weeks, during the summer of 1998, when Libby had her miracle of healing. Libby had been suffering from a number of benign tumours in her womb, which were causing her great suffering and discomfort, and she bled heavily. She was very swollen and distended. The surgeons had recommended some radical surgery to remove them. Some were as large as two fists held together. Pastor David Bell was preaching at Mountain Lodge that Sunday evening and, after the service had ended, my wife decided that she would go forward for prayer. He was a kind and patient man, who listened closely, and then prayed for healing in Jesus' Name for Libby. The prayer was powerful, and we went home in faith to wait on God.

When my wife was called to her next pre-surgery consultation, she was examined as usual. The surgeon, after a thorough examination and a deep scan, was unable to find any of the tumours. They were completely gone! The prayer of faith, prayed by Pastor Bell, had accomplished a miracle in Jesus' Name. She was completely and perfectly healed and had no further symptoms.

Some months later, attending Mountain Lodge one Sunday,

we noticed a poster advertising that people were going from the Church on a mission trip to China. Mr David Robinson and his son Glen were keen to do a great work for God over there, with the help of Mountain Lodge. My wife Libby had been on mission to China before and was keen to go again, now her health was restored. She volunteered and was greatly encouraged by Pastor David's wife Sally; indeed Sally herself went too, along with others from Mountain Lodge. They brought Bibles, medicine and other much needed things to the Chinese people. Thanks to the great miracle my wife received through Pastor Bell's prayer, she was able to go to mission again in October 1998 and to be part of a group of lovely Mountain Lodge believers who had a great desire in their hearts to serve the Lord. It was a privilege for her, and she humbly remembers their kindness and love towards her, that we still enjoy so much today when we meet anyone from Mountain Lodge.

Some 15 years later, my wife's disabled brother, Bert became very sick. He was very ill and was not expected to live over the weekend. I felt the Lord encourage me to call on my Christian brothers and sisters to pray that God would change the expected outcome for my brother-in-law Bert. I rang and emailed almost one hundred and fifty churches and pastors all over to rally round and help. Sadly, no one from Northern Ireland got back to me at all and I was becoming very discouraged.

However, I was checking my email very late that night and found a precious response from Pastor David Bell at Mountain Lodge Pentecostal Church. He encouraged me and reassured me that he and his church would be praying. It was a light in the darkness; we had fresh hope - we were not alone, we had help from Mountain Lodge and the good people there!

In the middle of the next morning, everything changed. Bert began to recover - he turned the corner and began to come back to life again. He made a good recovery and is alive and well to this day - another miracle. Praise God! I still have the precious email from Pastor Bell:

'Thank you for contacting me, Tony. We will pray for Bert. Nothing is impossible to God; after all He is the one who created us in the first place. Pastor David.'

We have been blessed many times at Mountain Lodge, and we have so much to thank Jesus for and indeed all the good people who worship there. We give thanks for their kind prayers over the years. We owe them a great debt. Tony and Libby Hamilton."

(Following Tony's email, for the next few weeks the church family at Mountain Lodge took Bert's need faithfully to the Lord in every meeting, believing God for a miracle.)

Chapter 41

Camp Meetin' Time in the Darkley Hills

Long before the arrival of computers and mobile phones, a communications network existed between the various independent Pentecostal churches and fellowships that extended not only across the UK and Ireland but, in fact, around the world! As itinerant preachers would travel from one continent or country to another, they would share stories of revival meetings that had occurred in the churches where they had just previously ministered.

People like Eddie Smith, Ken Harwood, Jackie Ritchie, Brian Smithyman and other preachers would visit the various churches, just as Peter, Barnabas, Paul and the other apostles had done in the scriptures. Thus, those present in the meetings felt that they already intimately knew the fellow believers of whom they spoke, although they had never met.

It was in one such meeting at Hollybush Camp in North Yorkshire that Wilbur Jackson, a preacher from the USA, recognized Pastor David's accent as being distinctively 'Irish', and he asked him which area of Northern Ireland he was from. Assuming that an American would never have heard of the small town of Keady, never mind the backwater village of Darkley, Pastor David opted for what he considered to be the safest option, and answered that he pastored a small Pentecostal church in County Armagh. The United States preacher replied that he did not know where County Armagh was, but asked if that county was near a place called Mountain Lodge!

Imagine his surprise when he discovered that he was actually conversing with the pastor of that very church. It transpired that the American preacher had ministered there, some thirty five years previously! That's how the Pentecostal communication system works!

Many connections were made between Mountain Lodge and various other fellowships around the world at Hollybush Christian Fellowship camp meetings, and Jim and Cynthia Wilkinson, pastors of Hollybush, became good friends of Pastor David and his wife Sally.

It was at one of those Hollybush Camps that the Bells would meet the France family; however that would not be for a few years yet.

The Conventions at Mountain Lodge, traditionally held each Easter and Christmas, were always great times of blessing as folk travelled for miles to be in the Lord's presence. However in more recent years numbers attending had begun to decline and so the decision was taken to reduce the number of meetings from two days (Easter Sunday and Easter Monday, and Boxing Day and the day after) to just the one day at Easter and Christmas, with two meetings and tea between.

Then as numbers continued to decline, the decision was taken to abandon the Christmas meetings, and just hold the two meetings on Easter Sunday. It just seemed that folk didn't have the same desire to come out for special meetings like these; so many other things appeared to preoccupy their minds.

Pastor David sought the Lord much, as to what to do about the convention meetings. It seemed pointless to carry on with something just because it had always been done that way, yet it is always difficult to let go of something that had previously been successful for so long.

Pastor David finally made the decision: he was going to advise the leadership at the next meeting that he had decided to not organise any further convention meetings. However, it is in those moments of our final decisiveness that God very often speaks in the most remarkable way.

Just a few days before the next scheduled meeting, God sowed a thought in Pastor David's spirit that just simply wouldn't go away. Yet it seemed totally ludicrous. It was an impossible and incredulous thought. People were no longer attending one day conventions. God's solution to the problem? Scrap the ONE DAY convention in favour of a ONE WEEK camp!

This was something that Pastor David did not want to hear. Surely it would never work. If folk failed to turn up for one day of special meetings on Easter Sunday, what would possess any one to think that a week-long camp at Easter would be a success?

A battle of the mind ensued over the next few days. Pastor David knew first hand something of the work involved in planning and organising camps (and the team of willing volunteers that would be needed to man such a venture) for he and his family had attended the Family Camp at Hollybush in North Yorkshire many times. He had even taken across teams of young people from Mountain Lodge, so they could enjoy the spiritual experience. He knew such a venture would amount to 'hard graft.'

People would be required to prepare meals all day, from breakfast through to supper. Others would be needed to vacuum the carpets and clean the toilets. A team would be needed to man the sound system and song projection. Those engaged in all these activities would almost likely be required in the praise and worship team. Pastor David was right to think it could never work!

And so the time for the monthly committee meeting came around, and Pastor David found himself beginning to explain to those assembled how the Lord had spoken to him, how he had seen the inner workings of a family camp when at Hollybush, and how he believed this was God's solution to ailing convention meetings!

The committee unanimously backed the pastor's plan, for it would soon prove to be God's plan. The incredulous, the unimaginable, the impossible became a reality during the Easter week of 1998 - a one week camp! Those camps have continued to be a real blessing each year right up to the present time.

God never leads us to do things by halves. His plan is always perfect. And so it was, that during that first Easter Camp in 1998, we felt God lead us to plan a full week of children's meetings along side the adult meetings! We hired a 53 seater coach to collect children at various pick up points planned throughout the area. Four thousand flyers were distributed throughout the locality. You can therefore imagine our disappointment when night after night, the coach turned up at the church with not a single child on board! Andy and Tracy Newlove and their family had travelled over from England to run the Children's work for us. The meetings continued in a small marquee (during very cold weather!) with just a few local children who were escorted to the meetings by their parents, many of whom were coming to the adult meetings anyway.

One could have so easily become disillusioned and have given up but the following year, after much prayer, we felt that the Lord would have us to run with the children's work again. While at Hollybush Camp in Yorkshire the previous year, Pastor David and his family had met the NET Team, a group of young people headed up by Nigel and Sushila Lawrence, who had a passion for reaching out to children with the Good News of the gospel, in an engaging, fun and interactive way. Pastor David invited them to come to Ireland for the Easter 1999 Camp at Mountain Lodge.

This time we decided however, that we would send a car into each individual housing estate to collect the 'few' children that might turn up, rather than incur the expense of a large coach. We could never have envisaged what would happen next, but the story is best told in Nigel and Sushila's own words:

"It was with some fear and trepidation that we loaded into our Nissan Micra and set off from Lancashire to Mountain Lodge Church. The car was absolutely packed out with guitar, sketch board and luggage for a week, as well as the five team members – it was a miracle we made it there in one piece!!! Our journey took us up to Stranraer in Scotland, where we caught the ferry over to Belfast, and then a couple of hours drive up to the church. Our limited knowledge of Mountain Lodge was that it was set in the heart of the 'murder triangle'.

We'd been invited over by David Bell, to run a children's mission alongside their Easter camp. We would run meetings parallel to the adult meetings, morning and evening over the Easter weekend, and the idea was that we would seek to bring children in from the local housing estates, These estates were comprised of mainly Catholic families, and therefore the children had previously not been to the church, so there was an uncertainty as to how many we would get coming along.

The children's club was based on a pirates theme so, all dressed up in our costumes, we headed down to the local estates in the single decker coffee bus, armed with leaflets to give out. We expected that parents may be suspicious of what we were about and would probably call their children in and close the doors. We knew we were potentially heading for some challenges, but full of faith and up for the adventure, we began knocking on doors. The response was one that only God could have engineered. As we began to give out leaflets and talk to parents, doors were opening further down the street and children were being encouraged out to come over to the bus and find out what was going on. This happened in each area we went into, raising the faith and expectancy of us all.

After lots of practical preparations and plenty of praying, the time arrived for the first meeting to take place. The plan was that the church would take the bus down to make a visual impact, along with a car, to pick up the children and bring them back in time for the children's meeting to start at the same time as the adult meeting began. However, God had other plans! As the team arrived at the first pick up point, it was clear we'd underestimated the response we were going to get! We didn't have enough space for the first group of children to be transported up to the church, let alone the other pick ups that were planned. Messages were sent and all the drivers with cars at the church, (including the visiting speaker!), were sent down to the estates to pick up the very enthusiastic children.

So, the first meeting began with over 50, mainly Catholic, lively children! Extra helpers were drafted in from the adult meeting to help manage the numbers and we had a lot of fun! We did two meetings a day, morning and evening and the numbers remained steady throughout. We taught scripture based songs and verses from the Bible. At every meeting there was a clear presentation of the Gospel. On the Saturday evening, we gave the opportunity for anyone who wanted to become a Christian to do so and approximately half the children responded.

We found during our time there, that God really burdened us for the area and for the lives of the young people we were working with. As the meetings went on, our prayers for these young lives increased in passion and fervency. God really honoured the faith of the church as they reached out to their local community and they reaped an amazing harvest. We felt incredibly honoured and blessed to be a part of it.

On the morning that the team set off for Ireland, one of them had been woken with a word from God that said, *'I'm going to send a fire like you've never seen before.'* He was faithful to His word as His Holy Spirit moved in power through young lives that week.

We did another three missions with Mountain Lodge following that first one in Easter 1999. We returned later that year over the August bank holiday and then the following two Easters, each time seeing God building on the awesome foundation He'd laid in the children's lives."

Easter 2013 saw the fellowship at Mountain Lodge host its 20th camp in fifteen years, and this is what some of those who visited had to say:

"Easter Camp ... well what can I say - it was an amazing, blessed weekend!!! We all had such a great time, great preachers, fantastic singing and worship!! Then there's the yummy food and the fun as well. Kids also loved the Easter Bunny visiting. God willing, we will be there for Easter Camp '14!!! Yayyy!!!" J.G.

"For our first experience as a family at Mountain Lodge Camp, we didn't know what to expect, heading up the road. We had an idea it was going to be good, but never thought we could feel so at home in just a few hours. The church itself is so warm and homely, with the best of good food served by busy workers all weekend.

The thing that tops it all off was the lively praise and worship. You can feel the presence of God in the building. The preachers who preached the Word of God and ministered in song were powerful.

Another point was the love that flows out to the lost, with both sections of the community in worship together. To sum up Mountain Lodge's camp in one word for me would be 'Alive!'" M.G.

"Had a wonderful time at camp this year! Food was great! Music was great! The Word was great! The friends were great! Looking forward to seeing you all again!" M.H.

"We had a brilliant night tonight with John Gaughan, what a way to kick off Easter Camp. Greater things are on the way!!" A.L.

"I loved being part of Mountain Lodge Easter Camp weekend. It was wonderful to see everyone joining in worship and praise, and having the opportunity to hear God's Word from preachers from all over the world. The Camp passes so quickly! The presence of God is wonderful and the fellowship before and after each service, when folks make you feel so welcome." N. R.

"I really enjoyed Easter Camp. The fellowship was great, with a good choice of speakers and singers. The presence of God was so real, a wonderful opportunity to share with others and to be ministered to. The food was good and there was plenty of fun and fellowship at Julie's chippy in the evenings!" S.B.

Chapter 42

'A Different type of Church'

As previously stated, the majority of the kids who came along to those early children's meetings during camp were from a Catholic background. Young Andrew Leonard was among those children who came from the nearby village of Darkley. Andrew remembers those meetings very well:

"I grew up in a loving Roman Catholic home in the village of Darkley. My first encounter with Mountain Lodge was during the kids' club outreach, that the church ran around 1999. This was a different type of church; we sang fun songs like, 'Who's the King of the Jungle.' There were dramas, mimes, games, competitions and lots of other fun activities. Among the kids bussed in to the church, there were some rowdy characters to say the least! Some came to disrupt the meeting and cause chaos, but others came to listen. In later years, Pastor David told me that he remembers me popping my head out the window of the bus and saying, 'Hey mister, I went to first mass this morning, so I could come to this kids' meeting!' Looking back, it was at these children's meetings that a seed was first planted, that would be harvested seven or eight years later.

The kids' club ended after a few years, and I did not regain contact with the church until 2006. Life, for me, took a drastic turn in March 2006, when I was just 13. I had some very serious allegations made against me. I was arrested and the investigation lasted ten long months. Suddenly this fun-loving big kid had a lot of growing up to do. The ten months that followed would change my life forever. Due to the seriousness of these allegations, a lot of my friends turned their backs on me, and I lost my trust in people. It was a very dark and trying time in my life.

In the summer of 2006, I took part in a cross community summer scheme, where people from different backgrounds met up together, to learn more about each others beliefs and cultures. It was at that summer scheme that I came back into contact with some young people from Mountain Lodge. After the summer scheme ended, I kept in contact with the young people from Mountain Lodge, Esther Bell in particular. I began to confide in Esther and I explained what had happened to me earlier in the year, and she understood. She hardly knew me, yet she trusted me, and was on my side, which was such an encouragement.

Esther began to tell me of my need to be saved and at the beginning, becoming a Christian seemed unthinkable to me - what would people say? Esther invited me to the youth club at Mountain Lodge, and to a weekly youth meeting in Armagh Elim Church. I went along, and enjoyed these youth events. I got to mix with young people who just accepted me from day one. Esther then invited me to go to the evening service at Mountain Lodge, on Sunday 26th November 2006. I went to the service, and David Kenny was the speaker. He spoke about the hymns of Fanny Crosby. Through Esther, the youth club, and the youth meeting at Armagh Elim, I had become aware of my need to be saved. I was reluctant, but in that Sunday evening service as David Kenny began to sing these words,

'Pass me not O gentle Saviour, hear my humble cry;
While on others Thou art calling, do not pass me by.'

I suddenly knew in my heart that I needed to be saved, I didn't want Jesus to 'pass me by'. The next night, Monday 27th November 2006, I accepted Jesus as my Lord and Saviour. From then on I began to attend the church every week. In January 2007, I was proved innocent of the allegations that were made against me.

2006 was a challenging year for me as a young person. At times I felt like life wasn't worth the struggle and the stress. But the words of the hymn are so applicable to me:

"Through it all, I've learned to trust in Jesus:
I've learned to trust in God."

Mountain Lodge is a church where, if you are willing, you will be given something to do, and before too long I was helping out with the technical side of things, like operating the sound desk and the projector. The following year Esther Bell, Gillian and Kyle Morton and I began a youth praise team. This led to us beginning a monthly youth meeting in the church, in April 2008, to which we would bring in guest speakers each month. The name of the monthly youth meeting was Lifestyle. Our slogan was *'Being a Christian isn't a hobby, it's a Lifestyle.'* The youth praise team then began to lead the praise and worship in alternative meetings with the senior praise team.

For anyone who attends Mountain Lodge, the highlight of the Church year is always the Easter camp. In 2008, I decided that I wanted to get baptised. During the Easter Camp that year there were seven of us baptised during the Monday evening service. Getting baptised was an amazing experience, one that I will never forget.

In more recent years, the youth of the church have been involved in various outreaches, including an annual Fun Day. This event is held in August each year. We have bouncy castles, pony rides, face painting, a barbeque and lots of other fun activities for the surrounding area. This event has proved to be a huge success each year and we see a lot of people coming in from the local community. In March 2011 we ran our first youth weekend. This outreach was entitled 'Reach.' The weekend consisted of three meetings with a praise band and a different speaker each night. Through this outreach we saw three people come to know the Lord which was brilliant.

Since becoming a Christian my life has not been perfect. Life still has challenges, and it still has its ups and downs. However in the midst of any storm, I know that I have the One who calms the storm, by my side."

In the spring of 2012, Andrew asked Esther Bell, Pastor David's daughter, to marry him. They had been going out together for over five years. She said yes!

Esther shares a little of her own story below:

"I was brought up in Mountain Lodge. My parents are David and Sally Bell, and so I have been the pastor's daughter the majority of my life, and I wouldn't have it any other way! Mum and Dad have been a wonderful example of dedication, service and Godly love to me and to those around them. I was brought up going to church, and attended Sunday School every week. I have to give great credit and thanks to my two Sunday School teachers, Doreen Robinson and Violet McFadden, who taught me the truth from the Bible faithfully every week. It's because of them, and my parents, that I became a Christian at a young age. I have been baptised in water and in the Holy Spirit at Mountain Lodge. I've always been involved in church life, and now lead praise and worship, and I also am a youth leader. To me, Mountain Lodge is much more than a church - it is home!"

Miss Violet McFadden and Mrs Doreen Robinson taught Sunday School faithfully for many years, and a great number of young (and not so young) adults gained a good knowledge of the scriptures through their godly ministry, a work presently carried on by Mrs Kathryn Thompson.

Chapter 43

Kays Farm Fellowship
:: Going in the Purposes of God ::

Pastor David, his wife Sally and their young daughter Esther have been frequent visitors to Hollybush Family Camp for many years. For a number of years, they took a number of young people from the fellowship at Mountain Lodge with them. As many as twenty crossed the Irish Sea on the ferry, complete with camper vans, tents and enough luggage for a round the world trip, bound for the flat terrain of North Yorkshire.

It was on one such occasion, during the week of Hollybush Camp in August of 1998 that Pastor David observed Lucy France from Kays Farm Fellowship in Lancashire, assisting a few times in the morning worship at the piano.

Lucy takes up the story and relates the events that followed:

"David approached me and asked if I would be willing to come over to Mountain Lodge in Northern Ireland, and lead the praise and worship for their Easter Camp the following year. After discussing the invite with my husband Mervyn a few days later, we were both thrilled to accept the invitation. For many years we had known about the fellowship at Mountain Lodge, and quite often visiting speakers to our Monday night meeting at Kays Farm Fellowship would tell us of their experiences at the Darkley church a few nights before. Having heard so much about the fellowship over in Northern Ireland had put a desire in our hearts to meet them, and we had often prayed for an opportunity to go.

Easter came round the following year and we found ourselves on board the ferry for Northern Ireland. We were filled with anticipation and a real sense that we were going in the purposes of God. We will never forget driving off the boat on to this land that we had heard so much about, and all the troubles that had dominated the news. We felt that this was going to be a day of new things for us. Little did we realize at this point just how much God was going to intertwine our hearts and our lives with everyone within the fellowship at Mountain Lodge, and especially so with David, Sally and Esther Bell.

We arrived at the church early on Good Friday morning excited to be there, but also apprehensive as we would be spending the next three days and nights on the very spot where the Darkley Massacre had taken place. This was their second Easter Camp. We had heard about the previous year's camp and had decided that we would go sometime, and now here we were as invited guests.

The meetings were fantastic with one meeting almost merging into the next. However the ladies of the church prepared lovely meals in between the meetings, so the whole place was a hive of activity with meetings, meals and washing up. Mervyn soon found a job washing up in the kitchen, and I helped to prepare tea, so we soon got to know everyone as we worked together. We were really impressed with some of the youth, how they were so willing to muck in and help. We struck up great bonds of friendship in those early days with Julie and Sharon, Jill, Jenny, Esther, and now many more over the years, as we have seen them grow up.

On the Easter Monday afternoon of that first visit, Trevor Caldwell arranged to take Mervyn to visit the victims' families of the Omagh bombings and pray with them. This was going to be one of those experiences for Mervyn that would take him right out of his comfort zone. That day, he met Doreen McFarland, whose sixteen year old daughter was murdered in the bombing. Chatting with Doreen, he learnt about Samantha and her ambition to go to Nepal as a charity worker. Mervyn then told Doreen of our children's home in Nepal, and after praying with her, Mervyn and Trevor left. A few weeks later, we received a gift from Doreen for the children's home in memory of Samantha. Since then Doreen has become a lovely friend and has raised tens of thousands of pounds for the children's home in Nepal, in Samantha's memory. A few years ago, we planted a tree in the garden of the children's home, as a memorial to Samantha. It is lit up every Christmas, and the children are told Samantha's story.

Over the years there have been many highlights at the Easter Camps. Precious times of fellowship with David Greenow, Herbie Stewart, Nancy Kerchoff and Tané Miller to name but a few, but a real gem was the year when Pastor David invited brother and sister Rodney and Esther Wilson to come along and sing one evening. Having heard much of their story, it was a blessing to meet them on their first visit back to Mountain Lodge since their father, who had been an elder in the church, had been shot and killed on that tragic November 1983 Sunday evening. Listening to them practice in the afternoon, and seeing their out and out love for Jesus, and the touch of God on their lives was absolutely overwhelming. They both walked straight into our hearts. Since then it has been our privilege to have them stay in our home on several occasions and it was a great joy to attend Esther's wedding in Canada.

Since that first visit we have never missed an Easter Camp and we also started to go to Mountain Lodge for the August Bank Holiday weekend as well. It was during one of those early August Bank Holiday visits that Pastor David asked us if we had ever thought about printing a newsletter for the children's homes. He said he would be willing to come alongside us and help design, print and post it out as a gift to the work. To us this was absolutely brilliant, as it had been on our hearts for some time to send out an informative newsletter, but we really didn't know where to begin.

Sometime prior to this, when Nancy Kerchoff and Tané Miller were ministering in a meeting, they had called me forward, and prayed and prophesied over me that 'God would bring someone alongside to help Mervyn and me in the work.' This is a wonderful example of how God engineers circumstances to fulfill

His purposes. Mervyn and I are very grateful to David and Sally for all the resources that they have poured into the newsletters down through the years, and now we find ourselves more often than not jumping on to a plane and visiting Northern Ireland five or six times a year.

To us, Mountain Lodge has become home; we love each and every one of its church family. We have shared both happy and sad times, we have enjoyed seeing the youth grow up and mature in God, baptizing many of them. We have attended weddings and child dedications. Now we are seeing a new generation grow up in Mountain Lodge Church. We thank God for all the fellowship down through the years, which first began at that Easter Camp in 1999."

(Mervyn and Lucy France are the pastors of Kays Farm Fellowship at Lancaster, England. The Fellowship pioneered a Christian work in Asia thirty five years ago, primarily among children, and they presently operate and maintain five children's homes and a bible school. They have also sponsored the building of churches in Asia).

Chapter 44

The Highways and the Byways

*'Go out into the highways and hedges, and compel them to come in,
that My house may be filled.'*

Luke 14:23

There has always been a real spiritual desire among the people of Mountain Lodge to reach out to others in whatever way possible with the message of the gospel. Door to door visitation, open-air meetings, tract distribution, radio programmes, crusades and any other means available have been used over the years to propagate the gospel.

It therefore came as no surprise when, in 2004, Mrs Iris Walker came forward with a burden the Lord had given her. She initially shared her thoughts with some of the ladies in the congregation, before bringing her desire to the pastor. This is the story, as Iris told it:

"It was Saturday 11th December 2004 at approximately 11.30pm when God spoke to me very definitely about visiting elderly, single, needy people in our area with a gift for Christmas.

The following day - Sunday 12th December - in the back room of the church I and four other ladies said yes to God's call and the following week we started. We thought it was a one off visit but God had other plans. Contacts made before Christmas saw us back again and again on a regular basis. You see we had met lonely, needy people whom God was giving us a heart and a love for. Many have been touched by God's love and have come into a real relationship with Him.

Since then we have come along side people with addictions, many of whom have been at the church at different events and we have seen God at work in their lives. We count it an honour and a privilege to be part of the work of God in our land. We believe, as a church, God is going to set many people free from all sorts of sicknesses, addictions, problems etc."

The following report has been compiled by some of those presently serving on the team:

"Following the vision God gave to Iris in Dec 2004, about visiting needy people in the community, we set out in pairs and visited the elderly and housebound with a little gift for Christmas. We received such a warm reception from both sides of the community that we felt this was something we could do as a means of outreach, so we started week by week, usually on Thursdays, and went into a different area each week.

What began as visitation to the elderly and house bound, soon extended to the sick, and to those with emotional and spiritual needs in their lives. We also visited the nursing homes in the local area and befriended folks there, and had some real opportunities to share the gospel with them. One man we spoke to said he should have become a Christian long ago and there, in his chair in the dayroom, he prayed the sinner's prayer. Today he is in Heaven.

Another lady we met for the first time was just there recovering for a few weeks, so we went back to visit her again. As we talked about spiritual things, she shared a lot of her hurts in life and we had a real opportunity to talk things over together. We never know sometimes what people are going through, or the reasons for their attitude towards God. She moved on again, so we really do not know what happened next, we had to leave it in God's hands. We also visited a lady who had been a very devout church goer all her life, but never had a born again experience. She also prayed the sinner's prayer. We have continued to visit and pray with her.

A Christian lady whom we visited in her own home for quite a long time just loved the fellowship and would always ask us to pray, no matter who was visiting with her at the time. Sometimes that can be daunting! Another young woman, who was just out of hospital, invited us into her home and we talked for some time about spiritual matters. It seemed we must have covered every subject as she asked a lot of questions. She had no knowledge of the scriptures, so we called again with a new bible for her. We just trust that the seed sown will bring forth fruit in due season.

Another lady, who suffered a lot of heartache throughout the troubles and other tragedies, talked to us through her tears. Her friend came in one day while we talked, and he too entered into the conversation, and when we went to the car to fetch a booklet for him, before we knew it, he was standing by our side, waiting for what we had to give. We visited with another man and shared the gospel with him, but he felt he was ok. However one day when we called, he expressed concern about a sore on his leg that the nurses had been dressing, but which did not seem to be getting any better. We asked him if he would like us to pray with him. We prayed a simple prayer, and the next time we called he was proudly showing us how it had healed up! Praise the Lord! To God be all the glory!

We give out the 'Word for Today' (a daily devotional) to a lot of people and those who receive it really look forward to receiving their copy on a regular basis. Such comments after reading the booklet include, 'you know what you need to do', and 'I couldn't find my book because he had it in his room,' (referring to her son).

Another young woman, whose elderly relative we were visiting, expressed an interest in the book, so we gave her a copy of her own. Later, she said, 'Now I order my own copy.'

We also knocked on doors and distributed the Gospel of John into all the local housing estates and received a very warm reception.

Just as Jesus understood the safety of sending the disciples out two by two, we work together in pairs with people who have alcohol, as well as other addictions. Many of them have great needs in their lives. We have witnessed people come to God and come to church, who have never come before. It is a rewarding work, and a work for all Christians to do. We should endeavour to win the lost at any cost.

> Our motto for the outreach work is:
> *Rescue the perishing, care for the dying;*
> *Snatch them in pity from sin and the grave.*
> *Weep o'er the erring ones, lift up the fallen,*
> *Tell them of Jesus, the Mighty to save.*
> *Rescue the perishing, duty demands it,*
> *Strength for thy labour, the Lord will provide.*
> *Back to the narrow way, patiently win them,*
> *Tell the poor wanderer, a Saviour has died.*

We decided to spread the message further, so we rented a room in the Dobbin Street Community Centre in Armagh, for quite some time, as a drop in centre and others from the church joined us. A number of people saw it advertised, and came in for a chat. People expressed how they had been helped and ministered to; others stated how family situations had turned around. One young woman, although she did not make a public confession of faith, we believe she found the Lord, after much prayer and discussion. She passed away quite suddenly but we believe we will meet again in Heaven.

It had been on our hearts to do something similar in Keady, but up until this time it had not materialised. Then one day out of the blue, we got a telephone call from Tané Millar in the USA, asking if she could come and spend some time with us, as she had made a new CD. Tané has a beautiful singing voice and a wonderful ministry. She felt she wanted to come about two weeks before Christmas 2010. We thought this was probably not a good time so close to Christmas, however we said 'yes'. The day she arrived it was snowing so heavily that traffic was almost at a standstill! She was booked to speak and sing at a ladies' night in Enniskillen that evening, but it soon became obvious that few people if any would venture out on such an evening, and so the service was cancelled.

We had also scheduled her in for a ladies' night in our own church, but the snow continued to fall. Those who know where we are situated would not expect anyone, especially lady drivers, to turn up. It looked like everything was against us and that this trip was a mistake, but we decided to look for a new venue. We went into Keady and rented a room in the Old Mill Heritage Centre and at very short notice, and after a few quick phone calls, some forty people turned up, and we had a really good evening and a supper afterwards. We felt this was a God-ordained opportunity. We also were able to take Tané into the Nursing Home in Keady where she sang Christmas carols to the residents, as they joined in with some of the older carols, and had a great evening.

We felt this was something we wanted to continue to do on a regular basis, to provide somewhere that people from the town could drop in. Many folk from both sides of the community come and enjoy a good evening, listening to various speakers share real life stories, or sometimes enjoying a concert evening. People continually ask, 'When is the next night going to be?'

One young man recently committed his life to the Lord and he has since said his life was really changed that night. We believe that no matter what our background, Jesus loves us and died for us, and everyone deserves to know the way to Heaven."

Iris continued to invest her time, her money and her home in this work, right up until her home-call to Glory, in February 2012. However, the rest of the team continue to fulfil the vision Iris initially received, right up to this day.

A Bible School is currently being built in Asia in her memory, a fitting tribute to one who lived her life for the Saviour she loved.

Chapter 45

"It Sounds Lively!"

"I know the plans I have for you, declares the Lord"
Jer. 29:11.

In true fulfilment of Tommy's vision of the 'Ark', families continued to come. One such young couple, who first arrived in May 2008, were Kenny Nesbitt and Elinor Brownlee. Kenny tells how they both were drawn to Mountain Lodge:

"The above scripture is very true to me as I reflect on how my family and I came to be members of Mountain Lodge. I first heard the words 'Mountain Lodge' through overhearing a conversation between my mum and a good friend of hers, Olwyn Keys. The both of them, on occasion, would have gone along to some of the meetings in the church.

'The praise and worship is just awesome!'
'The presence of God is so real!'
'I don't know of any other church like it!'
These were just some of the phrases they would be saying!

From a child, I was brought up in a Baptist Church where I was faithfully sent along to church, Sunday school, children's meetings, and then prayer meetings. My fiancée Elinor had also been attending the Baptist Church for the past six months, but had originally been brought up in a traditional Church of Ireland. A move to the Baptist for her was therefore quite a change, but nothing compared to what was yet to come! We had been engaged for some months and wedding plans were well underway with the Baptist Church, and the reception at the Killyhevlin Hotel was also securely booked for 20th August 2009.

> 'In his heart a man plans his course,
> but the Lord determines his steps.' Prov. 16 v 9.

Elinor by now was starting to express interest in becoming a member of the Baptist Church, but after giving it some prayerful thought, it was my wish that we should hold off until we were married and then join as husband and wife.

One night while having tea, I overheard my mum and her friend discussing the up and coming Sunday night meeting in Mountain Lodge; there was a special guest speaker and singer to attend. God brought a spirit of curiosity and discontentment upon me - I wanted to go and check this place out for myself. I said to Elinor and we both agreed to go along, but due to my work situation our plans fell through.

I was disappointed but all hope was not lost. As the following week rolled by, I came across an advertisement in the local paper. It said, 'Lifestyle Youth Meeting in Mountain Lodge Pentecostal Church on Friday Night.' Something inside me jumped with excitement - finally - an excuse to go and check this place out, see what it was like.

Friday night came, and off we went, not knowing much with regard to location, apart from 'head in the Keady/Darkley direction'. So after being up and down a few little roads, we finally arrived. With just a few cars around the church, we wondered if we had got the date right and, feeling a bit apprehensive, we debated whether we would venture in or not. But there was this tug, this longing in my spirit wanting to be in this place. Only now as I look back, I know that it was God at work in my life. 'I know the plans I have for you to give you a hope and a future.'

We slipped into the seats at the back and tried to take in the new surroundings. A young lady started to speak from up near the front; her name was Andrea. She was sharing her testimony of how, on Tuesday night past, some of the youth from the church had laid hands on her and prayed with her. She had been suffering from irritable bowel syndrome. I could relate to this only too well, as I also suffered from the same condition, meaning that I had a wheat free, dairy free and low sugar diet. She told how God had healed her of this irritating condition! I don't remember much else about the meeting that night, other than the welcoming friendship shown to us by some of the young people from the church.

As Elinor and I headed home that night there was only one thing very much on the forefront of my mind, and that was if God could heal Andrea, could He not also heal me? Up until now, I had never realised or been taught from scripture that there is healing power in the name of Jesus Christ, through the laying on of hands and praying the prayer of faith. *'The prayer offered in faith will make the sick person well; the Lord will raise him up.' James 5:15.*

A few weeks went past, and Elinor and I attended a meeting over in Moneymore, at which a man named Angus Buchan was the speaker. He was preaching and praying for the sick and, as he did so, I took a step of faith and believed that Jesus had healed me. From that night on, my dietary problems have become a thing of the past! 'Hallelujah, all glory to Jesus!'

We attended Mountain Lodge the following Sunday morning. I did so with some expectancy that I needed to share the testimony of my healing. Sister Iris Walker was leading the praise and worship that particular morning and as she drew it to a close, she said that the Holy Spirit was prompting her to give opportunity for someone whom she felt had something to share. As no one else moved I knew only too well it was me. It was a nerve-racking few moments but a gloriously memorable one as I shared something for the first time publicly to the church.

By this time, Elinor and I regularly attended the morning

and evening services, but there was one meeting we still had to experience - 'the prayer meeting'. So off we went one Tuesday night! I can remember going in through the front door and Elinor saying, 'I wonder where they have it,' but by the time we got into the main building we had no trouble knowing! We could hear them! We just followed the sound coming from the balcony. 'It sounds lively,' Elinor commented. Our early memories of the prayer times were special to us. Not only was God's presence so real, but the love and encouragement we got from the Pastor and other members as they laid hands on us, and prayed with us was a real blessing. It was during one of these prayer times, that we both received the Baptism of the Holy Spirit.

The Wedding date was fast approaching and we both, at this time, really felt that we would like to get married in Mountain Lodge, instead of the Baptist Church that we had already pre-booked. We prayed that God would confirm it to us, which He soon did through the word the Pastor spoke that Sunday morning. It was a wonderful day and a real blessing to have had our wedding in the church that God had led us to, and with many from the church taking part in our special day.

During the summer of 2011 God started to put something on both of our hearts. He had drawn to our attention the need for the young people of the church to have something to do, and somewhere to go to on Sunday nights. So with much prayer and confirmation from the Pastor, we started up a youth meeting once a month, on a Sunday night after church, called Ignitable. It's during these nights that we have bible studies, times of prayer, and some informal fellowship with the young people. It has been a real encouragement to us both, as we have seen God blessing the young people, watching them grow in the faith and their walk with God, as they attend Ignitable.

We have not only seen the youth of the church growing spiritually, but Elinor and I have been adding to the numbers also, as over the past four years God has blessed us with three beautiful children, Emily, Caleb and Daniel, who have all been dedicated to God in the church.

As I end my story, I'd like to take you back to where I began. Jer. 29:11, *'I know the plans I have for you,' declares the Lord, 'plans to prosper you and not to harm you, plans to give you a hope and a future'*. His ways are much higher than our ways, He is a wonderful God!"

~~~~~~

'A word fitly spoken is like apples of gold in pictures of silver.'

Proverbs 25:11

~~~~~~

Chapter 46

A Timely Word
from our Oldest Member!

Mrs Margaret Bain, the oldest member of Mountain Lodge, is the widow of the late Pastor Bob Bain. She has always been someone of a quiet disposition but nevertheless, a real 'Mother in Israel', seeking God in prayer for the needs of others and providing personal words of encouragement. She has been a stalwart member over the years and many a preacher has enjoyed a good meal at her table, and in earlier years quite a few were treated to a bed for the night! Having just celebrated her ninety-fourth year, she is a perfect example of how to live the Christian life, rarely missing a single meeting and certainly never without good cause. Her voice is seldom raised so it is a rare treat for you, the reader, to be privy to her thoughts, as she puts her pen to paper:

"It has been my privilege to be Pastor Bain's wife. We had two boys and five girls, who have all been saved from an early age. All of our family were behind us in the work, and still are. In our house we had always an open door with people coming from far and near, seeking for prayer and spiritual help.

Many people came to the church needing prayer. Families also came from south of the border and joined us in the church. Well, these were mountain top times but we had also valley times, when we had the fire and the shooting, but God was with us as we went on in His strength. I thank God for the prayers of God's people that kept us in His plan.

Even from our ministry in the home we had the privilege of raising spiritual sons and daughters, who are still today pillars in our church. (You are very special).

David Bell came into the church at that time, a young man eager for God. David came alongside to help, and now has been the Pastor for many years. (David is married to my daughter Sally). My husband, Pastor Bob, passed away in May 1994.

I would like to encourage Pastor David and Sally in the work they are doing, and I would like to give a word to the congregation to be in there, and give full support, and we will see the work grow from strength to strength. Like as the hymn says;

> *Raise up a people, holy and free*
> *Hearts with a vision like unto Thee*
> *Souls that would rather die than give in*
> *Hearts with a passion, victory to win.*

I would also like to pay tribute to my daughter Iris, who passed away on 11th February 2012. She was a worker and a worship leader, and an inspiration in the church and to all of us. Times have been hard but we have to keep going on till we meet again."

Chapter 47

What of the Future?

In the introduction to this historic record celebrating sixty years of faithful ministry in Mountain Lodge, I stated that:

> *'My sincere desire is that this book will serve to re-kindle a fresh flame within those more mature souls among us, who have worshipped faithfully in this place over the years, as we remember some of the mighty visitations of the Lord in our midst. I also hope that it will also be a source of inspiration and encouragement to our younger members, as they discover the rich heritage that the saints have sought to preserve for them through overcoming various trials and tribulations down through the years'.*

So what of the future? Well, the future of this historic Pentecostal fellowship is in Safe Hands. During this sixtieth year, the main kitchen has been upgraded to commercial standards fit for any hotel; a bulk gas supply has been installed; we have purchased part of the farm adjacent to the church to allow for future expansion of the work and the next item on the agenda is the installation of a passenger lift to service the upper floors of the building at some point in the near future, as funds permit. And that's only the practical side of things.

Spiritually, this independent Pentecostal fellowship continues to press forward, helping the broken, lifting up the weary, ministering to the sick, encouraging the saints, reaching out to the lost and preaching Jesus. Souls are being saved, entering into a personal and meaningful relationship with the Lord Jesus, and receiving assurance and peace of mind concerning their eternal destiny. The Word of God is faithfully taught week by week, while those present are encouraged to seek the daily blessing of God upon their lives.

A new generation of young people is emerging up through the ranks of the church, many of them uniting in marriage, and raising families of their own whose young lives are dedicated to the Lord's service.

Yes, the future is in safe hands.

Now thanks be to God who always leads us in triumph in Christ, and through us diffuses the fragrance of His knowledge in every place.

2 Cor 2:14. (NKJV)

For more information about

FIRE ON THE MOUNTAIN
&
MOUNTAIN LODGE PENTECOSTAL CHURCH
please visit:

www.mlpc.co.uk
pastor@mlpc.co.uk

....

For more information about
AMBASSADOR BOOKS AND MEDIA
please visit:

www.ambassadormedia.co.uk
info@ambassadormedia.co.uk